Response to Intervention (RTI) and English Learners

Using the SIOP® Model

Second Edition

Response to Intervention (RTI) and English Learners

Using the SIOP® Model

Jana Echevarría

California State University, Long Beach

Catherine Richards-Tutor

California State University, Long Beach

MaryEllen Vogt

California State University, Long Beach

PEARSON

Boston • Columbus • Indianapolis • New York • San Francisco • Upper Saddle River
Amsterdam • Cape Town • Dubai • London • Madrid • Milan • Munich • Paris • Montréal • Toronto
Delhi • Mexico City • São Paulo • Sydney • Hong Kong • Seoul • Singapore • Taipei • Tokyo

Vice President, Editor in Chief: Jeffery W. Johnston
Senior Acquisitions Editor: Julie Peters
Editorial Assistant: Andrea Hall
Director of Marketing: Margaret Waples
Executive Marketing Manager: Krista Clark
Project Manager: Annette Joseph
Project Coordination and Text Design: Electronic Publishing Services Inc., NYC
Photo Researcher: Electronic Publishing Services Inc., NYC
Operations Specialist: Linda Sager
Electronic Composition: Jouve
Cover Design: Suzanne Behnke
Cover Image: Monkey Business Images/Shutterstock and Blend Images/SuperStock

Credits and acknowledgments borrowed from other sources and reproduced, with permission, in this textbook appear on the appropriate page within text.

Library of Congress Cataloging-in-Publication Data
Echevarria, Jana
   Response to intervention (RTI) and English learners : using the SIOP® model / Jana Echevarría, Catherine Richards-Tutor, MaryEllen Vogt. — Second edition.
     pages cm. — (SIOP series)
  Includes bibliographical references and index.
  ISBN 978-0-13-343107-0
  1. English language—Study and teaching—United States—Foreign speakers. 2. Language arts—Remedial teaching—United States. I. Richards-Tutor, Catherine. II. Vogt, MaryEllen. III. Title.
  PE1128.A2E25 2015
  428.0071—dc23

                                  2013039123

ISBN 10: 0-13-343107-X
ISBN 13: 978-0-13-343107-0

For Grace

About the Authors

Jana Echevarría is Professor Emerita of Education at California State University, Long Beach, where she was selected as Outstanding Professor. She has taught in elementary, middle, and high school in general education, special education, ESL, and bilingual programs. She has lived in Taiwan, Spain, and Mexico where she taught and conducted research. Her UCLA doctorate earned her an award from the National Association for Bilingual Education's Outstanding Dissertations Competition and subsequent research and publications focus on effective instruction for English learners, including those with learning disabilities. She has presented her research across the U.S. and internationally including Oxford University (England), Wits University (South Africa), Harvard University (U.S.), South East Europe University (Macedonia), and University of Barcelona (Spain). Publications include the popular SIOP book series and over 50 books, book chapters, and journal articles.

Catherine Richards-Tutor is an Associate Professor in the special education program at California State University, Long Beach. Before receiving her doctorate from the University of California, Santa Barbara, Dr. Richards-Tutor worked as a classroom teacher, a reading specialist for students at-risk, and a behavioral consultant. In 2009 she was awarded the Early Academic Career Excellence Award at CSU Long Beach for her accomplishments in research, teaching, and professional service. Dr. Richards-Tutor has worked with many districts and schools with high percentages of English learners in implementing RTI in both academics and behavior. Currently, she is Co-PI on Project EQALS, Evidence-based, Quality Professional Development in Algebra for Learner Success, which is funded by the California Department of Education. Her research and publications focus on reading and math interventions and progress monitoring for English learners, particularly within a RTI model.

MaryEllen Vogt is Professor Emerita of Education at California State University, Long Beach. Dr. Vogt has been a classroom teacher, reading specialist, special education specialist, curriculum coordinator, and teacher educator. She received a doctorate in Language and Literacy from the University of California, Berkeley. Dr. Vogt is an author of over 60 articles and chapters, and is co-author of sixteen books for teachers and administrators, including Making Content Comprehensible for English Learners: The SIOP® Model (2013), and the other books in the SIOP series. Her research interests include improving comprehension in the content areas, teacher change and development, and content literacy and language acquisition for English learners. Dr. Vogt has provided professional development in all fifty states and in several other countries, including Germany, where she served as a Visiting Scholar at the University of Cologne. She was inducted into the California Reading Hall of Fame, received her university's Distinguished Faculty Teaching Award, and served as President of the International Reading Association.

Contents

Since we wrote the first edition of this book, implementation of RTI has grown across the United States and is used widely as a way to identify students who struggle academically and to offer the support they need to be successful. RTI may be particularly useful in the current era of high standards, including the Common Core State Standards (CCSS), since it is anticipated that more students will struggle to read rigorous texts and perform challenging math processes required by the standards. RTI offers a way for teachers and specialists to collaborate, support student learning, and assist those who are at-risk for academic failure. As a result, children and adolescents who formerly may have been assigned to special education classes through a refer-test-identify-place approach are finding that their academic problems and deficiencies are ameliorated with appropriate and effective intervention. Within effective RTI programs, those youngsters who need and deserve special education services are now being served by expert teachers in settings that are better designed to meet their needs. With many English learners, however, this scenario is not the case. These students whose home culture differs from the ways of school and whose home language differs from the language of instruction continue to be over- and underrepresented in special education. Some are referred for special education services, regardless of whether they have disabilities, in large part because many classroom teachers are ill prepared to meet their language and academic needs. In other cases, English learners are denied special education services because it is assumed their learning problems are due to their lack of language proficiency. These students languish without appropriate assistance either because of low expectations or because it is thought that they just need more time to learn English.

New To This Edition

This second edition of our book has been updated and revised to assist teachers and administrators to better meet the needs of the increasing group of English learners in United States schools. As implementation of RTI across the U.S. continues to grow and evolve, it is important to include updated research as well as classroom connections so that readers have the most recent information on research and practice. The first edition was intended to provide tools for effective RTI implementation such as forms and questions to guide development of programs. After several years of "field testing" the book, we offer an even more useful means for providing effective RTI in schools.

Some specific changes include:

- The first two chapters, "Using RTI With English Learners" (Chapter 1) and "The Big Picture: Cultural and Linguistic Realities" (Chapter 2) have been updated and recent research has been included.

- A new chapter on assessment, "Assessment and Data-Based Decision Making for English Learners" (Chapter 3) is included. In our work with schools across the country, questions about the assessment of English learners dominate discussions. In this chapter we address universal screening, progress monitoring, diagnostic measures, and data-based decision making. A sample class is presented and the reader is "walked through" the assessment process, including the use of Curriculum-Based Measures (CBM).

- Chapter 4, "Tier 1: What Is Best Practice for Teaching English Learners?" has been updated and includes a new SIOP lesson plan so that readers can see the features of high-quality instruction. New research has been added to the chapter as well.

- The chapter "Tier 2 and Tier 3 Interventions for English Learners" (Chapter 5) reflects the evolution of RTI implementation in schools. We suggest that the principles of intervention are similar across tiers or levels and the focus is on key elements of effective intervention, regardless of how many levels an RTI program includes.

- A new chapter, "How to Distinguish Disability from Linguistic Differences" (Chapter 6), is included. Drawing on information in the first edition, this chapter expands the previous discussion about issues surrounding English learners and decisions about learning disabilities, and provides guidance about what might be expected for students learning in a second language. Included are new recommendations for assessing English learners for learning disabilities and the role of the site-based decision-making team.

- The revision of the chapter "Special Considerations for Secondary English Learners" (Chapter 7) reflects changes in practice and research as related to RTI in the secondary grades. RTI initially was used mostly in elementary schools, but increasingly, secondary teachers are adopting RTI assessments and instructional practices as described in this chapter.

- Each chapter includes the feature From the Field, in which a teacher, administrator, school psychologist, or other specialist shares his or her insight about a topic. Half of the interviews are new to this edition.

- This edition includes a subscription to the PDToolkit for SIOP, an online site for readers that provides access to a variety of resources. Included in the PDToolkit for SIOP are video clips that illustrate ideas in the book, such as demonstration lessons or RTI team meetings, downloadable forms found in the book, and a sample IEP that addresses the needs of an English learner with learning disabilities.

We hope that this book will help educators design effective RTI programs that provide the appropriate type of instruction that English learners need and deserve in elementary and secondary schools. It is organized into seven chapters that include the following:

- **Chapter 1, "Using RTI with English Learners."** In this chapter, we introduce Response to Intervention and discuss its purposes, goals, and components, especially as they relate to English learners.

- **Chapter 2, "The Big Picture: Cultural and Linguistic Realities."** This chapter focuses on linguistic and academic issues for English learners, including educational, socioeconomic, and cultural factors that impact student success.

- **Chapter 3, "Assessment and Data-Based Decision Making for English Learners."** In this chapter, we discuss the three types of assessments that are used most often in RTI models, and how to use the data from these assessments to make decisions regarding instruction and intervention for English learners.

- **Chapter 4, "Tier 1: What Is Best Practice for Teaching English Learners?"** In this chapter, we discuss research-validated instructional practices for Tier 1 for English learners, including effective literacy instruction and the SIOP® Model.

- **Chapter 5, "Tier 2 and Tier 3 Interventions for English Learners."** Within the RTI framework, we discuss appropriate and effective interventions for English learners, including the five key elements for establishing Tier 2 and Tier 3 interventions across grade level and content area assessments.

- **Chapter 6, "How to Distinguish Disability from Linguistic Differences."** A vexing issue for educators is identifying learning disabilities in English learners. In this chapter we discuss research on second language learners and offer suggestions about identifying learning disabilities in English learners.

- **Chapter 7, "Special Considerations for Secondary English Learners."** In this chapter, we provide suggestions for how to develop effective RTI programs for English learners in middle, junior, and high schools, focusing on how these programs differ from those at the elementary level.

- **Appendixes and Glossary.** Pertinent text from IDEA 2004 is found in Appendix A. Frequently Asked Questions (FAQs) are asked and answered in Appendix B. The SIOP Protocol is included in Appendix C. Some student scenarios for reflection and discussion are found in Appendix D. The Glossary includes terminology for both RTI and second language acquisition.

eBook Options Available and PDToolKit

Look for availability of eBook platforms and accessibility for a variety of devices on **www.mypearsonstore.com** by inserting the ISBN of this text and searching for access codes that will allow you to choose your most convenient online usage.

Accompanying *Response to Intervention (RTI) and English Learners: Using the SIOP® Model,* Second Edition, is an online resource site with media tools that, together with the text, provides you with the tools you need to implement the SIOP® Model within an RTI framework.

The PDToolkit for SIOP is available free for twelve months after you use the password that comes with this book. After that, you can subscribe for an additional twelve months. Be sure to explore and download the resources available at the website.

Currently the following resources are available:

- Information About the Authors

- SIOP Research

- SIOP Resources, including RTI documents

- SIOP Lesson Plans and Activities, including Tier 2 and Tier 3 lesson plans

- SIOP Videos (Note: In this section there are a number of videos that specifically address aspects of RTI. In addition, there are videos that show SIOP lessons. These video segments were filmed in classrooms with real teachers and students. They have been edited for brevity so you will not see all SIOP features in every video. The teachers who agreed to share their SIOP lessons represent a range of teacher implementation from experienced, high implementers to teachers just learning the model. We hope you will find all the videos informative and helpful as you implement RTI in your school or district.)

To learn more, please visit:
http://pdtoolkit.pearson.com

Acknowledgments

We acknowledge and thank our reviewers for this book, including Gretchen Anderson, Pocatello/Chubbuck School District in Pocatello, ID; Susan D. Tillery, Clermont Elementary in Clermont, FL; and Annmarie Urso, the State University of New York at Geneseo. Their suggestions and ideas have enhanced our thinking and the recommendations we make in this book.

We offer great appreciation to our contributors Mardell Nash, Vivan Chinn, Susan Leonard-Giesen, Phil Giesen, Rebecca Canges, Candice Chick, and a special "thank you" to Jacob Seinturier. As always, we feel very fortunate to have Aurora Martínez as our editor, and we thank her for ongoing advice, support, and friendship. Finally, we offer special appreciation to our co-author, co-researcher, and dear friend, Dr. Deborah Short.

je, crt, mev

Response to Intervention (RTI) and English Learners

Using the SIOP® Model

1 Using RTI with English Learners

Monkey Business/Fotolia

In Ms. Caliari's class, Maribel tends to be a quiet but friendly child. One of 11 English learners (or former English learners) in the class, Maribel enjoys math and does fine, but lags behind the others in literacy. Ms. Caliari scaffolds instruction, uses teaching techniques to make the information understandable, and incorporates activities for developing academic

English proficiency. But Maribel continues to struggle. The RTI team at Rodriguez Elementary School considered Maribel's test scores, classroom performance, and English language proficiency when they assigned her to intervention for 30 minutes per day. During that time, Maribel receives focused instruction in reading comprehension with specific attention to vocabulary development skills that the team determined were below what they should be. Maribel's progress is documented regularly to ensure that the intervention is meeting her needs and that she acquires the necessary skills to participate successfully in literacy activities.

When students like Maribel struggle in school, an increasing number of districts and schools are using Response to Intervention (RTI) to provide support. RTI is an instructional delivery model that is designed to identify at-risk learners like Maribel early and to provide appropriate services to them. Since English learners are the fastest growing segment of the school population in the United States, our goal is to describe how RTI is most effectively applied to English learners.

In this book we promote the notion that RTI represents a way for schools to reshape general education into a multileveled system oriented toward early intervention and prevention of learning problems (Fuchs, Fuchs, & Compton, 2012; Kampwirth & Powers, 2012). Although RTI originated from the 2004 Individuals with Disabilities Education Act (IDEA) as a framework to both prevent mislabeling and overidentifying students as having disabilities and to identify students with learning disabilities accurately, it has had a significant impact on the design and delivery of literacy programs in elementary schools throughout the nation (Brozo, 2010) and has changed the way secondary schools address the needs of struggling learners (Reed, Wexler, & Vaughn, 2012).

RTI Is an Opportunity

With the implementation of the Common Core State Standards (CCSS) and Next Generation Science Standards, greater numbers of students may struggle as they are faced with more complex reading material, more challenging math and science concepts, and overall higher academic standards. There is growing concern about how to best serve English learners who are encountering new, rigorous content in a new language. High dropout rates—especially among Latinos—overall poor academic performance, and disproportionate representation of English learners in special education classes (both over- and underrepresentation) are some of the realities that contribute to this concern. In the current educational context, an RTI process offers school personnel an effective way to support student learning and make informed decisions about improving student performance. It provides a framework that enables students to receive the kind of education they need and deserve.

Click on SIOP Videos, then search for "What is RTI?" to find out about the origin of RTI and its purpose.

It may be tempting to consider RTI the latest "new thing" schools are required to do; however, since it is part of federal legislation RTI is here to stay. RTI came about because historically, when students experienced academic difficulty or behavior problems, the most common response was to wait until the problem was acute enough that they would then be referred to special education programs. This often meant waiting until students fell far behind or in some cases, until individuals had a long, documented history of behavior issues. Over the past 25 years, educators have proposed and experimented with a number of alternative approaches to strengthening the academic achievement of low-performing students as well as identifying more accurately students with learning disabilities (Fuchs & Deshler, 2007; Gersten & Dimino, 2006; Marston et al., 2007). Most recently, RTI has emerged as a more effective process for serving the needs of students with academic and/or behavioral concerns than the traditional "wait to fail" or "identify-test-qualify-place" procedure. Advocates were successful in having RTI included in the Individuals with Disabilities Education Improvement Act of 2004 (IDEA 2004) so that districts have a choice in how they attend to struggling learners (see Appendix A for IDEA Regulations).

We suggest that RTI be viewed as an opportunity to use a school's or a district's existing resources, programs, personnel, effective teaching practices, assessments, and data systems in a comprehensive way to offer an optimal learning environment for all students. A well-implemented RTI model establishes a closer working relationship among professionals who are engaged in the education of our most at-risk students. The kind of collaboration that RTI offers is commonly carried out through Professional Learning Communities (PLCs), which provide a structure for teachers and administrators to engage in an ongoing process of improvement. From our experience in schools, we've seen myriad ways that staff work together toward this goal. PLCs often have subgroups that meet as teams for specific purposes: grade-level teams for lesson planning, aligning curriculum and instruction, and planning interventions based on data, and an RTI team for implementing the model and overseeing professional development. In addition, a site-based team (also called student study team, teacher assistance team, school-based intervention team) analyzes student data and makes recommendations about more intensive intervention for students who struggle academically and may be considered for special education services.

Effective RTI is an overarching conceptual framework that guides the entire school improvement process for all students. It provides schools with an opportunity to reduce the number of students who experience academic and behavior problems, including those who eventually become labeled as having a disability. We might think of RTI outcomes even more broadly: "to prevent the kinds of life-limiting results of inadequate academic performance such as school dropout, unemployment, incarceration, and poor health" (Fuchs, Fuchs, & Compton, 2012, p. 270). RTI was founded on the principles that (a) all children can learn when provided with appropriate, effective instruction and (b) most academic difficulties can be prevented with early identification of need followed by immediate intervention (Fuchs & Deshler, 2007).

Study of human development confirms that all individuals can and will learn under the right conditions. RTI shifts the focus away from the child having a "problem" and onto the learning conditions of the classroom and school. Students benefit when teachers create a learning environment that promotes linguistic and cognitive development using materials, teaching methods, and settings that will facilitate learning for each student.

RTI in Practice

Let us begin by stating that there is no single, agreed-upon "model" for implementing RTI, particularly since IDEA does not provide specific guidelines and procedures. Across the country, states and districts require elements of RTI that may vary slightly from one another, but essentially all RTI approaches contain the components seen in Figure 1.1. Some districts prefer to call the process by other names such as "response to instruction" to highlight the important role of teaching in the learning process. In this example, it is called RTI^2, emphasizing both instruction and intervention. The intent of RTI is to move away from looking at poor learning outcomes as an indication that there is something wrong with the student and instead to think about what teachers need to do to make the student successful. It may be

Figure 1.1 Core Components of RTI[2]: Response to Instruction and Intervention

Source: http://www.cde.ca.gove/ci/cr/ri/rticorecomponents.asp.

1. High-quality classroom instruction
2. High expectations
3. Assessments and data collection
4. Problem-solving systems approach
5. Research-based interventions
6. Positive behavioral support
7. Fidelity of program implementation
8. Staff development and collaboration
9. Parent/family involvement
10. Specific learning disability determination

Figure 1.2 A Multi-Tiered Model of RTI for English Learners

Source: Modified from Echevarria & Hasbrouck.

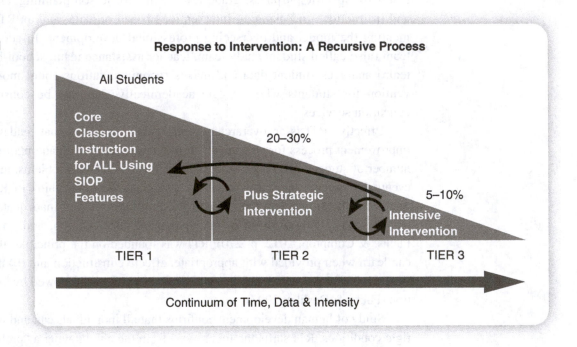

Response to Intervention: A Recursive Process

All Students

Core Classroom Instruction for ALL Using SIOP Features

20–30%

Plus Strategic Intervention

5–10%

Intensive Intervention

TIER 1   TIER 2   TIER 3

Continuum of Time, Data & Intensity

helpful to consider the process as "responsiveness of instruction" (Hiebert, Stewart, & Uzicanin, 2010), which rightly places responsibility for student improvement on teaching methods, materials, grouping, pace, and so forth.

Click on SIOP Videos, then search for "How Does the SIOP® Model Fit Into RTI Programs?" to listen to ways that a multi-tiered RTI model benefits English learners.

A Multi-Tiered Approach

Although commonly referred to as a three-tiered approach, more generally RTI is a multi-tiered approach because there may be more than three tiers or levels in an RTI process. As shown in Figure 1.2, the tiers typically represent the following: Tier 1 is the general education classroom where all students receive instruction in the core curriculum. Tier 2 provides intervention in a specific academic area for those students who need it. Tier 2 instruction is often done by general education teachers, and it supplements the core curriculum and classroom practice. Although Tier 2 provides additional support, general education teachers continue to be responsible for providing modifications in Tier 1 as needed to ensure student success. (Later in this chapter we will discuss specific modifications and adaptations that take place in Tier 1.) Tier 3 is usually provided by special education teachers, reading specialists, or a specially trained school professional. Teaching involves more intensive, individualized intervention and may or may not include students with identified disabilities who have an Individualized Education Plan (IEP). In some models, students with IEPs receive special education services in Tier 4.

In practice, RTI should be thought of as a continuum of services that increases in intensity based on student need and is recursive in nature. Students move in and out of tiered services depending on the level of intensity required to support specific skill development in language, reading, writing, or math. For example, a student may require Tier 2 intervention in math, but also receive Tier 3 intervention in reading. The duration of intervention and the decision about whether a student is dismissed from intervention or requires more intensive intervention depends on the needs of the learner. The number of levels or tiers offered is not as important as having a systematic approach in place that works best for students. When RTI is used with English learners some initial considerations include:

- how instruction (and intervention) are provided to students
- who provides this instruction
- how these students learn most effectively

The goal for English learners—and all students—is to achieve positive academic outcomes using the elements described in the rest of this section.

Provide High-Quality Instruction

RTI begins with solid, evidence-based instruction in the general education classroom provided by a highly qualified teacher and includes regular assessment of student progress. In the case of English learners, we propose that the research-validated SIOP® Model (Sheltered Instruction Observation Protocol) is the most effective approach to general education instruction because it has been shown to improve the achievement of both English learners and English speaking students alike when implemented with fidelity (Echevarria, 2012; Echevarria, Richards-Tutor, Canges, & Francis, 2011; Echevarria, Richards-Tutor, Chinn, & Ratleff, 2011; Echevarria, Short, & Powers, 2006; Honigsfeld & Cohan, 2008; McIntyre et al., 2010; Short, Fidelman, & Louguit, 2012).

Sheltered instruction is a method of teaching that uses strategies and techniques to make instruction comprehensible for learners while promoting academic language development at the same time. The SIOP® Model is a lesson planning and delivery system that is composed of eight components, each of which reflects research-based practices that should be used systematically and regularly in the general education classroom, as discussed in detail in Chapter 4. Many of these practices are widely known, such as scaffolding, differentiating instruction, providing clear instructions and explanations, and using repetition, but they are not consistently practiced in every lesson. Using the SIOP® Model is a way to ensure that best practices become habitual.

From the Field Best Practice for Using RTI with English Learners

Price Elementary has a diverse student population, consisting of 85% Hispanic, 9% white, 2.2% Asian, 1% African American, and 2.7% other ethnicities. Nearly 56% of the 760 students at this urban K–5 school are socioeconomically disadvantaged and 29% are English learners. There were 143 fluent English-proficient students (former English learners) with 30 English learners having been reclassified during the 2008–09 school year. The school places an emphasis on English language development in all classes; each day, a minimum of 30 minutes is set aside to work specifically on English language development, including oral language practice and vocabulary development.

The RTI process at Price is called *Team Up*, a name that accurately connotes school-wide collaboration. Representatives from general education, ESL, and special education meet regularly to analyze progress monitoring data and make decisions about students. All teachers receive ongoing professional development in the SIOP® Model to ensure that the features of best practice for English learners are present in instruction and intervention school-wide.

In observing classes at Price, English learners are engaged in rich, meaningful discussion and activities around text, which develops important oral language skills. Teachers use techniques designed to encourage active participation, and they provide students with the support they need to be successful in each lesson. Lessons are guided by content and language objectives, and are differentiated to meet the needs of students of varying ability levels. English learners work alongside English-speaking students on engaging tasks and assignments.

Specific RTI support in literacy occurs one period each day at the same time for all students. Students across grade levels (K–1, 2–3, 4–5) are grouped based on progress monitoring results and decisions made by the RTI team. Students with the greatest need (Tier 3) have a lower student-teacher ratio than others receiving intervention (Tier 2), which provides varying levels of intensity based on need. For example, children in grades 2 and 3 receiving Tier 3 intervention might be in a group consisting of three students working on a specific skill area (e.g., reading comprehension) with a special education teacher while another group of two students is instructed by a paraprofessional. In both Tier 2 and Tier 3, intervention is provided by both general education and special education teachers and personnel assignments are based on student need. While Tier 2 intervention might typically be delivered by a general education teacher, a particular group may require the expertise of a special education teacher for a period of time. ESL teachers also provide support since English language development is an area of emphasis during intervention in both Tier 2 and Tier 3. In other words, the composition of groups and personnel assigned to groups is fluid; one week the ESL teacher may work with a group of students in Tier 2, and the following week she may teach another group, depending on student need and available personnel. Students reading at or above grade level work together with a general education teacher during this period.

While they are aware of the sociocultural influences on students' lives, such as poverty and linguistic differences, Price's staff nevertheless convey high expectations and instill confidence in students by communicating their belief that all students can meet academic standards. In-class observations reveal that class assignments challenge students yet provide support and encouragement. In one lesson observed by researchers, students including English learners were eager to share their work during oral presentations at the end of the period. The same positive atmosphere is apparent in Tier 2 and Tier 3 intervention. Teachers encourage students to learn skills by modeling, moving at a brisk but reasonable pace, and providing feedback to responses in a way that communicates confidence in students' ability to succeed: "Excellent, try another example. [Student makes error.] Ok, listen again and repeat what I say. [Student repeats accurately.] Good, I knew you could do it."

At Price Elementary, and throughout the district, there is a commitment to ongoing professional development. A cohort model is used as a way to ensure that over time, every teacher in the school (and teachers at the other 19 schools in the district) learns to implement the SIOP® Model of instruction. Each school in the district has a designated SIOP coach, a person who provides support and guides implementation at the school site, which is important for teacher practice to take root. All coaches meet once a month at the district office with the SIOP coordinator for continued professional development of their own. Additional professional development around RTI is conducted regularly with teachers, as well as paraprofessionals. Topics include conducting intervention with fidelity and effective progress monitoring. These professional development sessions also provide an opportunity for collaboration as teachers discuss issues together.

With the implementation of a school-wide RTI program, Price Elementary students appear to be making improvements academically. Each year, schools in California receive an Academic Performance Index (API) score (ranging from a low of 200 to a high of 1,000) which reflects a school's, or a student group's performance level, based on the results of statewide testing. Its purpose is to measure the academic performance and growth of schools. After the second year of *Team Up*, their increase in API scores was noteworthy: school-wide (+35), socioeconomically disadvantaged (+42), and English learners (+29). School personnel stated that the *Team Up* program provided the support they and the students needed to make academic progress.

A well-implemented RTI model acts as a "prevention system" when teachers create a learning environment that catches difficulties early and they provide the type of instruction and modifications that supports student learning. With implementation of Common Core State Standards, it is particularly important that teachers be alert to learning struggles. With the proper supports, students who struggle can make the progress necessary and in some cases, learning difficulties can be ameliorated. In either situation, the goal is maximizing student achievement and reducing behavior problems.

Unfortunately, this is not always the experience of struggling students and their families. As one parent recently emailed:

> If only we could get everyone who is involved in the education of our children to think about what the adults need to do to help students succeed instead of labeling children who struggle as defective and in need of fixing. My daughter has a nonverbal learning disability, which affects every aspect of her life (and mine), so I am a veteran of the special ed process. Our school district has been very good to us overall, and I am grateful for the special ed services that Cassie receives. She needs them in order to be successful in the general ed classroom. But we have encountered too many teachers along the way who seemed to feel that the onus was on Cassie to learn to do things their way rather than figuring out how they could adapt their ways to better meet Cassie's needs.

The foundation of RTI lies squarely in Tier 1, or general education. As Brozo (2010) asserts, "Within RTI, the frontline of prevention is Tier 1, or the general education classroom, where every student regardless of ability is to receive high-quality instruction. Thus, the preventive possibilities of RTI are only as good as the Tier 1 supports classroom teachers provide students" (p. 147). Even when students receive intervention, it is a small part of the day. During the majority of the school day, English learners are in general education and should be engaged in rich, meaningful discussion and activities around text. Teaching techniques are used that encourage active participation and provide students with the support they need to be successful in each lesson. Even if English learners receive Tier 2 and Tier 3 intervention, instruction in their general education classroom must reflect best practice for English learners.

Figure 1.3 What RTI Is/Is Not About

RTI is A/An . . .

- Process that begins **by focusing effective instruction** in the general education classroom. Emphasis is placed **on what the teacher needs to do to make the student successful,** providing instructional intervention in reading and mathematics, immediately upon recognition of student need.
- **Data-driven process** (using progress monitoring and assessments) to improve reading and math skills.
- **Collaborative effort** implemented within the general education system, coordinated with all other services including special education, Title I, ESL, Migrant Education, and School Improvement.
- **Alternative approach** to the diagnosis of a Learning Disability.
- Process that determines if the child responds **to scientific, research based intervention** as a part of the evaluation procedures.

RTI is NOT A/An . . .

- System for **identifying what is "wrong"** with the student.
- **Pre-referral system only.**
- **Holding place for students** with behavior and academic challenges.
- **Special education** placement.
- **Curriculum.**
- **Additional period** of ELD, math, or reading.
- **Adjective** (to describe students, teachers, or classes).

From our experience, the most effective programs are those that focus on finding out what students CAN do and searching for the type of instruction, modification, or accommodation that works for them, regardless of whether they have been diagnosed with a language/learning disability. Figure 1.3 shows that there are a number of misconceptions about the purpose of RTI and its role in a school or district. It is not merely a "new way" to refer students to special education, as some teachers have called it. Although some aspects of the RTI process may be similar to conducting and documenting pre-referral interventions, RTI is not a path toward special education services. In fact, it can prevent students from being referred unnecessarily for costly services if what they need is academic skills development (Ehren, 2013). Further, RTI is not a single classroom set aside where students are sent when they experience behavior and academic problems. Rather, RTI is an approach that involves all school personnel and, as mentioned previously, presents an opportunity for collaboration. Using this school-wide process, the success of students is the responsibility of everyone, not one teacher in one location. An RTI process searches for what will work most effectively to support each individual student's learning. Nor does it rely exclusively on a set of curricular materials developed for "intervention." While materials are an important part of instruction, RTI requires decision making based on data that reveal students' strengths and specific areas of need, not the same "packaged" intervention lessons for all students. Finally, please do not use RTI as an adjective to describe students, teachers, or classes (e.g., Mr. Cavale is the RTI teacher, or Miguel is RTI). Using the term as an adjective relegates the responsibility for successful RTI to one specific teacher or classroom and unnecessarily labels students who receive services.

RTI is not all about intervention—it is about focusing on effective instruction in the general education classroom and then using intervention effectively for students who continue to struggle. We want to prevent problems from occurring at the first sign of risk.

Identify Areas of Concern and Monitor Progress

Early identification and support for students at risk for poor learning outcomes and behavior problems is critical, especially given that in the past schools waited for students to fall significantly behind their peers before services were provided. Alba Ortiz, an expert in the field of bilingual special education says, "RTI may help us more quickly identify other factors contributing to low performance. It's important to respond early. You sometimes see third graders referred to special education, but once you examine their records, you realize they have been struggling with language since kindergarten. The more time passes, the harder it is to tell ESL issues from learning disabilities" (Council for Exceptional Children, 2008, p. 2). In high school, it is not uncommon for students to be referred for special education assessment when records indicate they have experienced learning difficulties throughout earlier grades.

The RTI process begins with high-quality instruction and universal screening. Universal screening is used to determine the performance or skill level of every student and to make decisions based on the findings. For students who are underperforming, further evaluation may be necessary to determine the exact nature and scope of the problem. Language proficiency should always be considered. Perhaps the student requires increased, focused ESL or English language development rather than intervention.

When ongoing monitoring data indicate a lack of progress, an appropriate research-based intervention is implemented. The interventions continue at increasing levels of intensity as needed to accelerate students' rate of learning. Progress is monitored closely to assess both the learning rate and the level of performance of individual students. Tier 2 and Tier 3 intervention are intended to be short term, lasting a specified number of weeks. Most students will be dismissed from Tier 2 services once they have acquired the skills they need. Students receiving Tier 3 intervention may need intensive support for a longer period of time, after which they may move to Tier 2 intervention for less intensive support. Some students may be dismissed from intervention altogether, but their progress is monitored regularly in case further problems arise.

It is important to remember that Tier 2 and Tier 3 interventions are not designed for students who are just having difficulty in meeting grade-level standards such as interpreting tables and graphs in math or finding a theme in a novel. Intervention is for students who have difficulty with key skills that impact more global success in content areas. For students who have difficulty in meeting specific standards, RTI provides an opportunity for educators to examine the general education classroom to ensure that research-validated instruction is in place and that teachers are meeting their students' needs. Some general practices for improving students' performance that supplement teaching include the following:

- conferencing with a parent or guardian
- conducting a health screening to check vision and hearing
- moving a student to another seat or to a carrel to reduce distractions
- allowing another student to translate using a student's native language
- designing a behavior or academic contract with a student and/or family
- reducing the number of math problems or questions in any subject area for a student
- conferencing with the student, using an interpreter if needed
- providing the student with assistive technology
- adjusting the level of difficulty of an assignment
- providing sentence frames, outlines of a text or lecture, or other scaffolds
- permitting students to complete an assignment using their native language
- giving a student extended time to complete an assignment or take a test

These would not be considered interventions. These practices are part of a teacher's repertoire for differentiating instruction as needed—the kinds of things "good" teachers do because they know these modifications and accommodations will facilitate their students' learning. In Figure 1.4 we illustrate the distinction between accommodations, modifications, and interventions. Modifications are changes a teacher makes so that the student can be successful, such as adding a word bank to an English learner's test. Accommodations are supports that a student has to have in place in order to be successful. such as taking a test orally instead of in writing. Whatever modifications or accommodations are provided, it is important to document them so that a comprehensive record of the student's education is created. The Record of Modifications and/or Accommodations (Figure 1.5) is useful for a number of purposes.

1. It provides a record of what was tried previously, for how long, and its effectiveness with the student that teachers can refer to as they think about how to modify instruction.

2. It provides a historical record for teachers in subsequent grades that might guide their instructional decisions.

3. It provides a record of Tier 1 classroom modifications that might help inform decisions if a student is considered for Tier 2 or Tier 3 intervention.

4. It may be useful when conferencing with parents to show the type of things that work well or to offer an account of modifications that were provided before their child was referred for more intensive intervention.

Figure 1.4 Clarifying RTI Terms

Accommodations	Modifications	Interventions
Use assistive technology	Simplify directions, providing picture support, if needed	Form small groups consisting of students with similar academic profiles (3–5 students, depending on intensity required)
Record reading assignment for homework and/or review	Reduce number of correct responses required (e.g., math problems)	Focus on specific skills, e.g., fluency and comprehension
Give a test orally so student can express knowledge without reading and/or writing	Slow the pace of instruction	Develop targeted vocabulary, using words in context with sufficient repetition
Provide peer tutoring	Adjust the level of difficulty of an assignment	Select materials appropriate for student's ability
Move the student's seat to reduce distractions	Give an outline for an assignment (in the native language, if needed)	Provide immediate, explicit feedback on responses
Pair student with a partner who speaks the student's native language	Provide sentence frames for oral participation and writing tasks	Increase intensity by lowering number of students in the group, providing intervention more frequently, and moving at a brisk pace

Figure 1.5   Record of Modifications and/or Accommodations

Student (Last Name) _____   First Name _____

Teacher Name _____

Modifications/Accommodations Note date(s) used, and outcome	K	1	2	3	4	5
Access to Recorded Books/Text						
Adapted Texts						
Assessment by Psychologist (informal)						
Behavior Contract						
Classroom Instructional Aide						
Cross Age Tutoring						
English Language Development/ESL						
Extended Time to Complete Assignment						
Health Screening						
Homework Helper						
In-School Counseling (Straight Talk, etc.)						
Kids Korner/Homework Time						
Language Proficiency Assessment						
Learning Specialist Support						
Modified Assignments						
Modified Class Assessments						

(continued)

Figure 1.5 (continued)

Modifications/Accommodations Note date(s) used, and outcome	K	1	2	3	4	5
Parent Contact Re: Absences/Tardies						
Peer Tutoring						
Primary Language Instruction						
Private Tutoring						
Psychologist Observation						
Retention						
RSP (Special Education Support)						
Small Group Math Instruction						
Small Group Reading Instruction						
Reading Intervention						
Special Classroom Seating						
Multidisciplinary Team Meeting						
Student Planner Monitored						
Summer School						
Tutoring from Adult Volunteer						

5. It provides documentation of each step of the RTI process, which is particularly important if a student eventually receives special education services. The outcomes of fair hearings and other legal challenges are often based on documentation or lack thereof (Kampwirth & Powers, 2012).

Remember that screening and progress monitoring are done for a purpose: to make instructional changes for those students identified as at-risk. So, we conduct screening and progress monitoring—and then do something with it. Students who make progress are moved out of groups, which creates more time for those who need it.

Provide Evidence-Based Intervention

For approximately 20%–30% of English learners, Tier 1 instruction alone is not sufficient for them to be successful academically. These students require Tier 2 and/or Tier 3 interventions. The intensity and nature of interventions are adjusted depending on a student's responsiveness. Interventions will vary by grade level and content area (i.e., reading, writing, and mathematics), but there are key elements for effective implementation across grade level and content areas. These elements are discussed in detail in Chapter 5 and include how to best group students and how to design and conduct effective interventions. Although there is limited research about which specific interventions are effective with English learners, it appears that some of the same interventions that are used with native English speakers can be used to improve the outcomes for English learners who receive core literacy instruction in English (Vanderwood & Nam, 2007).

Identify Learning Disabilities

As we have mentioned previously, the under- and overidentification of English learners and other diverse students for special education services makes RTI appealing for reaching more accurate eligibility decisions. During referral and eligibility decision making, well-implemented RTI takes into consideration the classroom context, including quality of instruction (particularly with regard to early literacy), teacher qualification to teach English learners, students' language proficiency match to materials and instruction, and other factors that have not typically been considered. In the past, school personnel have "seemed quick to attribute a child's struggles to internal deficits or the home environment" (Klinger, Sorrels, & Barrera, 2007, p. 225).

If English learners have received high-quality instruction in general education that is research-validated for English learners (Chapter 4), if their language proficiency and sociocultural context has been considered (Chapter 2), and if appropriate intervention has been tried and well documented (Chapter 5), yet they are not making progress with appropriate intervention (and other factors have been excluded as influences on their learning), then identification of a learning disability would be considered.

As one veteran teacher commented about identifying students who have not responded to intervention, "Be sure you've tried everything before referring a student for testing. It is very costly in terms of money, time, and labor. The special education teacher isn't teaching while she's testing; the school psychologist can't do other things when testing. You want to avoid unnecessary referrals." Well-implemented RTI holds promise for providing English learners with adequate opportunity to learn so that we can more accurately identify those who have learning disabilities and provide appropriate special education services to eligible students.

RTI Models

In addition to variations in the number of tiers used to deliver RTI services, schools also employ different approaches in implementation. The most common are a standard treatment protocol, a problem-solving model, and hybrid approaches. Although RTI components such as universal screening and using a multi-tiered process look similar under both standard treatment and problem-solving protocols, the approaches vary in how interventions are implemented.

Standard Treatment Protocol

In the standard treatment protocol, one standard intervention is given for a fixed duration to a group of students with similar needs. This approach assumes that providing the same research-based intervention to similarly grouped students introduces a level of quality control (National Association of State Directors of Special Education, 2005). For example, in Roosevelt School, students who test at the "struggling" level are automatically placed in one hour of supplemental literacy (or math) instruction. This Tier 2 intervention is in addition to general education literacy instruction. Students who test two grade levels below are placed in Tier 3, which is intensive intervention. (Tier 4 is special education.) Tier 3 curriculum and instruction typically supplants the core curriculum because it is intended to offer students something different to move them at an accelerated pace. One drawback is relying on assessment results to automatically place students in Tier 2 and Tier 3 interventions. With English learners, some assessments are questionable and may not be accurate for this population (Figueroa, 2002; Hosp & Madyun, 2007; Ortiz & Yates, 2002; Vanderwood & Nam, 2007).

In addition, teachers may not provide adequate modifications and accommodations in the general education classroom because they have come to rely on automatically sending struggling students to intervention. They do not have the level of support that problem-solving teams provide to assist teachers with ideas for modifications, instructional techniques and strategies, progress monitoring, and interpreting data.

Finally, we run the risk of beginning to think of RTI as a curriculum that students are plugged into rather than considering all options for making the student successful. Ultimately, the teacher always provides the intervention, not the materials.

Problem-Solving Model

In the problem-solving model, a team of practitioners identifies and evaluates the problems of an individual student and designs and implements flexible interventions to meet that student's needs. This model typically has four stages: problem identification, problem analysis, plan implementation, and plan evaluation. This model assumes that no one intervention is effective for all students (National Association of State Directors of Special Education, 2005). A key feature in successful RTI programs is teachers working together and examining data as a team, which may reduce the likelihood that a student will be misplaced (Haagar & Mahdavi, 2007). The team examines data and considers numerous possibilities for resolving the student's issues. Student progress is constantly monitored, and the team takes the results and discusses options.

In some schools, grade-level teams meet with others who provide intervention such as special education and ESL teachers and reading specialists to analyze student data and plan interventions. If a student fails to make progress, she would be referred to the site-based team, which includes a school psychologist, administrator, and other staff as appropriate.

For example, in Bellevue School the grade-level team analyzes student data and brainstorms ideas for improving the performance of underachieving students (typically the lowest 20%). For some students, the classroom modifications that the team suggests and the teacher implements provide the support they needed and the process ends. If a student's progress isn't adequate after receiving modifications/accommodations, the team revisits the problem-solving process. The student would most likely be recommended for Tier 2 intervention, which supplements classroom instruction. A student who is in Tier 2 will require a detailed plan about the intervention to be implemented. For example, in addition to the core curriculum and methods already in place, a student will meet with the teacher in a small group three times a week (frequency). During that time, they will work for 30 minutes (intensity) on phonemic awareness for a period of 6–12 weeks (duration of the intervention).

When the grade-level team is concerned that a student isn't making sufficient progress in spite of Tier 2 intervention, the student's teacher meets with the site-based team and presents documentation about the issue and what has been tried thus far. The team reviews the information and discusses the student (problem identification and problem analysis) (see Figure 1.6, RTI Intervention Record). They offer suggestions for intervention that are specific for addressing concerns about the student. The recommended interventions are used with the student (plan implementation), documenting the duration and outcome. Then the team examines the documentation and makes decisions about the appropriateness of those particular interventions based on how the student responded (plan evaluation). This team problem-solving process continues as long as the student experiences difficulty and is used when making decisions in both general education and special education, creating a well-integrated system of instruction and intervention guided by student outcome data.

The drawback of this model is that it is time and labor intensive. Also, to be effective, the problem-solving model requires a level of sophistication in terms of understanding instruction for English learners, recommending appropriate intervention based on specific student need, verifying accurate data collection and interpretation, and ensuring fidelity of intervention implementation.

Hybrid Approaches

The two approaches discussed above are not necessarily mutually exclusive, and in many cases a combination or hybrid of the two is used. Although there are various ways schools might implement RTI, in all cases it should involve a collaborative effort for making data-based decisions and efficiently allocating resources to improve student outcomes.

Making RTI Work

To begin using an RTI approach or to enhance the effectiveness of the one you are currently using, there are a number of issues to consider.

First, fidelity is critical. In education research, fidelity is defined as the degree to which an intervention or model of instruction is implemented as it was originally designed to be implemented (Gresham, MacMillan, Beebe-Frankenberger, & Bocian, 2000). Fidelity in the RTI process involves:

- **Instruction**—All students, including English learners, receive systematic, research-based teaching that is consistent and effective. Many districts commit to professional development to ensure that all teachers are highly qualified for teaching content area subjects as well as understanding effective instruction for English learners.

- **Intervention**—For students who struggle, intervention is implemented with high fidelity and in the specific way the approach was intended. Intervention involves research-validated instructional techniques and implementation approximates as closely as possible the original model used in the research.

● **RTI process**—Assessments are used accurately for benchmark/screening, skill diagnosis, and progress monitoring. Data are used effectively for making decisions about placement, instruction, and program evaluation. These aspects of RTI cross all tiers and are essential.

Second, an important aspect of effective RTI is documentation. Developing a comprehensive record of student performance—and how the school responded to assessment data—will provide critical information for decision making. Figure 1.6 shows a sample form that may be used to document initial concern (based on universal screening and/or teacher recommendation), the kind of modifications the teacher used in the classroom with the student,

Figure 1.6   RTI Intervention Record: A Problem-Solving Approach

RTI Record

Student: _____ Grade: ___ DOB: _____ Date of Meeting: _____

Teacher: _____ School: _____

Reading: _____ Math: _____ English Proficiency Level: _____

Home Language: _____

Area(s) of Difficulty (Check)

☐ Articulation	☐ Writing	☐ Social Emotional
☐ Language	☐ Math	☐ History/Health Concerns
☐ Listening	☐ Motor Skills	☐ Attendance
☐ Reading	☐ Academic English	☐ Behavior

Specific Difficulty _____

Student's Strengths _____

Teacher Accommodations and/or Modifications (use a separate line for each

modification/accommodation) _____

Date Began: _____ Duration: _____

Outcome: _____

Specific Interventions Developed by RTI Site Council

Describe the intervention(s) _____

Frequency _____

Duration _____

How will effectiveness be measured? _____

_____

Date of RTI Site Council Follow-up Meeting: _____

Summary of intevention effectiveness (after _____ weeks)

and the recommended intervention, duration, and outcome. This form reflects a problem-solving approach to RTI as noted by the "RTI Site Council."

Third, effective RTI requires administrative support to ensure it is implemented well. In Figure 1.7 we have provided some questions for administrators to consider for implementing high-quality RTI. Teachers and other school personnel need to be aware of effective instructional practices for all students, including the research for teaching English learners presented in Chapter 4. In addition, the development of procedures for accurate assessment of students and collection and interpretation of data are critical since these results will be used to inform instructional decisions. Figure 1.8 provides some questions for teachers to consider during the planning phase when developing assessments and collecting student data. We want to create optimal

Figure 1.7 Questions to Consider: Administrative Support

- Are you supervising the RTI process by going into classrooms, checking lesson plans, observing instruction with English learners, reviewing data, and monitoring intervention?
- Are you using all your staff effectively by encouraging collaboration between general educators, ESL and bilingual personnel, special educators, and other specialists?
- Have you provided adequate time for teachers to discuss at-risk students? Where in the schedule could you fit that in? Is there a specific room to discuss RTI? (Not the lunch room!)
- Do you oversee the foms needed for the process? (For example, are they updated, are they accessible for teachers, are there enough copies?) Do the forms specifically address issues related to English learners (e.g., language development, cultural considerations)?
- Are your teachers qualified to work effectively with English learners?
- Are the student assessments used appropriate for English learners?
- What kind of professional development do your teachers need? Do you have a plan that prioritizes topics (e.g., providing effective instruction for English learners, understanding second language acquisition, implementing the RTI process, and monitoring progress and interpreting data)?
- Have you established relationships with culturally diverse families? Have you made sufficient effort to involve them in the RTI process as valued partners?
- Are you following through on certain students who require it? Do you contact families who aren't following through with agreements? Is someone checking on a student who has poor attendance?

Figure 1.8 Questions for Teachers to Consider: Preparing Assessments and Collecting Data

- Are you giving ample time for the student to complete the task?
- Would another day be advantageous for testing the student because s/he is tired or ill?
- Are you testing in a place with minimal distractions?
- Are you doing the testing yourself, or are you relying on someone unfamiliar with the student?
- Will a tester unfamiliar with the child recognize progress since that person may not be aware of the child's English proficiency level or areas of difficulty, e.g., articulation problems?
- Is the language demand too high for the student's English proficiency level?
- Are you repeating the directions as needed? Are you checking for understanding? Can the student explain to you what you want him or her to do on the test?
- Does the student need the instructions translated into his/her home language?
- Have you pre-taught the vocabulary of the task you're testing the student on?

conditions for students to demonstrate their knowledge and skills. Collaboration among school personnel facilitates understanding of student data results and increases the likelihood that the results will be interpreted accurately and used effectively. As the questions for administrators imply (Figure 1.7), time needs to be set aside for collaboration.

Further, effective RTI requires substantial professional development. Districts should create a long-term professional development plan that addresses the fidelity of both the instruction and intervention and the implementation of the components of RTI. Professional development needs to be ongoing and sustained to support teachers in:

- providing high-quality instruction and intervention
- selecting and accurately administering assessments for benchmark/screening, skill diagnosis, and progress monitoring
- using assessments for decisions about placement, instruction, and program evaluation

Finally, in Appendix B we provide answers to some frequently asked questions (FAQs) about implementing RTI and making it work effectively for English learners.

Final Thoughts

In this chapter we have discussed that RTI is a multi-tiered instructional delivery model designed to identify at-risk learners early and to provide appropriate services to them. In the current era of high standards, including the Common Core State Standards (CCSS) and Next Generation Science Standards, RTI offers a process for supporting students' academic progress and for systematically addressing the needs of those students who struggle with the skills required to meet high standards. In the remainder of this book we will elaborate on many of the ideas presented in this chapter, preparing readers to implement RTI effectively. In the next chapter we will discuss factors that impact learning for English learners and should be part of the discussion whenever an English learner struggles academically or behaviorally.

For Reflection and Discussion

1. Why is RTI especially important with the advent of CCSS and Next Generation Science Standards?

2. In the Standard Treatment Protocol, what is the drawback to relying on assessment results to automatically place students in Tier 2 intervention? What about Tier 3?

3. The students at Cabrillo Middle School are supposed to be assessed every four weeks to make sure they are making adequate progress academically. However, due to absenteeism, school activities, teacher apathy, and other factors, the practice isn't consistent. The idea of RTI is to provide a quick response to academic problems, but these students are falling farther behind without intervention, consistent documentation, and progress monitoring. If you were a district administrator in charge of implementing an RTI model, what recommendations would you make to the school administration and staff?

4. Why is fidelity such a critical issue for RTI? How might you ensure that a school staff is implementing the process with fidelity?

2 The Big Picture: Cultural and Linguistic Realities

Diego Cervo/Fotolia

The challenge for English learners is that they are learning rigorous, standards-based content in a language in which they are not yet fully proficient. They attend schools with practices and expectations that they may not understand completely and that may not reflect the values of their home. So, English learners are learning the language of English at the same time they are studying curricular content, learning how to express their ideas, and trying to understand the ways of a school environment—all through English.

As schools implement the Common Core State Standards (CCSS), many educators are concerned that English learners will struggle to meet these more academically demanding standards and may end up being labeled as having learning problems. To give you an idea of what it is like to try to make sense of a difficult concept, the following explanation of how to use formulas for converting radians to degrees and back might suffice. Could you explain this formula to a colleague in your own words?

> A radian is the measure of an angle that, when drawn as a central angle of a circle, inter-cepts an arc whose length is equal to the length of the radius of the circle. The length of 1 radius stretches out to a portion of the circle. That portion is 1 radian of the circle. There is a simple formula to convert radians to degrees: 1 radian = 180. Therefore you can easily convert from one unit of measure to the other.

For some of you, the task was easy. For others, you tried with some difficulty to make sense of it, perhaps using your academic background. Some of you undoubtedly disengaged—lost interest immediately and didn't even attempt to decipher the text. Other readers may have been moderately successful in making sense of the text but with lots of energy expended. This task represents the experience of millions of students in our schools every day, except that for them the task is presented in a language in which they are not yet proficient.

The intent of this chapter is to help educators understand that in our efforts to assist students in reaching benchmarks, attaining standards, and passing standardized tests, we may lose sight of the child as a whole person. There are myriad influences and realities that impact learning, especially for English learners. Some realities to keep in mind as we dis-cuss the education of English learners include:

1. Immigration almost inevitably includes (at least temporarily) issues such as loss of status and difficulty communicating. Students are put in the position of interpreting for their parents, which can impact family roles and lead to feelings of inadequacy. Imagine your own feeling of incompetence if you had to depend on your own child to communicate with officials, doctors, teachers, and other people you encounter in everyday life. One of the teachers with whom we worked in our research had been a physician in Mexico, yet in the United States was teaching remedial science classes in a rough inner city high school. Over the years we have met many school staff such as teacher aides who held professional positions in their home country.

2. Poverty impacts learning. More than 60% of English learners come from poor families (Garcia & Jensen, 2007). The impact of poverty on learning is significant and includes the following realities for poor children: They have a greater risk of exposure to lead, which causes lower IQ, learning disabilities, and behavior problems; they suffer from hunger and poor nutrition; their parents typically do not engage in talking and reading with them, reducing language development and early literacy opportunities (at 36 months old, the vocabulary of children in professional families is more than double that of children in families receiving welfare); and they tend not to participate in summer enrichment programs, resulting in reading losses (Barton & Coley, 2009). Poverty is also the largest correlate of reading achievement. The number of students receiving free or reduced-price lunch in a school can provide a fairly accurate estimate about test scores.

3. Separation from loved ones, even their own parents, can lead to depression, feelings of isolation, and sadness. "The separation of children from their family members during immigration is a complex and long-lasting process that generates lingering long-distance emotional ties" (Suarez-Orozco, Suarez-Orozco, & Todorova, 2008, p. 69). English learners born in the United States may be separated from parents or significant family members because they have returned to the home country for extended periods of time or they did not immigrate with the rest of the family.

4. Household and family responsibilities may interfere with education. Low-performing students were more than three times as likely to report missing school to help with their families than high-performing students (Suarez-Orozco, Suarez-Orozco, & Todorova, 2008).

5. Hispanic children account for the largest percentage of English learners, yet they are the least prepared to begin their school careers. Hispanics between the ages of 3 and 5 years old were less likely to have parents involved in home literacy activities and were less likely to have school readiness skills than White or Black children (Simon et al., 2011).

6. Teacher attitudes affect student achievement. Teachers want students to behave in certain ways, and it is well documented that they give higher grades to those students they like and who behave in ways that suit their preference. These attitudes and expectations also extend to parents: Those who have time to participate in school activities are considered interested in their child's education and those who do not participate are deemed uninterested. Thompson (2008) concluded that her study of low-performing schools illustrated "the culture of low expectations and disrespect that prevails in schools that serve many Black and Latino families" (p. 52). When minority students perform poorly on tests and earn low grades, teachers often blame the students, their parents, and their circumstances. They attribute poor performance to being lazy, not valuing education, and having parents that don't care (Hale, 2001; Rodriguez, 2010; Thompson, 2004).

7. The challenges youngsters face when they enter American schools are particularly difficult for those who come during the middle school and high school years. They must not only learn English quickly so they can participate in interpersonal communication with teachers and peers but also acquire enough English to learn rigorous subject matter when instruction is conducted exclusively in English (Valdes, 2001).

We begin this chapter by discussing some issues to keep in the forefront of your mind as you read the remainder of this book. English learners—like all children—come to school with their own experiences, home values, and ideas. They "see" schooling through this cultural and experiential lens. We cannot cover all the issues English learners face in this chapter; indeed entire volumes are devoted to their impact on learners (e.g., Cummins, 2000; Glen & de Jong, 1996; Nutta, Mokhtari, & Strebel, 2012; Valdes, 2001), but we touch on some sociocultural and linguistic factors that impact learning and some critical issues for educating English learners.

We also discuss how effective schools can help mitigate outside-of-school factors that impact learning so that English learners experience success in school. The learning context for English learners presents a unique set of issues, and an RTI process will be more effective when educators are aware of these issues and adjust the process to accommodate these realities.

Issues Faced by English Learners in School

For more than three decades, researchers in bilingual special education have focused on the educational needs of culturally and linguistically diverse populations, the reasons many struggle in school, and the services provided to this group of students (Artiles & Trent, 1994; Baca & Cervantes, 1984; Cloud, 1993; Cummins, 1984; Echevarria, 1995; Figueroa, 2002; Gersten, Brengelamn, & Jiminez, 1994; Ortiz & Yates, 2002; Rueda, 1989; Ruiz, 1989). Over the years, this pioneering work has continued to influence the discussion around issues that impact student achievement and well-being. In particular, we discuss the issues of language proficiency, background knowledge and experience, and cultural values and norms and their impact on schooling for English learners.

Language Proficiency

Overall, English learners underperform in school compared to their English-speaking peers (Simon et al., 2011) and English proficiency is the greatest predictor of academic success for English learners—more than all other factors combined (Suarez-Orozco, Suarez-Orozco, & Todorova, 2008). When we refer to *academic English proficiency,* it is more than simply "learning English." The social, conversational speaking ability that one learns through exposure to a language is different from the academic language proficiency required in classroom settings and on standardized tests.

Academic language development is particularly important since academic English proficiency is highly predictive of educational success. Academic language is defined in a number of ways, such as the language of the classroom, the language of academic disciplines (science, history, mathematics, literary analysis), and the language of texts and literature. It is more abstract and decontextualized than conversational English and is not typically found in everyday settings. The ability to perform on tests, to extract meaning from text, and to argue a point verbally and in writing are essential skills for high levels of academic attainment. These and other language skills are required by the Common Core State Standards and are an essential part of schooling. Inherent in these skills is oral language proficiency which, in addition to being the foundation for participation in academic tasks, is significantly correlated with higher grades and even more strongly with achievement test outcomes (Suarez-Orozco, Suarez-Orozco, & Todorova, 2008).

A large part of academic language development involves vocabulary (Nagy, 2012). General academic vocabulary crosses curricular areas (Coxhead, 2000; Zwiers, 2008) and domain-specific vocabulary is associated with each content area. General terms include those found in all academic texts such as *analysis, cooperation,* and *definition.* Domain-specific vocabulary is associated with a discipline and includes terms such as *divisibility, histogram, unit conversion, variability,* and *expanded notation* in math; *conflict, colonization, interpret, relief map, longitude,* and *plateau* in social studies; and *magnetism, attraction, consumers, investigation,* and *igneous rock* in science. Although English Language Arts (ELA) would seem to have terms for general language development, in reality the study of ELA includes specific terms such as *homographs, characteristics of nonfiction, citations, text features, conjunctions,* and *logical fallacies.*

Research findings highlight the importance of providing high-quality English language development (ELD) for English learners (August & Shanahan, 2006). Effective teaching includes both content and language objectives in every lesson to ensure that there is an explicit focus on language development along with the topic or skill being taught. Further, ELD may be accelerated by providing a separate period in which the instructional focus is solely on language development (Saunders & Goldenberg, 2010).

Background Knowledge and Experience

Students come to school with a wealth of knowledge, and their previous cultural, language, and literacy experiences influence their ways of learning. In a culturally diverse classroom, students' background knowledge and experiences don't always align with the materials and

Click on SIOP Videos, then search for "Background Experiences and Knowledge" to listen to an example of the importance of acknowledging what students bring to the classroom.

content of the curriculum. Here is an example. This is a high stakes test you must pass. What are these sentences referring to? You have one chance to answer:

1. This type does not have a high cantle.

2. It is designed to provide optimal movement, including classical dressage.

3. A piece of equipment may vary in style based on discipline, but most feature some type of cavesson noseband.

4. Most standards require, as a minimum, jodhpurs.

If you don't have background in English horseback riding, then you most likely did not pass the test! So much of what we understand is based on our background experiences—or lack thereof. English learners are responsible for learning and understanding content that is based on assumptions of common experiences and may be, quite literally, foreign to them and their background experiences. Effective instruction for English learners connects new concepts with students' experiences and past learning. When students have knowledge of a topic, they have better recall and are better able to elaborate on it than those with limited knowledge of the subject (Chiesi, Spilich, & Voss, 1979; Marzano, 2004).

Some educators mistakenly think that the Common Core State Standards call for the elimination of linking text to students' background. As reading expert P. David Pearson pointed out, asking students to read without using background is like telling someone "You can breathe but don't use oxygen." The intent of the CCSS is for lessons to be more text driven with less time spent on general discussion, predicting, or "sharing" as prereading activities. Teachers ensure that English learners understand the topic or idea in the text and may spend a few minutes making it relevant for students, but the bulk of the lesson is grounded in the text, asking students for text evidence as a basis for discussion comments, for example, "Tell me why you think that" or "Show me where it says that in the text." Prereading preparation should focus on providing students with the tools they need to make sense of the text on their own (Shanahan, 2012/2013). Since rereading text is a prominent feature of the kind of lessons CCSS call for, English learners, like all students, will pick up some meaning on their own and the teacher will fill in the gaps as the text is read again.

Cultural Values and Norms

Cultural values are deeply engrained in us, although they may appear in subtle ways. They influence the way we interact with others, make sense of our environment, and deal with conflict. In fact, they permeate many aspects of daily life. Cultural norms and values are influenced by any number of factors including one's racial or ethnic group, the family's religious beliefs and practices, educational level, and socioeconomic status. Figure 2.1 shows other possible influences on one's culture.

School values and expectations are sometimes at odds with those found in the home and it may not be easy for students from culturally diverse families to adjust to these differing expectations. For example, the Common Core State Standards call for students to develop and use argumentation skills, a type of communication that may be in conflict with the student's cultural norms. Also, English learners may feel distant from peers and teachers because of differing parental expectations. In one study, 80% of immigrant students acknowledged that their parents had different rules than those of American parents (Suarez-Orozco, Suarez-Orozco, & Todorova, 2008). Other examples of cultural norms and values include notions of modesty and concepts of beauty, ways that language is learned and used, approaches to problem solving, order of time, and incentives to work (Hamayan, 2006).

Figure 2.1 Influences on Culture

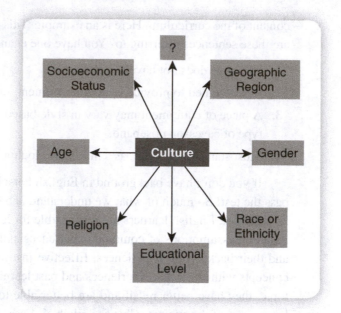

Education professionals who are knowledgeable about individual students' cultures should be included in the decision-making process of RTI because culturally appropriate interpretation of behavior and of data is critical when examining the academic progress of English learners.

The influences on learning discussed above are at the student level. We now turn to institutional influences, both those that impede learning and those that facilitate academic achievement.

Factors Associated with Underachievement

Researchers specializing in the status of English learners and children of immigrants suggest a number of factors that impact these students' well-being (Padron, Waxman, & Rivera, 2002; Rumberger, Gandara, & Merino, 2006; Suarez-Orozco, Suarez-Orozco, & Todorova, 2008).

Lack of Qualified Teachers

English learners, particularly those from low-income backgrounds, continue to have poor academic, social, and postsecondary outcomes (Barton & Coley, 2009; McCardle et al., 2005). There are many reasons that account for these outcomes including quality of teaching. Although teacher quality is strongly related to student achievement (Cochran-Smith & Zeichner, 2009; Darling-Hammond, 2000), teacher preparation programs in general education and special education have not kept pace with the need for more teachers who are qualified to work effectively with these students (Trent, Kea, & Oh, 2008). Few programs provide the kind of courses and experiences that adequately prepare new teachers to work effectively with English learners. Less than one-sixth of pre-service teacher preparation includes training on working with English learners (Ballantyne, Sanderman, & Levy, 2008).

One key factor beyond actual preparation for the job is the amount of experience teachers have in the classroom. It has been established that five or more years of teaching is considered the turning point in effectiveness. Hispanic students tend to have less experienced teachers, which impacts student achievement. Twenty percent of White 8th graders had teachers with four or fewer years of experience while 30% of Hispanic 8th graders did (Barton & Coley,

2009). Further, schools with high concentrations of English learners are less likely to have fully certified teachers than those with low concentrations of English learners, even after accounting for differences in poverty (Rumburger, Gandara, & Merino, 2006).

Finally, teacher turnover has a significant and negative impact on student achievement in both math and English Language Arts, and it is particularly harmful to the achievement of students in schools with large populations of low-performing and Black students (Ronfeldt, Loeb, & Wyckoff, 2013). This finding is important for English learners because teacher turnover rates are especially high in schools serving low-income, non-White, and low-achieving student populations. Nationally, about 30% of new teachers leave the profession within five years, and the turnover rate is about 50% higher in high-poverty schools as compared to more affluent ones (Darling-Hammond & Sykes, 2003).

All of these factors combine to provide a picture of English learners as disadvantaged, not because of their language, economic status, or cultural differences, but because they have not had the benefit of teachers who have the professional preparation and experience to teach them effectively.

Inappropriate Teaching Practices

English learners require adjustments to teaching (discussed specifically in Chapter 4) that enable them to understand the instruction. Too often English learners find themselves in classes where instruction is presented as if they are native English speakers. This kind of teaching hampers their access to the subject matter and their acquisition of the academic English they need to be successful in school.

In studies where researchers observed classrooms with English learners, instruction tended to be in whole-class settings with students generally doing passive activities, such as watching and listening. Teachers spent more time explaining than questioning, cueing, or prompting students, and they didn't encourage students to extend their oral responses, inadvertently denying them the opportunity to practice using academic English. The lessons were teacher dominated and included few authentic activities and little content that related to the students' lives outside of school (Ramirez et al., 1991; Rothstein & Santana, 2011; Waxman, Gray, & Padron, 2003).

Further, separating students by ability level for their classes (or by school) continues to be common practice, creating a "poverty of learning" for less advantaged students (Futrell & Gomez, 2008). Studies confirm that minority students and low-income students of all ability levels are overrepresented in the lower tracks and underrepresented in the higher tracks. In our own experience in mostly urban schools, we have witnessed the inequitable situation that research bears out. Segregating English learners from middle-class native English-speaking peers may be particularly harmful because the native language-speaking peers serve as language models, which facilitates English language development (Rumberger, Gandara, & Merino, 2006).

RTI has the potential to ameliorate entrenched practices of tracking students by monitoring each student's progress, changing grouping accordingly, and providing effective instruction tailored to the individual's level of English proficiency.

At-Risk School Environments

English learners are heavily concentrated in urban areas and attend schools that are often under-resourced and in which the school climate may be volatile. Students' perceptions about violence have been found to be highly related to their academic achievement

(Suarez-Orozco, Suarez-Orozco, & Todorova, 2008). This finding is significant given that between 2001 and 2005, Hispanic students reported an increase in the presence of gangs in schools (38.8% compared to 16.6% of White students) and Hispanic students were more likely to be involved in physical fights (18.3% compared to 11.6% of White students) (Barton & Coley, 2009).

In highly unstable environments where students feel at risk, threatened, or detached from a chaotic school climate, they are less likely to connect with peers, teachers, and staff. The impact on achievement is an interesting one. Positive relationships in school are important for the academic adaptation of students. Relational engagement is strongly correlated with behavioral engagement, defined as students doing their best on class work and homework, turning in assignments on time, paying attention and behaving appropriately in class, and maintaining good attendance. Not surprisingly, behavioral engagement is highly correlated with grades (Suarez-Orozco, Suarez-Orozco, & Todorova, 2008).

Factors Associated with Educational Success

English learners do well in some schools and poorly in others (EdSource, 2007). There are a number of factors that contribute to a student's performance in the classroom; in the following section we discuss some of the factors associated with success.

High Expectations for All Students

Student performance and achievement tend to rise and fall according to teacher expectations (Dudley-Marling & Michaels, 2012). Years of research have focused on the self-fulfilling prophesy in the classroom, where teacher expectations affect student achievement and behavior (Brophy & Good, 1970). In our own work, we have seen that when there is a school climate that values all students and expects each individual to achieve high standards, students outperform similar schools that do not hold high expectations (Echevarria, Short, & Vogt, 2008). The misperception of immigrant students as "pobrecitos" (poor little things) may lead to coddling of nontraditional students, which robs them of challenging learning experiences and prospects for achieving success (Adger & Locke, 2000).

High school is a critical time for college preparation or vocational and technical studies, yet in many urban areas students and staff alike have all but given up on the idea of achieving standards and graduating. Some high schools are beating the odds by offering to all students opportunities that are usually reserved only for the "best" students. Providing a rigorous program of study along with other features that engage students, these "High Schools That Work" are seeing positive outcomes as a result of having high expectations (Bottoms, 2007). In another successful program, even reluctant readers in high-poverty schools were taught to use critical thinking skills to discuss, argue, and write about topics, overcoming the misconception that these students "aren't up to" the challenge of a demanding curriculum (Schmoker, 2007).

Effective Teaching Practices

Specific, proven teaching practices discussed in detail in Chapter 4 provide the kind of instruction English learners require and deserve. Overall, highly effective teaching for English learners has a number of characteristics (Kelly, Gomez-Bellenge, Chen, & Schultz, 2008).

First, instruction is differentiated for learners so that they are provided with many opportunities to use reading, writing, and oral language in numerous ways across multiple academic content areas. In addition, teachers scaffold students' literacy attempts so that they will feel free to take risks. Effective teachers respect students' "funds of knowledge" (Moll et al., 1992) and integrate students' own experiences into lessons, which provide motivation to learn. Finally, use of small group instruction, one-to-one tutoring, extensive reading, and cooperative learning also enhances learning for English learners.

Within an RTI framework, when students struggle academically, the effectiveness of teaching is examined as a starting point. Jeanette Klinger and colleagues (Klinger & Edwards, 2006; Klinger, Sorrells, & Barrera, 2007) propose that decisions about instruction and intervention are guided by questions and concerns such as:

- How do we ensure that the child has in fact received culturally responsive, appropriate, quality instruction?
- How do we account for language and culture when designing interventions, conducting research, and generalizing findings?
- What do we mean when we say that instruction or intervention is "evidence-based"? What criteria are applied?
- In considering "evidence-based" interventions, what works with whom, by whom, and in what contexts?
- What does it mean when English learners do not respond to "research-based" instruction?
- To what extent might students be struggling because of limited English proficiency?
- Has adequate support in English language development been provided?
- To what extent has the "research-based" instruction been validated with English learners?
- Are most of the English learners in the classroom succeeding, while just one or two are not? Or are most English learners struggling?
- How should we decide what additional support to provide?

These questions and the issues they represent highlight the importance of effective teaching practices. Fundamentally, these questions point out that RTI isn't only about how students respond to instruction and intervention, but is also about how teachers and other personnel respond to English learners' needs.

Relationships of Respect

In her research about ways to help raise achievement for low-income students, Ruby Payne (2008) found that establishing positive relationships with students is a critical factor. She cites the following actions that indicate a teacher has respect for students, which were identified by students themselves:

The teacher calls me by my name.

The teacher answers my questions.

The teacher talks to me respectfully.

The teacher notices me and says, "Hi."

The teacher helps me when I need help.

These seemingly simple acts of respect toward students, coupled with awareness of the sociocultural influences on students' lives and the diversity of their life experiences, enhance communication and build positive relationships (Villegas & Lucas, 2007).

The Important Role of Parents

The importance of parent support is indisputable. Parents' involvement in their child's education is a factor that contributes to student achievement. Parents are also an important support to schools; they create a sense of community between the school and neighborhood, they offer assistance to staff, they are often our best informants about students, and they provide critical insights into cultural attitudes and practices.

Sometimes educators are puzzled when parents of English learners don't participate as fully as expected. Actually, culturally and linguistically diverse parents care very much about their children's success in school and want them to obtain as much education as possible, even through college (Goldenberg, 2006). A study that examined immigrant parent attitudes found that many parents make significant sacrifices in immigrating to the United States, with aspirations of a better life for themselves and their families. Seventy percent of the parents interviewed said that opportunity for their families was the main motivation for immigrating, with 18% explicitly stating that their children's education was the primary reason for coming. Further findings revealed that students themselves value education and recognize the importance of school. The overwhelming majority of students interviewed stated that school prepares you to get ahead and that studying hard leads to success (Suarez-Orozco, Suarez-Orozco, & Todorova, 2008).

Why Don't They Come?

If parents hold such high hopes for their children and communicate to them the value of education, then why is it a common teacher perception that parents are apathetic about their children's education? What are some barriers to active participation? The following are some of the many reasons that parents of English learners may not be as fully involved in the school as teachers might expect:

- **Language.** An obvious barrier to participation is not speaking English proficiently. It is likely uncomfortable for parents to be in a situation where they cannot understand the speaker and, in turn, are not understood themselves.

- **Unfamiliarity with the way schools function.** Culturally diverse parents may not understand the importance school personnel place on activities such as back-to-school night, parent-teacher conferences, and open house. Even if they are informed about such activities, they may think it is a courtesy letter and not realize that participation is expected. Further, parents may have responsibilities that preclude their participation, such as work or providing care for elders or young children.

- **Intimidation.** Many parents of English learners have low education levels and often find the level of discourse used and amount of information communicated overwhelming. Further, they may feel that they don't have much to contribute to a discussion with highly educated professionals, particularly in cultures that hold educators in high esteem. Finally, they may have had the common experience of immigrant parents who have been made to feel powerless against the "system."

- **Lack of awareness of their important role.** Parents in general are not familiar with the research on the influence they have on their child's learning. This is especially true with immigrant parents. In many other countries, parents are not encouraged to actively engage in their children's education, and it is the unspoken norm that this is the teacher's job (Sobel & Kugler, 2007). Once parents understand their role, they generally become willing participants (Goldenberg, 2004).

- **Economic circumstances.** Most immigrant parents arrive in the new country with very few resources. The poverty rate for children growing up in immigrant homes is double that of native-born families in the United States. These parents most likely cannot take time off work to attend meetings and activities.

- **Student's ability/disability.** Having a child who struggles in school because of academic and/or behavior issues can be painful for parents. Conferences that focus almost exclusively on the student's poor performance associated with a disability are a reminder of the dashed hopes and dreams these parents had for their child. Parents may avoid attending meetings so that they aren't put on the defensive or aren't made to feel like their parenting is being criticized by school personnel. Teachers need to be sensitive about depending on parents to "fix" the student's behavior, motivation, and academic issues because most likely the parents deal with many of the same problems at home—and look to the school for solutions. We want to work in partnership with parents, not overburden them with additional responsibilities. Further, parents respond to having a child with a disability in many different ways. You may know someone whose child struggles academically or socially, yet embraces the attitude that all kids have different strengths and they consider their child's difficulties a part of life. You may know someone else in the same situation who is constantly looking for the right teacher, doctor, or therapist to "cure" the problem. Just as individuals differ in their responses, there are also various cultural tendencies. In some cultures, having a disability brings shame on the family, whereas parents from other cultures may consider disability simply a fact of life. School personnel must be aware of cultural attitudes toward disability and, in every case, be extremely sensitive in their interaction with parents of students with disabilities.

What Can We Do?

The characteristics of effective schools include a welcoming attitude toward parents and formation of connections with the community (Shannon & Bylsma, 2007). We want to create a school environment that welcomes parents as partners, supports their needs, and provides opportunities for family and community involvement. Following are a few suggestions for garnering the support of families of English learners:

- **Be respectful.** School personnel must be welcoming to parents in word and deed. Some front offices in schools are toxic because the staff's attitude is unfriendly at best and sometimes even hostile. Administrators have the responsibility to set a positive, respectful tone in the school that is reflected by all staff. In particular, parents are affected by the attitude of their child's teacher.

- **Create a sense of community.** With the goal of shared responsibility for the school's success, parents and the school engage in a number of ways. Some schools have sophisticated programs that provide leadership training for immigrant parents, English as a Second Language classes, and parent resource centers. If that level of resources isn't available, there are other options for establishing an interdependent relationship between families and schools. Relatively simple yet important events such as weekly Coffee with the Principal communicate to parents that they are essential partners in the schooling endeavor.

- **Make specific suggestions for helping children academically.** Despite low levels of education, most families have at least one adult or older sibling who can assist children with homework. Also, parents can take their child to the library, look through books and talk about the pictures using the home language, and show enthusiasm for books and reading. In one school where we conducted research, parents attended regularly scheduled after-school "make and take" sessions where they learned, for example, the importance of using flash cards for memorizing math facts and vocabulary words. During the session, parents created a set of materials to use at home.

- **Encourage parent volunteers.** Even parents with low levels of education can have a role in the classroom. They may assist the teacher, work in small groups reviewing math facts or vocabulary cards, volunteer to share an experience or talent (music, cooking, or crafts), and participate in field trips and other events. This kind of participation helps bridge the home-school cultural divide that often exists.

- **Have interpreters available.** Students are often unreliable interpreters because they may screen information (Sobel & Kugler, 2007). Schools should invest in having reliable, trustworthy interpreters on hand both to provide information to parents and to assist parents in communicating with school personnel. The relationship is most effective when it is two-way, instead of just having school personnel unilaterally communicating with parents. Interpreters must be trustworthy because often the information being communicated, especially around the RTI process, is sensitive and needs to remain confidential.

- **Maintain regular communication.** Effective schools regularly send home newsletters that inform parents of what is happening at the school and include resources for parents. The National Center for Learning Disabilities has excellent resources for parents in Spanish to encourage early language and literacy development (http://www.getreadytoread.org/) as do the websites Colorín Colorado (www.ColorinColorado.org/families) and Reading Rockets (http://www.readingrockets.org/article/18935). In addition to written communication, regular phone calls to report a child's success and home visits are ways to establish good working relationships with families.

Parents and RTI

With effective RTI, parents are informed about their child's progress on a regular basis and their help is enlisted to support the instructional program at home. The From the Field box on page 33 features the insights shared by a veteran special education teacher who for many years team taught elementary students with a general education teacher in an inclusive setting called A Community of Learners. Students who are old enough should also be part of the process since participation by the student creates buy-in that improves the result of intervention (Hosp & Madyun, 2007). During a meeting, the student and parent are given an opportunity to offer their perspective and to discuss whether they agree with the school's assessment of areas of difficulty and suggested intervention. Documentation of each participant's input is important (see Figure 2.2) and a contract among the student, teacher, and parent helps ensure optimal results.

Figure 2.2   Parent/Student/Teacher Contract

K–8 Intensive Intervention Plan: Parent/Student/Teacher Contract

Student's Name: _____

Grade: _____   Birth Date: _____

School: _____

Date of Meeting: _____

To be completed by teacher:

1. Basis for determining the academic concern (Circle all that apply):

    ✓ Standards Test

    ✓ Classroom Assessment

    ✓ Report Card Grades

    ✓ Classroom Work Samples

    ✓ Other

2. Language Arts

    ✓ Phonemic Awareness

    ✓ Phonics

    ✓ Reading Comprehension

    ✓ Vocabulary Development

    ✓ Language Development

    ✓ Writing

    ✓ Spelling

3. Mathematics

    ✓ Number Sense

    ✓ Addition

    ✓ Subtraction

    ✓ Multiplication

    ✓ Division

    ✓ Skill Application

    ✓ Other

4. Performance Goal (state expected outcome from intervention):

    _____

    _____

5. Describe the intensive intervention program that would best achieve the performance goal:

    _____

    _____

Completed by: _____

(continued)

Figure 2.2 (continued)

To be completed by the parent and student:

6. As a parent I agree with the intervention plan and will be responsible for:

- Finding out how my child is progressing by attending conferences, looking at schoolwork, and/or calling the school.
- Providing him/her with a quiet place to study, free of interruption.
- Supervising my child's homework daily.
- Providing at least 20 minutes daily for my child to read silently and/or aloud.
- Providing additional instruction for my child (family member, neighbor, friend, tutor).
- Sending my child to school every day and on time.
- Monitoring the Minder Binder/Student Planner.
- Other plans to assist my child: _____

7. State the dates of implementation: _____

Start Date: _____

Completion Date: _____

I approve the Intensive Intervention Plan for this student:

Teacher's Signature _____

Date _____

Principal/Designee Signature _____

Date _____

I approve the Intensive Intervention Plan for my student:

Parent/Guardian Signature _____

Date _____

I agree with the Intensive Plan, will follow it and will put forth my best effort and cooperation with my teachers and parents.

Student Signature _____

Date _____

Parents should be informed about what progress monitoring is and what it means for their child. (See http://www.studentprogress.org/family/factsheet.asp for family resources and a fact sheet in English and Spanish.) As mentioned previously, a community worker or other person may be enlisted to assist families in understanding the process and in holding schools accountable. The following questions are important for parents to ask, particularly if their child is being considered for Tier 3 or special education services.

1. Is my child's teacher trained in effective instruction for English learners so that I know my child has been provided sufficient opportunities to learn?

2. What research-based instructional programs are being used, and what research supports the effectiveness of the program(s)?

3. Have the programs been validated on culturally and linguistically diverse populations?

From the Field | RTI and Parent Involvement

All parents want their children to succeed in school both academically and socially. However, for many parents involvement in their child's education is a daunting and uncomfortable process. Numerous factors influence this such as: limited understanding of the English language, lack of education, or feelings of intimidation about participating in the school process. Many parents depend on older siblings to navigate the educational path for their younger siblings, which at times is an unrealistic expectation placed upon the sibling.

How can we as educators help parents become more involved with a child who is struggling in school and become active participants in their child's education? For research has time and again shown that a parent's involvement in their child's education is a key factor in that child's success in school.

The Response to Intervention Model (RTI) provides levels of support for students before they begin to fail. The No Child Left Behind Act of 2001 and Individuals with Disabilities Education Improvement Act of 2004 both address the issue of helping students before they fall too far behind in school. With the RTI model educators are now examining a more comprehensive approach to early intervention in the classroom as well as outside of the classroom setting.

One of the key components of RTI in schools across the nation is assisting parents in recognizing the areas where their child is struggling and participating in an integral way in their child's progress in school. Many times parents express concern when the school district wants to "put a label" on their child, for fear that the child will be placed in special education classes and characterized as a child who needs extra assistance throughout his or her education. Without the knowledge behind them, many parents feel intimidated about contacting their child's classroom teacher and approaching the school district for help. They feel frustrated when they see their child failing in school but do not have the necessary expertise to assist the child through the various academic and behavioral supports that are necessary for him or her to succeed.

With the new processes in place using the RTI model, it is important for educators to inform parents in the early stages of a child's education and to be specific about the areas that the child is having difficulty with. They need to provide research-based data to back up their reporting and to inform parents of the interventions that will be employed to assist their child. Educators need to value parent input and realize that most parents really know their child and want to help him or her succeed.

A timetable needs to be clearly defined and parents need to see what the regular education expectation is for that particular skill that is deficient and impeding the child's progress. ... Parents need to be assured that the specific intervention will be done in a timely manner. The district should also provide parents with written material about their data collecting and the various programs being used to help their child improve his or her academic performance.

It would be beneficial for the district to provide parent workshops led by knowledgeable professionals with hands-on training for parents. The workshops could possibly provide parents with specific activities on how they can assist in helping their child succeed at home as well as in the school setting.

On a personal note as an educator I remember a meeting with parents of a special needs student and the parent later told me "I felt like I was at a meeting where no one really cared about my opinion. I felt like everyone was drinking out of ceramic mugs and I was given a Styrofoam cup." Educators need to be aware of the sensitive nature of dealing with both parents and the child who is struggling in school.

4. What process is used to match the intervention(s) to my child's academic, cultural, and linguistic needs?

5. How many weeks and minutes per day of instruction will my child receive in this program?

6. Given my child's English proficiency level, will this amount of time be sufficient?

7. How is my child's progress being assessed?

8. Is my child's English proficiency being taken into consideration in the assessment?

9. Is a written intervention plan provided in my home language as part of the RTI process?

10. How can I know that the interventions are being carried out as intended (with fidelity)?

11. What training is required to effectively teach the research-based programs?

12. Is my child's teacher trained in the intervention program as recommended by the publisher?

13. Does the training also include issues related to effective teaching for English learners?

Once parents are informed about and understand the importance of high-quality instruction and progress monitoring, some type of communication about the student's performance is sent home regularly. If the student is receiving Tier 2 or Tier 3 intervention, parents need to be informed of the results every couple of weeks (or more frequently) as data are collected and interpreted.

Final Thoughts

Understanding the issues that impact English learners is important, but perhaps never more so than in the current era of high academic standards, including the Common Core State Standards. There has been a long history of underachievement for English learners and the reasons are numerous. While there are factors outside of school that contribute, schools have not always supported culturally and linguistically diverse students in the ways they have needed in order to be successful academically. It is our hope that educators will learn and implement practices that respect students and their families, which will result in effective instructional programs for all students.

For Reflection and Discussion

1. The importance of having background knowledge and experiences that align with the content of lessons is undisputed. In your own learning, what are the conditions that facilitate understanding of new concepts or material, and what are impediments to learning?

2. Given the various facts about English learners and their families presented in this chapter, what do you consider to have the greatest impact on teaching and learning?

3. In what ways might you change your approach to working with English learners and their families after reading this chapter?

3 Assessment and Data-Based Decision Making for English Learners

Monkey Business/Fotolia

In an RTI model the purpose of assessing students is to make data-based decisions. Assessment allows us to identify students who need intervention, pinpoint specific areas of need, determine if intervention is effective, and ascertain which students are responsive to intervention. Without assessment, schools are not actually "doing" RTI. There are three types of assessments that typically are used within an RTI model: (1) universal screening measures, (2) progress monitoring measures, and (3) diagnostic measures. Each type of measure serves a different purpose within the model. In this chapter we will describe these three types of assessment and explain how to use the data from each one to make instructional decisions within an RTI model. We will follow Ms. Caliari's class and the grade 5 team at her school, Rodriguez Elementary School, as they gather assessment data and make decisions based on this data.

Accurate assessment has long been a concern of teachers with students who are English learners. For example, many assessments are not normed with populations of English learners, and often even assessments in students' native language are normed on populations of native-speaking students, for example in Spanish, and not on students who may not have fully developed primary languages, which is the case for many of our students. Within an RTI model most often the assessments used for decision making measure specific skills and may not consider the multiple dimensions of language and literacy that are needed for English learners to be successful. However, if we keep in mind that these assessments are *indicators* of student performance, use multiple measures for making decisions, and are cautious when interpreting the assessment data, then we can see that these measures provide us with information that is useful for making decisions about student response within an RTI model.

Using CBM in an RTI Model for English Learners

Before we describe each of the three types of measures and how they are used in an RTI model, it is important to provide a detailed discussion about curriculum-based measures (CBM).

CBM are assessment tools that are often employed in RTI models because they can be used for universal screening as well as progress monitoring. CBM are widely available and well-researched tools for collecting ongoing data during intervention (Wallace, Espin, McMaster, Deno, & Foegen, 2007). These measures were created to be reliable, valid, and practical so that teachers can administer the assessments quickly and interpret the scores of the assessments easily (Deno, 1985). In addition, CBM provide educators with data to determine if an intervention is effective; that is, the measures indicate whether students are making progress.

CBM provide individual student data so teachers can adjust instruction to meet the needs of each student (Deno, 1985). CBM assess students' initial performance and show progress on a particular skill. Small changes in student growth are revealed even if the student has not yet reached mastery in the skill (Fuchs, Fuchs, & Hamlett, 1993). This distinguishes CBM from other types of assessments, which are often mastery measures. Mastery assessments only give students credit if they have mastered the skill, and therefore they do not show changes over short periods of time. CBM often have multiple forms, usually called *probes*, of the same measure so that teachers can administer screening and progress monitoring assessments multiple times. They generally have established benchmarks, which are based on extensive research, that can be used to make decisions.

In Tables 3.1, 3.2, and 3.3, examples of CBM for reading, math, and writing are provided, including the grade levels for which these measures are appropriate. In addition, the National Center on Response to Intervention has on its website a review of screening and progress monitoring tools that is very helpful. The Center has published tool charts that have

Table 3.1 Examples of CBM for Reading

Measure	Skills Assessed	Grade Levels
Dynamic Indicators of Basic Early Literacy Skills (DIBELS) Also available in Spanish–Indicadores Dinámicos del Éxito en la Lectura (IDEL) http://dibels.org	Phonemic Awareness Alphabetic Principle Reading Fluency Comprehension (Retell, Maze) Vocabulary (Word Use)	K–6 (English) K–3 (Spanish)
Curriculum-Based Measurement in Reading (CBM-R) http://www.rti4success.org /progressMonitoringTools	Alphabetic Principle Reading Fluency Comprehension (Maze)	K–7
aimsweb www.aimsweb.com	Phonemic Awareness Alphabetic Principle Reading Fluency (Spanish & English) Comprehension (Maze Fluency)	K–8 1–8 (Spanish Passage Fluency)

Table 3.2 Examples of CBM for Math

Measure	Skills Assessed	Grade Levels
aimsweb www.aimsweb.com	Early Numeracy Math Computation Math Concepts and Applications	K–8
mClass-Math www.wirelessgeneration.com	Early Numeracy Math Computation Math Concepts	K–3
Project AAIMS Algebra Progress Monitoring Measures www.ci.hs.iastate.edu/aaims	Algebra	7 and up
Monitoring Basic Skills Progress (MBSP) http://www.proedinc.com	Math Computation Math Concepts	1–6

Table 3.3 Examples of CBM for Writing

Measure	Skills Assessed	Grade Levels
aimsweb www.aimsweb.com	Spelling Written Expression (scored as total words written, correct word sequences, words spelled correctly)	1–8
Early Writing Measures http://progressmonitoring.org/probes /earlywriting.html	Sentence Copying Written Expression	1

been created by the Center's Technical Review Committee (TRC). Additional instruments are added periodically, and we encourage you to review the tool charts to see which may be appropriate for your students and educational context at http://www.rti4success.org /toolschartsLanding.

Although many CBM have been found to be reliable and valid measures, when using these measures with English learners, we need to be cautious in selecting and interpreting the results of these assessments. There is a small amount of research literature that supports using reading CBM, particularly oral reading fluency measures, with second language learners (Graves, Plasencia-Peinado, Deno, & Johnson, 2005; Wayman, Wallace, & Wiley, 2007). However, research has also found that oral reading fluency may not be a reliable predictor of reading comprehension for English learners. English learners who have reading fluency scores in the average range may have reading comprehension scores that are well below average because of lack of vocabulary and other oral language skills (Crosson & Lesaux, 2011). Therefore, reading fluency assessments may actually underidentify English learners who may need intervention. Additionally, measures such as letter naming fluency, phoneme segmentation fluency, and nonsense word fluency have been found to be useful in predicting later reading achievement for English learner populations (Oh et al., 2007; Vanderwood, Kinklater, & Healy, 2008). In addition, Richards-Tutor and colleagues (2013) found that the local benchmark norms for kindergarten English learners on measures of phoneme segmentation and nonsense word fluency were very similar to the Dynamic Indicators of Basic Literacy Skills (DIBELS) benchmark cutoffs.

CBM tools have not been researched extensively with English learners, however, and therefore established benchmarks and cutoffs may not be appropriate for this population of students. There are a couple of solutions to this problem. One is to assess students in both English and their native language. For example, there are reading fluency measures available in English and Spanish (i.e., DIBELS/IDEL and *aimsweb* measures). Assessing students in both languages can be useful since English learners may have certain skills in Spanish but they may not be able to demonstrate these same skills in English because they have not had enough time to develop them. On the other hand, by assessing students in both languages, teachers may find that the student struggles to read in both languages and is not developing English language skills as quickly as other English learners. These students are likely in need of intervention. If students speak a language other than Spanish or they have few reading skills in their primary language, this may not be an adequate solution. Alternatively, instead of using benchmark cutoffs provided by the measurement tool, it is possible to create local norms if assessments are done across a grade level in a whole school or district. Available programs such as *aimsweb* allow local benchmarks to be established easily with their data management systems.

Universal Screening Measures

In Tier 1 of an RTI model, students are assessed regularly, usually three to four times per year. This process typically is termed *universal screening* because *all* students are assessed to determine if they are making adequate progress. The National Center on Response to Intervention defines universal screening as follows: "Universal screening tests are typically brief, conducted with all students at a grade level, and followed by additional testing or short-term progress monitoring to corroborate students' risk status." (Retrieved on March 25, 2013 from www.rti4success.org/categorycontents/universal_screening).

Using the data from universal screening tools, teachers can determine which students are making adequate growth at their grade level and which may be at-risk and in need of more intensive interventions in Tier 2 and/or Tier 3. Although many schools and districts have measures that are given regularly to all students, often these are measures that determine if students have mastered grade-level standards that have been taught. They do not necessarily focus on measuring the growth of specific skills that impact more broad academic success such as reading fluency and comprehension, math computation, problem solving, spelling, and written expression.

To explore universal screening further, let's look at Ms. Caliari's grade 5 class at Rodriguez Elementary School. At this school all students in kindergarten through grade 5 are screened in both reading and mathematics. In grade 5 the reading measures include both oral reading fluency assessments and maze passage assessments. In mathematics, all students are screened on both math computation and math concepts and applications, which includes word problems. The school uses these measures because they have been found to be good predictors of more broad reading or mathematics achievement. However, the teachers at Rodriguez know that these measures are just indicators of student performance, and therefore they use data from other measures they give to more closely examine the multiple aspects of reading and mathematics. For the purpose of this chapter we will focus on the reading data from Ms. Caliari's class.

Gathering Screening Data

During the first two months of school, the 5th grade teachers administered both oral reading fluency and maze reading assessments to students. These screening assessments are indicators of more global reading proficiency for students at this grade level. These assessments require that the students be given three probes, with the middle score being used as the student's score. The middle score is then compared to the assessment benchmark. The fall trimester screening results from Ms. Caliari's class are on the data sheet in Table 3.4. This data sheet also includes both English language proficiency assessment information and the students' 4th grade state testing information. Examining students' language proficiency in conjunction with academic data is critical for English learners.

Ms. Caliari first reviews her assessment data before she and her team meet to examine the data more closely with the bilingual specialist, reading specialist, and special education teacher at the school site. In looking at the data, Ms. Caliari notices that five students (Gabriel, Maribel, Leann, Andy, and Francesca) are below the grade 5 benchmark in both oral reading fluency and maze reading, and four students (Triet, Andrew, Daniel, and Tatyanna) have met the benchmark on oral reading fluency but are below benchmark on maze reading. She also considers the students' English proficiency levels and state testing data. She sees that all of these students were below grade-level proficiency on the 4th grade state test at the end of the previous school year, except for Andrew, who was proficient. Further, Ms. Caliari notes that the students are at various levels of English proficiency: two students are English Only (EO), four are fluent English proficient (FEP), four are at the advanced level, and one is at the intermediate level. She will highlight these nine students on her data sheet as a focus for the grade-level team meeting. She will also highlight the two students who met benchmarks but did not score proficient or higher on the state test, Cindy and Perla. She plans to bring copies of their screening assessments and individual datasheets from the state assessment and English proficiency measure in order to more carefully examine their strengths and areas of need.

Table 3.4 Partial Data Sheet from Ms. Caliari's Grade 5 Class: Fall Trimester, Reading Screening (Students in bold are those that are below benchmark in one or more screening assessments or below proficient on the state test.)

Student Name	English Language Proficiency Level	State Testing Designation	Oral Reading Fluency Fall Goal = 114 words per minute (End of year = 143)	Maze Comprehension Goal =16 (End of year = 25)
Vanessa	Fluent English Proficient (exited from English learner status)	Proficient	117	22
Triet	Intermediate	Basic	120	7
Megan	EO	Proficient	120	28
Gabriel	Advanced	Below Basic	98	8
Maribel	Advanced	Basic	110	7
Juana	Fluent English Proficient (exited from English learner status)	Proficient	118	27
Leann	EO	Far Below Basic	68	2
Perla	Fluent English Proficient (exited from English learner status)	Basic	114	16
Joseph	EO	Proficient	137	28
Cindy	Fluent English Proficient (exited from English learner status)	Basic	114	17
Andrew	Advanced	Basic	117	14
Christopher	Fluent English Proficient (exited from English learner status)	Advanced	140	24
Andy	Fluent English Proficient (exited from English learner status)	Below Basic	96	10
Marissa	EO	Advanced	145	26
Francesca	Advanced	Far Below Basic	51	4
Arianna	Advanced	Proficient	118	20
Daniel	EO	Basic	115	10
Tatyanna	Fluent English Proficient (exited from English learner status)	Basic	125	8

Using Screening Data to Make Decisions

Click on SIOP Resources, then under *RTI and English Learners* find the "Data Decision Guide" form to use in making data-based decisions for students.

The grade 5 team at Rodriguez meets after school twice a month to discuss data and determine who needs intervention, make changes to the student intervention groups, and modify instruction within the RTI model. This team consists of grade 5 teachers, Ms. Caliari, Ms. Martinez, Ms. Nguyen, and Ms. Catwell; Mr. Correon, the bilingual specialist, Mr. Fuller, the reading specialist, and Ms. Shin, the resource specialist (special education teacher), also join the team for these meetings. Having professionals on the team who have expertise in second language development, literacy, and special education is useful in making decisions for English learners within an RTI model.

For this meeting the goal is to determine which students are at-risk and need either Tier 2 or Tier 3 reading intervention. Before coming to the meeting each teacher highlights students who are performing below the benchmark on oral reading fluency and/or maze reading. The teachers also highlight students who are below proficiency on the state test even if they are not below benchmark on the screening measures. Ms. Caliari highlighted the following students: Triet, Gabriel, Maribel, Leann, Perla, Cindy, Andrew, Andy, Francesca, Daniel, and Tatyanna. Of these students, Gabriel, Maribel, Leann, Andy, and Francesca are below benchmark on both reading fluency and maze reading. Triet, Andrew, Daniel, and Tatyanna are only below benchmark on the maze reading, and Perla and Cindy are below proficiency on state testing but they met benchmarks on the screening measures.

Looking at the scores of the students who are below benchmarks on both reading fluency and maze reading, the team sees that Leann and Francesca are far below grade-level benchmarks. The team next considers the students' English proficiency status. Mr. Correon reminds them that while they should consider each student's English proficiency level, it should not be the deciding factor about whether a student needs intervention. English learners can benefit from intervention even if they are not proficient in English (Gersten, et al., 2007; Geva & Farnia, 2012; Richards & Leafstedt, 2010). Leann is an English Only (EO) student (native English speaker), and Francesca is at the advanced level in English proficiency, which is the highest level of proficiency before being exited from English learner status. Francesca has been at this level for two years, and now appears to be stalled in her English development. She has been at Rodriguez since grade 1, and although she was keeping up with her peers in grades 1 and 2, by 3rd grade she began to fall behind. Ms. Caliari shares that both Leann and Francesca have difficulty in all aspects of literacy, and the data from their state testing corroborates this. Both girls' school records also indicate that they had Tier 2 interventions in 4th grade, and although they made some growth they are still far behind their peers. Based on their assessment data, performance in class, and history of progress in intervention, the team feels that these students would benefit from going straight into a Tier 3 intervention.

The team then looks at the data for Gabriel, Maribel, and Andy. They see that while Maribel is essentially a fluent reader of grade-level text (four words per minute below the benchmark), it appears she has more difficulty with comprehension, as evidenced by the much lower score on maze reading. Mr. Fuller, the reading specialist, points out that English learners often develop fluency skills rather quickly but that their comprehension skills frequently lag behind due to limited vocabulary and comprehension skills. The team decides that Maribel will benefit from intervention focused on vocabulary and comprehension strategies. Gabriel and Andy are below benchmark on both reading fluency and maze reading. The team decides they will receive Tier 2 intervention that targets both reading fluency, with a focus on accuracy and reading rate, and reading comprehension, with a focus on vocabulary and comprehension strategies. It is important to note that although the interventions are guided by data from the screening measures, they are not focused on just getting students to read more words in a minute or filling out maze passages. The interventions are comprehensive and are designed to improve overall reading achievement. By increasing overall reading achievement we should see growth on measures such as oral reading fluency that are indicators of overall reading performance. More discussion regarding interventions will be provided in Chapter 5.

The team then discusses the data for students who are below benchmark on maze reading: Triet, Daniel, Andrew, and Tatyanna. Ms. Caliari shares each student's areas of strength and areas of need based on the screening data and state testing data. Triet, Daniel, and

Tatyanna have strong decoding and fluency skills but struggle with vocabulary and comprehension strategies such as summarizing and predicting. The team decides that these students will be given a Tier 2 intervention focused on comprehension with an emphasis on vocabulary and comprehension strategies. The team then examines Andrew's data. He has met the benchmark in oral reading fluency and is just shy of meeting the benchmark for maze reading. He is also an advanced level English learner, and in looking at the data provided by Mr. Correon, the bilingual specialist, the team notices that Andrew has made progress in English proficiency since arriving at the school in grade 3 when he was designated a beginning level English speaker. Andrew also scored proficient on the grade 4 state test. After discussion, the team decides that they will not provide Andrew with Tier 2 intervention at this time. He will continue in Tier 1 only, and his growth will be examined carefully over the next couple of months. Ms. Caliari will administer progress monitoring measures twice monthly for the next two months to determine if he is continuing to make progress. She will also focus on emphasizing key vocabulary and teaching reading comprehension strategies in Tier 1.

Finally, the team examines the data of Perla and Cindy, because although they met benchmarks on both screening measures they were only at the basic level on state testing at the end of grade 4. Data from the state test shows that these two students really struggle with figurative language and various aspects of grammar. The team notices that data across the grade 5 classes show that many students struggled with these skills; therefore, they decide to focus on re-teaching these skills through mini-lessons that are delivered during differentiation of the core curriculum in Tier 1.

Progress Monitoring Measures

For students who are identified through universal screening as needing either Tier 2 or Tier 3 intervention, frequent ongoing progress monitoring is needed. "Progress monitoring is used to assess students' academic performance, to quantify a student rate of improvement or responsiveness to instruction, and to evaluate the effectiveness of instruction. Progress monitoring can be implemented with individual students or an entire class." (Retrieved on March 25, 2013 from www.rti4success.org/categorycontents/progress_monitoring). In an RTI model, progress monitoring is a scientifically based practice that is used to assess students' academic performance, to quantify a student's rate of improvement or responsiveness to instruction, and to evaluate the effectiveness of instruction. Currently the best method we have for collecting progress monitoring data during intervention is by using CBM. For English learners, monitoring progress on indicators like reading fluency and maze reading does not give us information on all aspects of literacy and language for these students; these measures are just "indicators." During intervention teachers should regularly assess the vocabulary and comprehension skills being taught to get additional information about student performance.

The frequency of progress monitoring will vary at each tier due to the instructional intensity of each tier. For example, universal screening is essentially how progress is monitored in Tier 1. We want to know if ALL students are making progress within the general education setting, and therefore assess students three or four times a year. For students at-risk and in need of Tier 2 interventions, progress monitoring takes place at least monthly, if not twice a month. For students in Tier 3, progress monitoring is even more intensive and occurs weekly. It is absolutely critical that student progress be monitored regularly during intervention in an RTI model, because it enables teachers to readily make changes to instruction based on current data. This is even more important for English learners who are rapidly developing both academic and language skills concurrently.

Determining Baseline

For students in Tier 2 and Tier 3 interventions, we need to know if they are responsive to the intervention. That is, we want to know if the intervention is working and if the students are making growth. In order to measure growth, we need to collect baseline data, which measure how the students perform before they receive intervention. Baseline data typically include the results of screening measures that include three probes, yielding at least three data points for a particular student; the middle score is used as the baseline data point for that student. To use a screening measure as baseline data for progress monitoring, it needs to be the same measure that is used for progress monitoring. For example, if your school is using the oral reading fluency measure through *aimsweb, R-CBM,* as one measure for screening and progress monitoring then this screening data can be used for baseline. However, if your school is using the *Group Reading Assessment and Diagnostic Evaluation (GRADE)* for screening and the *aimsweb R-CBM* for progress monitoring then you will need to collect baseline data using the *aimsweb* oral reading fluency tool. At Rodriguez Elementary School, *aimsweb* measures are used for both screening and progress monitoring. Therefore, the fall trimester screening data can be used as a baseline for students who need intervention.

Progress Monitoring Out of Grade Level: A Focus on Francesca

There is another case when screening data may not be able to be used as baseline data. Let's look again at Francesca. Francesca only scored 51 words per minute on her oral reading fluency screening and 3 words correct on the maze reading. On her reading fluency assessment she read 51 out of 64 words correctly, which means she read with about 80% accuracy. This tells Ms. Caliari that this passage is well above Francesca's instructional reading level (which should be about 93%–97% accuracy). It is not likely that Francesca will show much growth on a grade 5 progress monitoring measure during the next 8 weeks even with intervention. During intervention, Francesca will be provided practice with text at her instructional level. Additionally, the intervention she receives will focus on the foundational skills that she needs to master in order to eventually read at grade level. In this case, monitoring progress at Francesca's instructional level is appropriate, even though it will be with reading materials that are below her grade level. To find Francesca's instructional level, Ms. Caliari may need to administer the grade 4, and possibly grade 3, oral reading fluency measures to determine her instructional level (this means she needs to read the passage with at least 93% accuracy). Ms. Caliari finds that the grade 3 probes are at Francesca's instructional level. These grade 3 scores are used for her baseline data. Periodically, grade-level measures are administered to see if Francesca is making improvement at the grade 5 level. See her progress monitoring graphs that show data across the 8 weeks of intervention in Figures 3.1 and 3.2.

Figure 3.1 Francesca's
Reading Fluency Graph

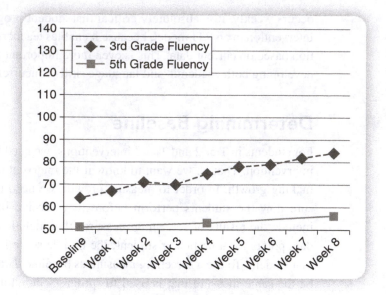

Figure 3.2 Francesca's
Maze Reading Graph

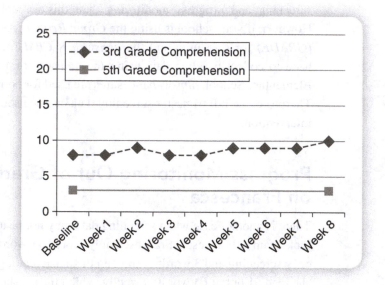

Graphing Data to Examine Growth: A Focus on Gabriel and Andy

Graphing data is a very useful way to see if students are making progress with intervention. When graphing progress monitoring data, we want to graph both the target, or goal, line and also the student's actual growth. The target line is based on the goal for the next quarter or trimester benchmark. At Rodriguez the winter target goal is 129 for grade 5 reading fluency and 21 for maze reading, and in Tier 2 intervention student progress is monitored every other week. In Figures 3.3 and 3.4 you will see Gabriel's progress monitoring graphs for reading fluency and maze reading during the 8 weeks of intervention. Notice that the dark solid line represents the goal line (needed growth) and the dotted line represents the trend line (which is actual student performance).

As the graphs show, after 8 weeks of intervention Gabriel is making progress but has not yet "caught up." Students who need intervention need to make more progress

Figure 3.3 Gabriel's
Reading Fluency Graph

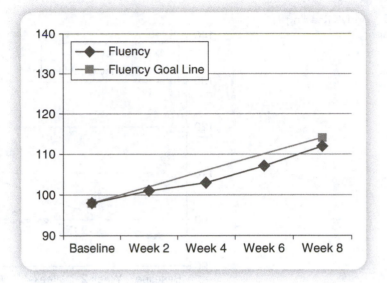

Figure 3.4 Gabriel's Maze
Reading Graph

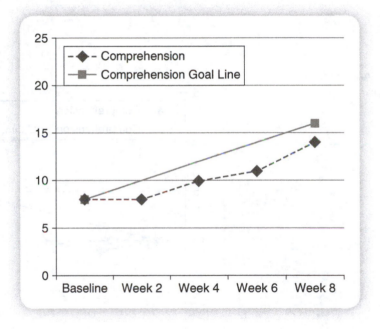

than their peers to meet these benchmarks because they start out at a lower point. For example, in grade 5, growth on reading fluency ranges from about .5–.9 words per minute (Hasbrouk & Tindal, 2006; Stecker & Lembke, 2005) and about .4 words per week for maze passage fluency (Hosp, Hosp, & Howell, 2007; Stecker & Lembke, 2005). Growth rates on CBM have been found to be similar for English learners, as research has shown they make the same if not more growth than their native English-speaking peers (Graves, Placentia-Peinado, Deno, & Johnson, 2005; Jimerson, Hong, Stage, & Gerber, 2013).

Let's look at another student, Andy. He had an average score of 96 on oral reading fluency and an average score of 10 on maze reading. Figures 3.5 and 3.6 show Andy's growth during intervention. Notice that the target line for Andy is similar to Gabriel's, but that his growth line is very different. Andy has a very flat growth line, and the gap between his actual growth and the growth he needs to make is widening.

Figure 3.5 Andy's Reading
Fluency Graph

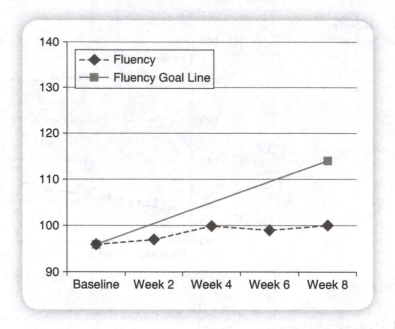

Figure 3.6 Andy's Maze
Reading Graph

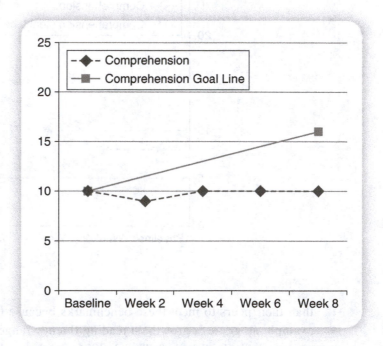

Using Progress Monitoring to Make Decisions: A Focus on Gabriel and Andy

Ms. Caliari and her team meet to discuss student data after they have at least four data points so they can look for trends in student performance. They then use this data to make decisions regarding student intervention. Essentially, there are four options for a student like Gabriel in Tier 2 intervention:

1. exit intervention and receive only Tier 1 support

2. stay in Tier 2 and keep up same intervention

3. stay in Tier 2 and adjust intervention

4. move to Tier 3 intervention

To help make the decision, Ms. Caliari and her team look at Gabriel's graphs, evaluate his errors on oral reading fluency and maze reading, and examine data from the decoding, vocabulary, and comprehension strategy assessments students are given periodically during intervention.

The graphs show that Gabriel made quite a bit of progress, but it was not enough to "catch up" to his peers. Additionally, Ms. Caliari shows data from assessments that she gave during intervention that indicate Gabriel has made progress on decoding and fluency as well as the vocabulary being taught, but he still struggles with several comprehension strategies they are working on. Because he has not "caught up," the grade 5 team rules out the first option of Tier 1 only. The team also rules out moving Gabriel to a more intensive intervention, Tier 3, since the intervention seems to be working for improving the majority of his skills. The team decides to continue to provide Tier 2 intervention to Gabriel. The majority of students in Gabriel's intervention group are also making progress on decoding and fluency skills, and therefore the intervention will be modified slightly to focus more time on vocabulary and comprehension strategies.

When the grade 5 team discusses Andy's data, they know right away that he needs a different intervention. In this case continuing with the same intervention is not an option because Andy is not making progress. For Andy either an adjustment to the Tier 2 intervention is needed or he needs a more intensive intervention at Tier 3. Again, the team reviews his graphs and assessment carefully and gets feedback from Ms. Caliari, who is delivering the intervention. Andy's assessments indicate that he is still struggling with decoding many words. Ms. Caliari states that Andy is really struggling with decoding multisyllabic words during the word study portion of the intervention and believes this is contributing to his lack of growth in both fluency and comprehension. The team decides to alter Andy's Tier 2 intervention to see if that will make a difference over the next 8 weeks. They decide to regroup him with other students who also are struggling with decoding multisyllabic words. This intervention group will spend a greater amount of time on word study during the 30-minute intervention but continue to also address fluency, vocabulary, and comprehension strategies. The team also decides that Andy's progress should be monitored weekly so they can determine sooner if he is making adequate progress. The team decided not to place Andy in a Tier 3 intervention because the Tier 3 intervention is 60 minutes each day, and this would remove Andy from Tier 1 for a longer amount of time. Ms. Caliari states that Andy is still benefiting from the differentiated instruction she provides in Tier 1.

Diagnostic Measures

Formal diagnostic measures are sometimes used in an RTI model to gain more information about a student in a particular academic skill area. This more detailed information is then used to more effectively design interventions. Often formal diagnostic assessments are only used when screening measures, progress monitoring measures, and other ongoing measures do not provide teachers with enough information in particular skill areas to design or modify interventions. For example, let's take a look at Francesca from Ms. Caliari's class.

Francesca's fall trimester scores are below the benchmark cutoff in both reading fluency and reading comprehension. The assessments sheets from one of her assessments are

Figure 3.7 Sample Assessment Sheets from Francesca's Fall Trimester Assessments

Oral Reading Fluency

Assessment Date: 9-10-13   Examiner: **Ms. Caliari**

Student: <u>Francesca</u>   Words Read Correctly: <u>51</u>   Errors: <u>13</u>

Baseball has been a part of Jake's family for generations. His dad played baseball in high
school, and now he is the coach of Jake's little league team. His grandpa played baseball, and
now he coaches too. Several of his cousins play baseball, and even his younger brother plays
baseball. Next year, Jake and his brother will play on the same team.
   Although everyone in Jake's family plays baseball, they all have their favorite positions.
Jake's favorite positions are catcher and third base. He likes the thrill of being able to tag
someone out at home plate.

Maze Passage

Assessment Date: 9-10-13   Examiner: **Ms. Caliari**

Student: <u>Francesca</u>   #Correct: <u>3</u>   #Errors: <u>5</u>

This summer we are going to our family cabin for vacation. The cabin is in the Sierra (mountain,
bicycle, work) range in California. It is right (of, on, fast) the lake, and we have a (flakey,
great, first) view of the lake and the (farm, country, mountains) from our deck. The drive is (right,
almost, by) six hours from our house, but (it, fine, my) is worth it because once we (get, fun,
most) there we have so much fun. (Next, My, Return) favorite activity . . .

Notes: These are only partial, rather than complete, passages. These passages are not actual
5th grade CBM passages but are used just as examples. If you are not using already developed
CBMs such as aimsweb, you can create your own on the CBM warehouse website http://www
.interventioncentral.org/cbm_warehouse#2. You can enter your own passages and create a
CBM probe for either reading fluency or maze.

seen in Figure 3.7. Francesca's reading fluency assessments indicate that she can read some
sight words and most one- and two-syllable words with short vowels. However, she struggles with multisyllabic words. She also does not appear to use a strategy for decoding the
words, but instead guesses. The maze passage results indicate that she may understand that
the paragraph is generally about the mountains. However, it appears that she lacks vocabulary that will help her understand the details of the passage. Additionally, her fluency assessments show that she is a slow reader and that she makes many reading errors, which
contributes to a lack of comprehension. Ms. Caliari and her team decide they should have
more information about Francesca's areas of strength and need before determining the intervention that would be most effective, especially since she reads so few words, it is really
hard to get a sense of error patterns. They also feel that her lack of English vocabulary may
be contributing to her reading difficulty. Ms. Caliari gives Francesca a formal diagnostic
reading measure that assesses phonemic awareness, phonics, fluency, vocabulary, and reading comprehension to examine her specific areas of strength to build on and her areas need
that are contributing to her overall low scores on the screening measures.
   For most students formal diagnostic measures are not needed because other assessments, such as screening measures, progress monitoring measures, and other informal

measures that teachers administer to examine student strengths and needs provide enough detail to determine both the intensity of intervention and the skills that should be taught during the intervention. Diagnostic measures often take quite a bit of time to administer, up to 90 minutes in some cases, and often need to be done individually, so they should only be administered when it is really necessary. For example, it could have been the case for Francesca that combining the grade 3 measures, grade 5 measures, and other ongoing assessment data would have provided the information the team needed to develop an effective intervention. Most often the combination of measures already in place provides the level of detail needed to design and modify interventions.

Final Thoughts

RTI is more than just assessing and providing intervention. It requires that a decision be made as to whether or not a student is responsive to an intervention; then next steps must be determined based on that decision. (See From the Field: Interview with a School Psychologist.) We do not want to rely on one measure alone to determine a student response to intervention. For example, with Gabriel and Andy, the team examined both reading fluency data and maze reading data. They considered input from the teacher who was conducting the intervention, data from vocabulary and comprehension assessments given during intervention, and English proficiency data. Multiple indicators provide the best picture of student growth and achievement. For grade 5 students like those in Ms. Caliari's class, teachers want to have indicators of fluency and comprehension. For younger students in kindergarten or 1st grade, a team would want to have data on concepts of print, letter recognition, phonemic awareness, phonics, word recognition, fluency, vocabulary, and listening and reading comprehension. For English learners, we also want English proficiency data for all grade levels.

Data-based decision making is a cycle. At the end of two 8-week intervention sessions, the grade 5 team at Rodriguez Elementary examines the progress monitoring data for all

---

From the Field | **Interview with a School Psychologist**

Interviewer: How do you determine if students are responsive to intervention?

School Psychologist: The classroom teachers and I hope students score at least 70% on their curriculum-embedded assessments; this data is gathered at least two or three times a month. Our school has adopted a school-wide database where students take assessments online and it is automatically uploaded to their student profiles, which has helped to streamline the process of gathering this data.

My interventionist and I review formative assessment data together. There is no cut score for this informal data. Instead, we look at whether students are struggling with specific aspects of grammar or vocabulary to inform small group instruction.

Interviewer: How do you determine when to move students to different Tiers?

School Psychologist: This determination is made between the classroom teacher, interventionist, and me.

Our team weighs the data with input from the classroom teacher and interventionist to identify students to be exited from the group. Our school has a high international enrollment, so new students are added to the groups throughout the year.

students who are in intervention and also administers and examines the second trimester screening data. A second trimester of screening data is conducted to determine if there are students who may have fallen behind and are now in need of intervention, even though they did not receive it during the first trimester. The team first considers progress monitoring data for students who previously received Tier 2 and Tier 3 interventions. The team discusses how to regroup students, considering both the additional students who now need intervention and the students who can exit intervention. The grade 5 team at Rodriguez Elementary illustrates how decisions can be made within grade-level teams; note how these decisions were made on an individual student basis. This is particularly important when considering English learners, because many factors impact both academic and language development for these students.

For Reflection and Discussion

1. How are universal screening measures used to make decisions about students for intervention?

2. Why are CBM useful for both screening and progress monitoring?

3. How can specialists such as a bilingual teacher and a special education teacher be helpful in making decisions about students?

4. How is regular progress monitoring useful for guiding intervention for individual students?

4 Tier 1: What Is Best Practice for Teaching English Learners?

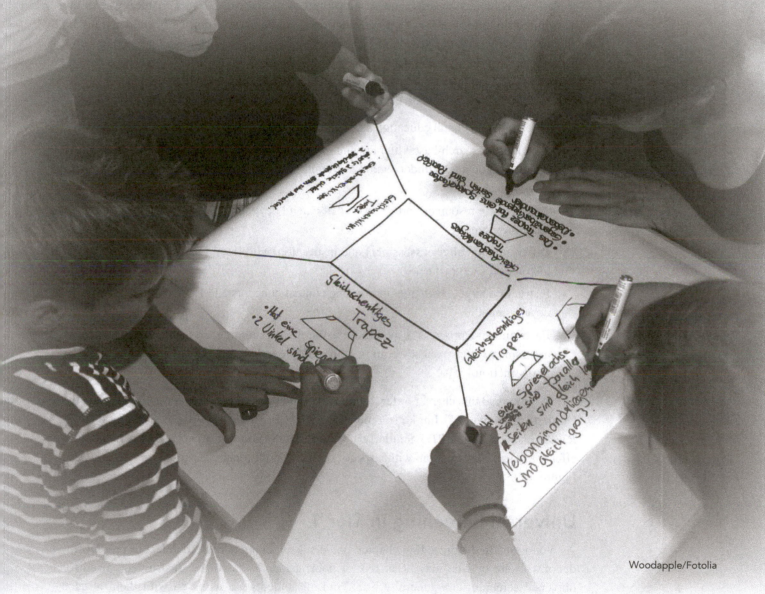

Tier 1 in RTI is referred to as general education because it is intended to serve the learning needs of all students in the general education classroom. We have known for years that expert teaching based on a high-quality curriculum is effective (Allington & Johnston, 2002; Echevarria, 2012; Echevarria, Richards-Tutor, Canges, & Francis, 2011;

Echevarria, Short, & Powers, 2006; Goldenberg, 2008; Pressley, 2005; Vogt & Shearer, 2011). Embedding research-based, sound practice within RTI exemplifies the interrelatedness between the RTI structure and high-quality instruction. This effective, core instruction can be characterized as both preventive and proactive because universal screening instruments and teacher observation provide data about a student's academic and language proficiency. These data guide instructional adjustments and modifications within the regular classroom.

For English learners, high-quality instruction requires particular modifications that are especially important if these students are to develop literacy skills and strategies, reach grade-level content standards, and develop English proficiency. In this chapter, we review the elements of effective Tier 1 implementation and propose an empirically validated model of Tier 1 instruction, the SIOP® Model. Intended originally for English learners and now proven effective for all students, the SIOP® Model includes necessary research-based modifications for effective general education instruction.

For English learners, Tier 1 within RTI includes the following principles:

- It occurs in a general education setting.

- It includes research-based literacy and math (and other) curriculums taught by high-quality teachers who understand the strengths and needs of all students, including English learners.

- Teachers use resources and methods that extend beyond the adopted reading and/or math programs.

- Differentiation aligns assessment and instruction, with flexible grouping for instruction and practice.

- Instruction targets both age-appropriate content concepts and English language development.

- Each student's progress is monitored with reliable, ongoing, and authentic assessments (universal screening), with multiple indicators that are linked explicitly to instruction.

Click on SIOP Resources, then under *RTI and English Learners* find the "Guide to Effective RTI Implementation" form to use with each tier of a multi-tiered RTI approach.

As you read this chapter, refer to Figure 4.1 and think about how you will complete the Guide to Effective RTI Implementation for Tier 1. In Chapter 1, you contrasted *What Is RTI?* with *What Is Not RTI?* Similarly, it is important to contrast aspects of what constitutes effective Tier 1 instruction with aspects of more traditional classroom instruction (see Figure 4.2).

Universal Screening in Tier 1

As mentioned in the preceding chapter, universal screening is used to detect or predict students who are or who may be at risk of poor academic outcomes. Instruments used for universal screening are generally brief, and all students are assessed with them at each grade level. Additional and more in-depth assessment and/or progress monitoring are necessary to substantiate those students who are identified as being at-risk. The results of screening are used to provide additional or alternative forms of instruction to supplement the general education teaching approach. The results may also inform decisions about grouping within the general education classroom so that students are receiving instruction at their own levels.

Figure 4.1   Guide to Effective RTI Implementation: Tier 1

Who Is Responsible?	
Necessary Professional Development (For whom and by whom)	
Modification(s) and/or Intervention(s)	
Length of Time	
Teacher-Pupil Ratio	
Assessments Needed	
Assessments Used	
Frequency of Progress Monitoring	
Treatment Fidelity Observation	

(*continued*)

Figure 4.1   (continued)

Review of Modification(s) and/or Intervention(s)	
Parent Involvement	
Forms/Resources	

Figure 4.2   Defining Tier 1

Tier 1 is...	Tier 1 is NOT...
Appropriate, effective, and research-based core instruction for all students (reading, writing, math)	Core instruction in which some students are successful and others are not, and this is perceived as reality
A process that includes formal, universal screening that occurs at least four times a year, focusing on specific skills, strategies, and content knowledge	In-class assessments that focus primarily on what is taught rather than what students know and are able to do
A process that includes formal and informal progress monitoring on an ongoing and continuous basis	Only about determining student progress every nine weeks and at the end of the school year
Instruction with specific adaptations and modifications based on assessment and progress monitoring	One-size-fits-all instruction
Targeted, intense instructional support within the classroom for students who are having difficulty	Reliance on other instructional support staff (e.g., Special Education) to determine a student's needs and to provide remediation
A variety of flexible grouping configurations for instruction and practice	Whole class instruction, or fixed instructional groups consisting of students who are high, average, and low achievers
A team approach with teachers, administrators, and parents working collaboratively	Teachers who work primarily on their own

High-Quality Instruction for Tier 1: Making Content Comprehensible for English Learners with the SIOP® Model

"Because teaching is complex, it is helpful to have a road map through the territory, structured around a shared understanding of teaching colleagues" (Danielson, 2007).

The SIOP® Model (Echevarria, Vogt, & Short, 2013; 2014a; 2014b) was designed and researched extensively to help classroom teachers systematically, consistently, and concurrently teach grade-level academic content and academic language to English learners. The SIOP® Model is effective with both English learners and native English-speaking students who are still developing academic literacy (Echevarria, 2012; Echevarría, Richards-Tutor, Canges, & Francis, 2011; Echevarría & Short, 2010; Short, Echevarría, & Richards-Tutor, 2011; Short, Fidelman, & Louguit, 2012).

The SIOP® Model consists of eight components and thirty features that when implemented to a high degree, have positively impacted the academic achievement and English language development for English learners (see Appendix C for the abbreviated SIOP protocol). The SIOP® Model is an instructional framework for organizing classroom instruction in meaningful and effective ways—and may be used across all Tiers (see Figure 1.2). Although the SIOP® Model is now effectively implemented in bilingual, ESL, and two-way immersion classrooms, it is primarily intended as a model of sheltered instruction for all content classrooms (pre-K–12) where the language of instruction is English. The SIOP® Model is now being implemented in all fifty states as well in numerous countries, and it represents the best hope for high-quality Tier 1 instruction for English learners.

The following overview briefly describes each of the SIOP components, followed by research and citations culled from research studies on English learner language acquisition and literacy. In Chapter 1, we introduced an RTI framework that includes high-quality classroom instruction with the SIOP® Model as ideal Tier 1 teaching for English learners (see Figure 1.2). If you have been working with the SIOP® Model for a while and are very familiar with it, this chapter will represent a quick but important review. If you are unfamiliar with the SIOP® Model, this chapter provides a brief overview of the eight SIOP components, but it is critically important that you read one of the core SIOP texts (Echevarria, Vogt, & Short, 2013; 2014a; or 2014b) before you look to the Model for Tier 1 instruction. Our research findings clearly indicate that fidelity to the SIOP® Model is imperative if English learners' academic and language proficiency is to be increased significantly (Echevarría, Richards-Tutor, Chinn, & Ratleff, 2011). Reading the core text and using the SIOP protocol for lesson planning, observations, and discussion results in higher levels of SIOP implementation (see Appendix C: SIOP Protocol).

Click on SIOP Resources, then under *RTI and English Learners* find the "Guide to Effective RTI Implementation" form to use with each tier of a multi-tiered RTI approach.

The SIOP® Model and the Common Core State Standards

The authors of the Common Core State Standards did not directly address the academic and language needs of English learners, and suggested that it is up to the individual states to attend to these needs by providing an appropriate curriculum and effective instruction that enables students to access and achieve the Standards. Whereas the Common Core State Standards represent requirements for what students should know and be able to do in the

Figure 4.3   The SIOP® Model and the Common Core State Standards

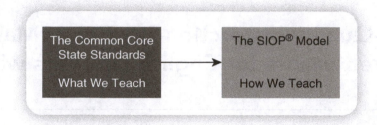

English language arts and mathematics, the SIOP® Model provides the "road map" for how to get there (see Figure 4.3). When teachers follow this road map and adapt their instructional practices to meet the academic and language needs of English learners, it is more likely that these students will be able to reach the rigorous Common Core State Standards. The Common Core State Standards, as well as other state content and language standards, are used along with the SIOP® Model to guide the development of highly effective lessons for English learners and other students.

The Eight Components of the SIOP® Model

Lesson Preparation

The focus for each SIOP lesson is content and language objectives that are clearly defined, displayed, and orally reviewed with students. These objectives are derived from content standards and are linked to the academic language that students need for success. For teachers, the goal is to help students gain important experience with key grade-level content and skills as they progress toward fluency in English. Because of content and language objectives, students know what they are expected to learn and/or be able to do by the end of each lesson. They have clear learning goals at the start of each lesson so that they can focus on what is important and take an active part in the learning process. Also within this component, teachers provide relevant supplementary materials (e.g., visuals, multimedia, adapted or bilingual texts, publisher-supplied summaries of literature selections, and study guides), because grade-level reading and math series may be difficult for many English learners to comprehend. Adaptations are provided through special texts, supportive handouts, audio-taped selections such as often come with reading series, and texts appropriate for varied English proficiency levels. Graphic organizers and illustrations are used for pre-reading activities and for teaching key points. Also, meaningful activities provide access to the key content concepts, and offer opportunities for students to apply their content and language knowledge.

Research Support for the Lesson Preparation Component

- English learners benefit from ELD (English Language Development) instruction, but they also need instruction in the use of English in the content areas. Because teachers find that teaching to both content and language objectives can be challenging, collaboration among teachers is beneficial (Short, Cloud, Morris, & Motta, 2012).
- "As a general rule, all students tend to benefit from clear goals and learning objectives . . ." (Goldenberg, 2008, p. 17). Teachers should incorporate into their

lesson plans objectives that support students' academic language development (Saunders & Goldenberg, 2010).

- An important theme in studies that investigated English learner literacy instruction is that of attending to students' individual needs, since English learners are not a homogeneous group. English learners need a variety of activities and instructional materials in varied settings (August et al., 2008) that are geared to their experiential and educational backgrounds, and their levels of English language proficiency (Echevarria, Short, & Powers, 2006).

- The more exposure students have to academic language and the more time they spend using it, the faster they will develop English proficiency (Saunders & Goldenberg, 2010). More progress will be made if all teachers on an English learner's schedule attend to language development and practice (Snow & Katz, 2010).

- When planning lessons for English learners, teachers must understand the context in which they develop as readers. The attributes a student brings to school (such as knowledge, beliefs, attitudes, motivations, behaviors, experiences with specific contexts and situations) impact how he or she deals with school. "The greater the differences in these attributes and the school experiences, the greater the hindrance to learning" (Goldenberg, Rueda, & August, 2008, p. 105).

Building Background

In SIOP lessons, teachers connect new concepts with students' personal experiences and past learning. Teachers build background knowledge because many English learners have not attended U.S. schools or are unfamiliar with American culture. At other times, it's necessary to activate students' prior knowledge in order to learn what students already know, to identify misinformation, and to discover when it's necessary to fill in gaps. English learners may have funds of knowledge different from native English speakers, and teachers can tap them as resources, perhaps in lessons related to short story characters or plots, poetry, native-language nursery rhymes, songs they have learned previously, universal themes in literature, and so forth. As teachers prepare lessons, they can examine the anthologies, novels, and other texts used for cultural biases and idiomatic speech so potential problems can be anticipated or potentially confusing concepts can be pre-taught. Granted, idiomatic expressions are generally taught as part of the language arts curriculum, but for English learners, teachers need to be especially sensitive to figurative language that may pop up in conversations, literature, and informational texts.

The SIOP® Model places great significance on building a broad vocabulary base for students. We need to pay more attention to vocabulary instruction across the curriculum so students become effective readers, writers, speakers, and listeners. Most language arts teachers explicitly teach key vocabulary and word structures, word families, and word relationships. Go further for English learners by helping them develop word-learning strategies beyond decoding. Share strategies such as using context clues, word parts (i.e., affixes), visual aids (e.g., illustrations), and cognates (a word related in meaning and form to a word in another language). Design lesson activities that give students multiple opportunities to use new vocabulary both orally and in writing. In order to move words from receptive knowledge to expressive use, vocabulary needs reinforcement through different learning modes.

Research Support for the Building Background Component

- English learners, including both immigrants and students born in the United States, may lack the academic language and key vocabulary necessary for understanding content information (August & Shanahan, 2010; Donnelly & Roe, 2010).

- Teachers can help English learners by having students read about topics with which they have some familiarity and by making sure they have adequate exposure to the topic prior to reading about it (Jiménez, Garcia, & Pearson, 1996).

- Vocabulary development, critical for English learners, is strongly related to reading comprehension and academic achievement (August & Shanahan, 2010; Lesaux, Kieffer, Faller, & Kelley, 2010; Zwiers, 2008).

- Studies of vocabulary instruction show that English learners learn more words through explicit instruction; by working with words that are embedded in meaningful contexts; by having many opportunities for repetition and use of the words in reading, writing, listening, and speaking; when the words are posted and reviewed; and when they are working with words in multiple texts and contexts (Beck, McKeown, & Kucan, 2002; Carlo et al., 2004).

- "A small but consistent body of intervention research suggests that English learners will benefit most from rich, intensive vocabulary instruction that emphasizes 'student-friendly' definitions, that engage students in meaningful use of word meanings in reading, writing, speaking, and listening, and that provides regular review" (Gersten et al., 2007).

Comprehensible Input

If information is presented in a way that students cannot understand, such as an explanation that is spoken too rapidly, or reading selections that are far above students' reading levels with no visuals or graphic organizers to assist them, many students—including English learners—will be unable to learn the necessary content. Instead, modify "traditional" instruction with a variety of ESL methods and SIOP techniques so students are able to comprehend the lesson's key concepts. Examples of these techniques are:

- teacher talk that is appropriate to student proficiency levels
- demonstrations and modeling of tasks, processes, and routines
- gestures, pantomime, and movement to make concepts more clear
- opportunities for students to engage in role-plays, improvisation, and simulations
- visuals and supplementary materials, such as pictures, real objects, illustrations, charts, adapted texts, audiotapes or CDs, perhaps in the native language, if needed and available
- restatement, paraphrasing, repetition, and written records of key points
- previews and reviews of important information
- hands-on, experiential, and discovery activities

Remember that academic tasks must be explained clearly and in steps, both orally and in writing for students. We cannot assume English learners know how to do an assignment because it is a regular routine for the rest of your students. Talk through the procedures and use models and examples of good products and appropriate participation so that students know the steps they should take and can envision the desired result.

The techniques mentioned above are particularly important as English learners strive to meet the Common Core State Standards for listening and speaking. Across the grade levels, the CCSS ask students to comprehend information presented orally and to express their understanding in a variety of ways, such as paraphrasing or summarizing information, and recounting key ideas and details. The way teachers present information orally will have a significant impact on the degree to which English learners will be able to achieve these standards.

Research Support for the Comprehensible Input Component

- While English learners benefit from many of the teaching practices that are effective for all students, these learners also require modifications to make instruction meaningful (August & Shanahan, 2010).

- For beginning English speakers, "teachers will have to speak slowly and somewhat deliberately, with clear vocabulary and diction, and use pictures, other objects, and movements to illustrate the content being taught" (Goldenberg, 2008, p. 23).

- Reducing the complexity of language is effective when used judiciously. Oversimplification of spoken and written language limits exposure to varied sentence constructions and language forms (Crossley, McCarthy, Louwerse, & McNamara, 2007).

- Visual representations, not just language-based explanations, provide students with needed, additional support (Scarcella, 2003).

Strategies

This SIOP component addresses student learning strategies, teacher-scaffolded instruction, and higher-order thinking skills. By explicitly teaching cognitive, metacognitive, and language learning strategies, teachers equip students for academic learning both inside and outside the SIOP classroom. Descriptions of each type of learning strategy follow (Echevarria, Vogt, & Short, 2013, pp. 117–118):

- **Cognitive strategies:** These help students organize the information they are expected to learn through the process of self-regulated learning. Examples: previewing, reviewing, re-reading, highlighting, underlining, taking notes

- **Metacognitive strategies:** These help students monitor their thinking, reading, and learning. Examples: predicting, inferring, generating questions, evaluating, summarizing, visualizing

- **Language learning strategies:** These help students increase their progress in speaking and comprehending a new language. Examples: skimming and scanning text, analyzing forms and patterns in English, making logical guesses, breaking words into component parts, substituting known words

Remember to capitalize on the learning strategies students already use in their first language because those can transfer to the new language.

SIOP teachers frequently scaffold instruction so students can be successful with academic tasks. Support efforts at their current performance level but also strive to move English learners to a higher level of understanding and accomplishment. When they master a skill or task, remove the supports that were provided and add new ones for the next level. The dual goals, of course, are the gradual release of responsibility and the increase of student independence, so that English learners can achieve independence one step at a time. (See Echevarria, Vogt, & Short, 2013, Figure 5.1, p. 121–122, for an explanation of the Gradual Increase of Student Independence.)

Teachers need to remember to ask English learners a range of questions, some of which should require critical thinking. It is easy to ask simple, factual questions, and sometimes we fall into that trap with students acquiring English, but we must go beyond questions that can be answered with a one- or two-word response. Instead, ask questions and create projects or tasks that require students to think more critically and to apply their language skills in a more extended way. Be sure to provide English learners with language support (such as sentence frames and sentence starters), so they can express their thinking orally and in writing. Remember an important adage: "Just because English learners don't speak English proficiently, doesn't mean they can't *think*."

Research Support for the Strategies Component

- The CREDE report (Genesee, Lindholm-Leary, Saunders, & Christian, 2006) suggests that instruction for English learners should combine both direct and interactive approaches. This includes a give-and-take between teacher and students, and also a teacher who encourages higher levels of thinking, speaking, and reading.

- Three types of learning strategies that have been identified in the research literature include metacognitive strategies, cognitive strategies, and social/affective strategies (August & Shanahan, 2010; Dymock & Nicholson, 2010; Echevarria, Vogt, & Short, 2013; O'Malley & Chamot, 1990).

- Students benefit from receiving explicit instruction in how to use a variety of learning strategies flexibly and in combination (Dole, Duffy, Roehler, & Pearson, 1991; Duffy, 2002).

- Teaching learning strategies has a long history of research supporting its efficacy (Echevarria & Graves, 2014; Vaughn, Gersten, & Chard, 2000).

- "One issue that emerges from . . . studies has to do with strategy use versus teacher's scaffolding of text as a mechanism for improving students' comprehension. For example, [the teacher] presumably focused on teaching students strategy use. However, [he] did many things that scaffolded instruction. . . . Future studies on strategy use would benefit from clearly distinguishing the two methods of building comprehension" (August et al., 2008, p. 153).

Interaction

We know that students learn through interaction with one another and with their teachers. They need oral language practice to help develop and deepen their content knowledge and support their second language reading and writing skills. Clearly, the teacher is the main role model for appropriate English usage, word choice, intonation, fluency, and so forth, but do not discount the value of student–student interaction. In pairs and in small groups, English learners practice new language structures and vocabulary that they have been taught and have seen modeled, as well as important language functions, such as asking for clarification, confirming interpretations, elaborating on one's own or another's idea, and evaluating opinions. Sometimes the interaction patterns expected in an American classroom differ from students' cultural norms and prior schooling experiences. We need to be sensitive to sociocultural differences and work with students to become competent in the culture that has been established in the classroom, while respecting students' values, backgrounds, languages, and cultures.

Research Support for the Interaction Component

- Second-language learning is a social process: Language develops largely as a result of meaningful interaction with others, much as first-language acquisition does (Saunders & Goldenberg, 2010).

- Structured interaction between English learners and native English speakers does not result in proficiency gains when it focuses primarily on "supportive and friendly discourse." Language proficiency gains were found when the EL–EO interactions focused more on negotiation of meaning or efforts to elicit comprehensible input (Saunders & Goldenberg, 2010).

- Researchers have found that English learners were more engaged academically when working in small groups or with partners than they were in whole-class instruction or individual work (Brooks & Thurston, 2010).

- Promising practices for improving English learners' comprehension include cooperative learning and discussion, such as instructional conversations (August & Shanahan, 2008).

- Interactive activities that effectively mix English learners with more proficient English learners or native speakers of English typically involve carefully structured tasks. The overall finding is that treatments with interactive tasks produced a significant and substantial effect on language learning outcomes (Saunders & Goldenberg, 2010).

- Oral language proficiency impacts all aspects of educational achievement, resulting in higher grades and achievement test results (August & Shanahan, 2006; Suarez-Orozco et al., 2008) and the acquisition of skilled reading (Lesaux & Giva, 2008).

- "Probably the most obvious instructional modification is to use the primary language for clarification and explanation. This can be done by the teacher, a classroom aide, a peer, or a volunteer in the classroom" (Goldenberg, 2008, p. 19).

- As noted in the Common Core State Standards, ". . . students must have ample opportunities to take part in a variety of rich, structured conversations" (National Governors Association Center for Best Practices and Council of Chief State School Officers, 2010).

Practice & Application

Practice and application of new material is important for all learners. Research on the SIOP® Model found that lessons with hands-on, visual, and other kinesthetic tasks benefit English learners because students practice the language and content knowledge through multiple modalities. SIOP teachers ensure that lessons include a variety of activities that encourage students to apply both the content and language skills they are learning. Additionally, they consider the structure of the task and degree of difficulty for the resulting product, the grouping configurations, the type of feedback that will be provided so it is geared to students' proficiency levels, and the expectations for student achievement (Vogt, 2012). For English learners to learn the language, it is imperative that they practice and apply literacy and language processes (reading, writing, listening, speaking) in every lesson.

Research Support for the Practice & Application Component

- It is well established that practice and application helps one master a skill (Jensen, 2005; Marzano, Pickering, & Pollock, 2001).
- For English learners at-risk for reading problems, teachers should provide intensive small-group reading interventions in which students have multiple opportunities to practice reading words and sentences (Gersten et al., 2007).
- Students benefit from opportunities to practice, apply, and transfer new learning (Goldenberg, 2008).

Lesson Delivery

A SIOP lesson is effective when it meets its objectives. Therefore, this component focuses on determining whether the delivery of a lesson supports the content and language objectives. Further, a well-delivered SIOP lesson engages the majority of students throughout the lesson. We know that lesson preparation is crucial to effective delivery, but so are classroom management skills. SIOP teachers have clear routines to follow, they make sure students know the lesson's content and language objectives so everyone stays on track, they introduce (and revisit) meaningful activities that appeal to students, and they provide appropriate wait time so English learners can process concepts. A lesson shouldn't move either too slowly or too quickly; student comprehension of key concepts is the goal, so teachers must monitor understanding throughout each lesson.

Research Support for the Lesson Delivery Component

- English learners need much richer and more extensive teaching procedures than are usually recommended in core curricular programs (August, Carlo, Dressler, & Snow, 2005; Blachowicz, Fisher, Ogle, & Watts-Taffe, 2006).
- Students benefit from "well-designed, clearly structured, and appropriately paced instruction; active engagement and participation . . . this is as likely to be true for English learners as it is for English speakers" (Goldenberg, 2008, p. 17).
- Written objectives allow students to know the direction of a lesson and help them stay on task. Schmoker (2011) recommends that "whole class lessons focus on a clear learning objective in short instructional 'chunks' or segments, punctuated by multiple cycles of guided practice and formative assessment (checks for understanding)" (pp. 20–21).

Review & Assessment

Each SIOP lesson needs time for review and assessment. Teachers do English learners a disservice if they spend the last five minutes teaching a new concept rather than reviewing what students have learned so far. Therefore, SIOP teachers revisit key vocabulary and concepts with students throughout the lesson and as a final wrap-up. They check on student comprehension frequently throughout the lesson period to determine whether additional explanations or re-teaching are needed. During formative and summative assessment, they provide multiple and differentiated indicators for students to demonstrate their understanding of the content and language instruction. Further, when designing their assessment and instruction, SIOP teachers consider how the interplay of contextual features (home, language, community, identity, culture, and school) influences school performance and operates within individual students (Vogt & Shearer, 2011).

Research Support for the Review & Assessment Component

- At-risk English learners benefit from clear feedback from the teacher when they make errors (Gersten et al., 2007).
- Students benefit from feedback on correct and incorrect responses, periodic review and practice, frequent assessments to gauge progress, and re-teaching when needed (August & Shanahan, 2008).
- "Data from screening and progress monitoring assessments should be used to make decisions about the instructional support English learners need to learn to read" (Gersten et al., 2007, p. 3).

Uses and Benefits of the SIOP® Model

While for purposes of RTI, we are suggesting that the SIOP® Model represents high-quality Tier 1 teaching for all students, it is also being successfully introduced in pre-service teacher preparation programs. The SIOP framework brings needed coherence to teacher preparation programs when new teachers are learning how to teach English learners (Vogt, 2009). Rather than viewing each content methods course as a separate entity, the SIOP® Model brings together all content classes in a systematic framework for effective classroom instruction.

Once in the classroom (pre-K–12), novice teachers are able to organize their teaching when the SIOP protocol (see Appendix C) is used for lesson planning, curriculum discussions, and observations with conferencing. For example, Lela Alston Elementary School in Isaac School District, Phoenix, AZ, a school in which all teachers have had extensive SIOP training, provides immediate SIOP professional development and SIOP mentors for all teachers who are new to the school (Echevarria, Short, & Vogt, 2008). It is very important to recognize and remember that the SIOP protocol is not an instrument intended to be used for teacher evaluation. Instead, SIOP lessons are observed and rated to determine the degree of implementation of each of the SIOP features.

Experienced teachers have found that the SIOP® Model has enhanced and refined their teaching practices through purposeful and principled decision making that is based on assessment of students' strengths and needs (Echevarria, Short, & Vogt, 2008, p. 175). The principal of Lela Alston Elementary School, Debbie Hutson, reported that she observed improvement in teaching including the way that teachers put forth more effort to keep students engaged. There was more active teaching. She also reported that lesson planning was more effective as a result of the professional development teachers received. They were more aware of the importance of including all the SIOP components in lesson planning and delivery.

We have seen average teachers become very good teachers, and very good teachers become excellent teachers when they implement the SIOP® Model. There is no question that substantive professional development coupled with study of the core SIOP text (Echevarria, Vogt, & Short, 2013; 2014a; 2014b) is essential if teachers are to become high-implementing SIOP teachers.

One of the advantages of the SIOP® Model for Tier 1 classroom instruction is that it provides a common language for instruction. In our work with educators who were committed to building wide reform and best practice, the common language that the SIOP® Model provides has often been cited as an important factor in a school's success (Echevarria, Short, & Vogt, 2008).

Differentiated Instruction

Most teachers agree that it is important to differentiate instruction to meet the academic needs of all students. However, making this happen on a consistent, systematic basis is considered by many to be very challenging, especially when a classroom consists of academically, linguistically, and culturally diverse students. High-implementing SIOP teachers have found that they differentiate their instruction frequently and naturally when they consistently incorporate the thirty features of the SIOP® Model in their lessons. SIOP teachers adapt and modify instructional materials and practices for English learners and other students. Appropriate differentiation does not imply that equality equates to fairness, or that fairness equates to equality (Diller, 2007), because what works for one student may not work or be appropriate for others. Within RTI, the goal is to provide the best instruction possible given a student's assessed needs. Therefore, differentiation can occur in the classroom in many ways through diverse content, processes, and products (Tomlinson, 1999), as long as assessment data and content and language objectives guide the way.

As you read the following From the Field feature, think about the suggestion that Ms. Nash makes regarding the powerful effects of relatively simple classroom differentiation. By asking Marco to identify his concerns, the principal was able to assist Marco's teacher in creating a learning environment more suitable to his needs. Sometimes teachers think that differentiation is complex and complicated, but in reality, often small adaptations can make the biggest difference for a child.

From the Field **A Principal's Classroom Observation**

Recently, I had the opportunity to observe a classroom with a group of students in 5th grade who had a wide range of abilities, but were all performing well below grade level and were recommended to summer school for a four-week intensive intervention program. Some of the students were there to work on their comprehension skills, and others attended to work on decoding and mathematical skills.

Of particular concern in one classroom that I visited was a student, Marco, who was constantly being referred to the office because he was distracting other students and was unable to finish his work. Marco continually got up and walked around the classroom to get a drink, sharpen his pencil, or get a tissue. When the teacher checked with him, he had only begun the assignment, while over half of the class had already completed the work.

I had Marco accompany me to the office and asked him what the problem was. His first response was that he was hungry and hadn't eaten any breakfast that morning. However, when I continued the line of questioning, Marco said that the classroom was too noisy for him to concentrate on his work. He specifically pointed out two students who sat by him and who were constantly talking. I then asked Marco if he could list some of the things that made learning difficult for him. I told him that he could list the things for me and I would write them down on a piece of paper. Here is the list of things Marco stated that made the classroom assignments hard for him:

1. The noise level of other students, especially ones who were sitting near him
2. His uncertainty about how to organize his work and decide on what he should do first
3. His uncertainty about the meaning of particular words when he was reading
4. He didn't think he was very good at the task and didn't find it fun or engaging.

We then took the list and brainstormed together solutions to help Marco be more successful in the classroom. I explained that he needed to take responsibility for his learning but that I would assist him in making the tasks less challenging. We looked over his assignments, decided which one was the most important, and figured out how we'd attack it before moving on to the next. We talked about the importance of completing one assignment before beginning another one. We also talked about putting his assignments on his desk in the order they are to be completed. I suggested that Marco keep a piece of paper by his desk and write down any words that he was unsure of when reading, and to show the teacher those words so she could explain them at an appropriate time. I asked the teacher if Marco could present the word list to her each day and if they could create a list of words that Marco could practice at home.

When examining his classroom, I discussed with the teacher a more suitable, far less distracting place for Marco to sit. I also asked her to pair Marco with a peer whose reading level was somewhat higher than his own. I suggested that when they read together, each student could read one sentence at a time, alternating between sentences, thus requiring both students to attend to the print. When I checked back with Marco and the teacher later on in the day, the teacher was impressed with Marco's ability to focus on his task and how the amount of disruptions was greatly reduced.

The simple accommodations described here are easy and effective techniques for any classroom teacher to use. At the end of the four-week period, Marco was experiencing success. He was completing his classroom assignments in an appropriate length of time and was not disruptive to his peers in the classroom.

A Glimpse into a Classroom: High-Quality Tier 1 Instruction for English Learners

To illustrate how Tier 1 instruction can be made meaningful for English learners, this section describes a classroom vignette in which English learners are engaged in an interesting and motivating writing lesson. From a classroom in Texas, Title 1 Specialist Vicki Roberts shares a process that she and teacher Lina Nino used throughout the year in Ms. Nino's grade 4 class where Ms. Roberts worked each Wednesday. In Shorehaven Elementary School, 80%

of the students are economically disadvantaged; 37.7% are designated as Limited English Proficient (LEP), and 58.9% are categorized as At Risk.

On the district writing test this particular year, 56% of the students in Ms. Nino's class were commended, meaning that they had received a score of 3 or 4 on a 4-point scale for their composition. In contrast, in the population of all students tested in the district, 34% were commended. The total LEP population in the district had a commended rate of 19%. This was the first year the students were tested in writing, so there are no comparison scores for this group. As you read about the process as described in the lesson plan and in the narrative that follows, think about what these educators did to enable their English learners to become successful writers. The lesson plan (see Figure 4.4) is from the first day the students were introduced to "My Treasure Chest."

Figure 4.4 "My Treasure Chest" Lesson Plan

Teacher: Vicki Roberts

SIOP Lesson: My Treasure Chest	Subject: Writing	Grade Level: 4th

Content Standards:

3. Write narratives to develop real or imagined experiences or events using effective technique, descriptive details, and clear even sequences.
   a. Orient the reader by establishing a situation and introducing a narrator and/or characters; organize an event sequence that unfolds naturally.
   b. Use dialogue and description to develop experiences and events or show the response of characters to situations.
   c. Use a variety of transitional words and phrases to manage the sequence of events.
   d. Use concrete words and phrases and sensory details to convey experiences and events precisely.
   e. Provide a concluding statement or section related to the information or explanation presented.

ELD Standard (Language Focus):
Writing Standards, Grade 4

Key Vocabulary:
Sequence words: First, then, next, later, soon, before, after, meanwhile, finally

Select an especially meaninfully event in your life. Create a storyboard that includes each of the things that happened. Write a story that describes the event, using signal words to put the details in sequence.

Supplementary Materials:
1. Sample Treasure Chest on chart paper
2. Students' personal dictionaries
3. Sample Storyboard
4. Chart paper and markers
5. Sample storyboard from Internet
6. Signal Words Poster for Sequence (see Vogt & Echevarria, 2008, p. 38)

Connections to Students' Background Experiences and Past Learning:
Teacher will share her Treasure Chest (on chart paper) and will relate several of her personal stories. TW share her storyboard, created from the events she selected from her Treasure Chest. TW share with students about how storyboards are used when making movies or writing stories. Students will examine the sample storyboard downloaded from the Internet. TW read the "boring" and "elaborated" examples of her own story.

Link to Past Learning:
TW review the Sequence Signal Words poster with students. TW review the elements of a short story: Beginning, Middle, End, Setting, Characters, Plot. TW review how to use the students' personal dictionaries while writing and afterwards to proofread spellings. Prior to the sharing of stories, the TW review how to read aloud with expression.

Figure 4.4   (continued)

Content Objective:

Students will put in sequence the details of an event.

Students will use their personal dictionaries to select words and check spellings.

Language Objective(s):

Students will write and read aloud their lists of meaningful life events.

Students will orally share their story ideas with a partner.

Students will write a story using a short story format, using a meaningful idea from their Treasure Chest.

Students will use Sequence Signal Words, as appropriate, in their stories.

Meaningful Activities:

Lesson Sequence:

1. Read and explain content and language objectives with students.

2. Read through the steps in the writing process that students will engage. These steps should be clearly written and explained. Briefly show the artifacts (Treasure Chest and Storyboard) when going through these steps.

3. Share with students the list of events collected in the "Treasure Chest."

4. Show storyboard created from the idea selected from the list.

5. Show the two examples of the resulting story: "boring" and "elaborated."

6. Ask students what's the difference in the two versions. How might they make the "boring" example more interesting?

7. Read the rest of the items on your list (Treasure Chest) as a model.

8. Working in groups, have each student create his or her own "Treasure Chest" of special life events. Ask what makes a particular event "meaningful."

9. When students each have a list of events (6–12), ask them to read their lists to their partners. If they think of other ideas during the sharing, it's fine to add more events to their lists. (For beginning English speakers, illustrations can be used as part or most of the list.)

10. From their lists, each student selects one event to write a story about.

11. Show the sample storyboards and explain how they're used.

12. Students each draw their storyboards, working with their partners, who can answer questions, provide suggestions, etc. Remind students to use the Sequence Signal Words on their storyboards. Students share their storyboards with group members when completed. If anything is unclear, group members are encouraged to make suggestions for revision.

13. Remind students of the elements of a short story (written on board). Students begin writing their stories, using their storyboards and personal dictionaries.

Review & Assessment:

As you read objectives, ask students to indicate with their fingers the degree to which they think they meet the objectives: 1 = I can meet it; 2 = I can come close to meeting it; 3 = I think this one might be hard for me to meet.

(Note: Most students will probably indicate #1. That's okay, especially because they're indicating "publicly." Students can also indicate privately, with their hands in their laps.)

Listen carefully to students' responses. Encourage elaborated responses, as appropriate.

Circulate and help as needed through steps 7, 8, 9. Lower language proficiency students may need assistance in articulating their events. Encourage these students to draw pictures to support their explanations if they're only able to produce 2–3 words orally or in writing. These students also may benefit from sentence frames, such as:

"I remember the time when

_____"

"One thing that happened to me was

_____"

"The first thing that happened was

_____"

"The next thing that happened was

_____"

Monitor students while they make their storyboards. Check to see if students are using Sequence Signal Words and the elements of a short story (listed on board).

Review and assess if students are on track.

(continued)

Figure 4.4   *(continued)*

14. Select a few stories to read aloud (without student names). Encourage "oohs" and "aahs" when students hear something they especially like.	Use a few stories to assess if students are meeting objectives. Use "teachable moments" to review directions and goals.
15. Note with sticky notes areas in students' writing that need re-teaching or mini-lessons.	Spot-check areas that require mini-lessons.
16. Teach necessary mini-lessons prior to students writing a second draft.	If time, re-teach mini-lessons or note what needs to be re-taught at another time.
17. Students continue working with partners, sharing, reading, and revising.	

Closing:
Have students share their Treasure Chests and post them on the wall. Ask students to say which signal words they used in their writing and how they used their personal dictionaries while working on their stories. Review content and language objectives and ask students to self-assess with their fingers the extent to which they met them: 1 = fully met; 2 = partially met; 3 = need more help

Vicki Roberts describes here some of the highlights of her collaboration with grade 4 teacher, Lina Nino, as they worked together with the English learners (and other students) while they created their own Treasure Chests and began this powerful and successful writing process. Her description begins as students started writing their individual stories, after they selected their ideas from their Treasure Chests (see Figure 4.5, My Treasure Chest), and had created their storyboards (see Figure 4.6, Storyboard).

Figure 4.5   My Treasure Chest

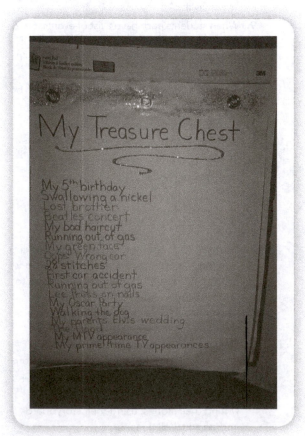

Source: Vicki Roberts

Figure 4.6 Storyboard

Source: Vicki Roberts

Note: Please read the lesson plan prior to reading Vicki Roberts's comments below so you can fully understand the writing process that she and Ms. Nino were using with the grade 4 students.

Using Students' Backgrounds for Academic Success

Vicki Roberts

The students began writing their stories in the same way they told their stories. To assist their writing, I provided the children with their own personal dictionary to use during the year. Although this dictionary contained many frequently used words, homophones, etc., it also had blanks for students to write in their own frequently used words. Writers have a tendency to use many of the same words over and over. By having their own frequently used words written correctly in their personal dictionary, they more readily take ownership of the words they use.

While they wrote, Ms. Nino and I walked around and talked with individual students, helping them through the process. In order to discourage their thought processes from being interrupted, they were told to spell difficult words the best they could, but to circle them, and Ms. Nino or I would help them with the spelling later. Relieved of having to be perfect, the students wrote without anxiety, and they were writing about their own real life experiences!

Once they finished writing their stories, the next step was to read them aloud to the class. I never told whose story I was reading, but I told them if they wanted everyone to know that they were the writer, then they could raise their hand and I would make the announcement. We talked about all the things we loved about the story. If there was something I particularly liked, I would stop and reread the part again, OOOHing and AAAHing over it. (The students immediately began using that "AAH" example in their next piece of writing.)

(continued)

As the stories were read aloud, Ms. Nino and I kept a sticky note handy to jot down mini-lessons the class could work on based on the problems they were having with their papers. We taught a mini-lesson by modeling the skill; then students practiced it to ensure mastery. We encouraged the students to use the new (or refined) skill in their next piece of writing.

We never assessed papers in private. If a child writes a paper and the teacher marks it up and hands it back, what has he learned? The teacher has learned that she can't teach writing, and the student learns that he can't write. My advice: Share their writing! If writers never hear a good piece of writing, they will never be able to create a good piece of writing. You will always get what you've always gotten. Sharing writing is valuable for everyone! The students begin emulating what they hear. They begin to become great writers.

Ms. Nino also had a Treasure Chest of stories from which to write. She always modeled her own piece before assigning a new piece of writing to her students. I think it is important for the teacher to write whatever she requires her students to write. Students need to see the thinking, the scribbled out revisions, the hesitations, and the mistakes (see Figure 4.7). Students need to see writing as a process. The finished product is really never written perfectly the first time. All writers go through a process of creation, frustration, and ultimately elation when the piece is complete (see Figure 4.8). Each time a new assignment was given, students had a choice to start on a new piece, or to use an old piece and "kick it up a notch!"

By modeling, talking, writing, and sharing, the results were astounding! However, I felt the most powerful factors were the modeling and the fact that the students wrote about their own experiences. Not writing from contrived writing prompts but instead writing about their own life experiences enabled them to be the expert in their experience. This created expert writers! 16/17 students passed, but 11/17 were commended! You must attain a score of 3 or 4 on the composition, 4 being the highest score, to achieve commended status! One of Ms. Nino's students even achieved a perfect score, meaning 100% on the objective part of the test (editing and revision) and a 4 on the composition! It still brings tears to my eyes!

Figure 4.7 *Boring* My 5th Birthday Story

It was my birthday. My friends said happy birthday to me. We had cake. It was good. There was a merry-go-round in the front yard. We rode it. It was fun. I opened presents. I gave my friends candy. It was a great birthday.

Figure 4.8 *Elaborated* My 5th Birthday Story

It was my birthday!

"Happy birthday!" shouted my friends. I couldn't believe it. I was finally five years old. I could go to kindergarten! I was grown up! It was the day I had been waiting for, and it was finally here.

We had cake.

In walked my mother with a chocolate birthday cake. It was the prettiest cake I'd ever seen. It was iced with white icing and big pink roses. I couldn't wait to bite into it! I could just taste the big pink rose melting in my mouth.

Figure 4.8   *(continued)*

There was a merry-go-round in the front yard.

"Look out the window," said my dad. When I looked out the window, I couldn't believe my eyes! There in my own front yard was a merry-go-round! It was red and white striped just like a candy cane with four beautiful horses. Pinch me, I must be dreaming!

We rode it. It was fun.

"Let's go ride the horses!" I screamed. We ran out the door as fast as we could. My favorite color is purple, so I jumped up on the purple carousel horse. It was beautiful with a gold saddle and ruby eyes. I felt like a queen on top of this magical horse. We all looked like royalty riding the magical horses. We rode round and round until we felt dizzy with excitement.

Then we opened the presents.

"Time to open presents," announced my mom. "Open mine first!" all of my friends shouted. I tore into the specially wrapped gifts. I received all my favorite things: four different colors of Play-Doh, a Barbie, the one with the black striped bathing suit and black ponytail, and a paint by number oil painting set. Was I a lucky girl!

Then I gave my friends a goody bag.

Now it was time for me to give my friends their goody bags. I gave them each a sack filled with all my favorite candy: miniature Hershey bars, Bazooka bubblegum, and Tootsie Roll pops. It had been an exciting day. Although this birthday happened forty-six years ago, it's one birthday I always remember.

Final Thoughts

In the past, many English learners who were unsuccessful at learning to read or write in English were referred to and placed in special education programs. At the same time, other English learners who perhaps needed special education services were not appropriately placed because of the difficulties in assessing the difference between a learning "problem" and a language "proficiency" issue. Common sense and assessment data suggest that the percentage of English learners in special education should be equal to the percentage of students representing all other demographics. However, this wasn't the case, in large part, because classroom instruction for English learners was ineffective, and the gap between their achievement and that of their native English-speaking peers was substantial.

The SIOP® Model has been found to be a reliable, valid, and empirically sound framework for teaching English learners (and others) in the mainstream classroom. At the heart of high-quality instruction for English learners is systematic and consistent attention to their language and academic strengths and needs. Effective Tier 1 instruction within RTI for English learners is exemplified through the SIOP® Model with the type of differentiated instruction as described in its eight components. We hope that you will consider the SIOP® Model for exemplary Tier 1 instruction within RTI and that your students' academic and language proficiencies are positively impacted from implementing the Model consistently throughout your classroom lessons.

For Reflection and Discussion

1. Tier 1 instruction requires that teachers provide high-quality, effective instruction for all students that is based on assessment, content and language standards, and regular monitoring of student progress. As you think about the professional development that will be required to bring this about, who are the key players (both faculty and administrators) who need to take leadership in this endeavor? What will be each of their responsibilities, and what is a reasonable timeline for putting the RTI pieces in place? What are some possible pitfalls? What are your collective, expected goals for determining success in Tier 1? Turn to Appendix D and select one of the three profiles, answer the questions, and discuss your responses with your RTI team members.

2. Becoming a high-implementing SIOP teacher is a process that requires professional development, planning, and time. Reflect on your answers to the questions in the preceding exercise. In what ways can SIOP professional development intersect with Tier 1 planning and your overall RTI goals? This intersection is critically important for English learners, but what might be some advantages for native speakers whose academic achievement and language proficiency are lacking?

5 Tier 2 and Tier 3 Interventions for English Learners

Annie Pickert Fuller/Pearson Education

For some English learners, Tier 1 instruction might not be enough for them to be successful academically. For example, despite the fact that Ms. Caliari uses the SIOP® Model and differentiates instruction in Tier 1 in her class, there are nine students for whom this instruction is not sufficient. For these students, Tier 2 and possibly Tier 3 interventions are necessary and can be effective at meeting their needs. Throughout this chapter, we will continue to follow Ms. Caliari's class and her grade 5 team at Rodriguez Elementary School. (Rodriguez Elementary School uses a hybrid approach within the RTI model, employing a combination of both standard treatment protocol and problem-solving approaches. (See Chapter 1 for more details.) You will notice that students in Tier 2 or Tier 3 receive a similar intervention, but that in making decisions about grouping students, the content of the intervention, and modifications to the intervention, the team takes into account individual students' strengths and needs.

At Rodriguez Elementary School, Tier 2 interventions are supplemental interventions that are provided in addition to the core curriculum (see Figure 5.1). These interventions build on students' strengths and focus on targeted areas of need. The interventions are used to build core foundational skills that are aligned to grade-level standards, and are not used as a studies skills class or as a way to reteach students who have not mastered a specific grade-level standard. Roughly about 25% of the students at Rodriguez need Tier 2 interventions. If teachers notice that more than 30% of students at a particular grade level have gaps in certain areas, they make changes to Tier 1 instruction to meet the majority of the students' needs.

Tier 3 interventions at Rodriguez are designed for students with the most intense needs. These interventions are more intensive than Tier 2, which means that they are more teacher-directed and explicit, conducted in smaller groups, and provided for a longer period of time (see Figure 5.2). They are tailored to meet individual student needs even within a small group. Tier 3 is not a "place" where students spend their school careers. At Rodriguez, students who receive Tier 3 intervention still participate in part of the core curriculum, and student groups

Figure 5.1   Defining Tier 2

Tier 2 is...	Tier 2 is NOT...
Supplemental instruction.	A replacement of core curriculum (if students are not getting core program, they will only fall farther behind).
Focused and targeted on core skills that are associated with broader academic successes.	A studies skills class.
Designed for students who are not making adequate progress on core skills that are aligned with grade-level standards, but associated with broader academic success.	Designed for students who have not mastered some of the specified grade-level standards, such as comparing settings or converting centimeters to meters. (These students need to receive differentiated instruction and reteaching in Tier 1; see Chapter 4.)
Explicit instruction that emphasizes key instructional features we know to be important for English learners: opportunities for developing and practicing oral language, key vocabulary emphasis, interaction, learning strategy instruction, etc.	A replacement for English Language Development (ELD).
For approximately 20%–25% of the students in a given class, grade level, or school.	For more than 30% of the students in a given class, grade level, or school. (If it is the case that more than 30% of the students need Tier 2 interventions, it is time to rethink Tier 1—what can we do to improve this level of instruction?)

Figure 5.2 Defining Tier 3

Tier 3 Is...	Tier 3 Is NOT...
Instruction that promotes learning for each student (including English language development), based on individual need. It is more intensive than Tier 2; is more teacher-centered, systematic, and explicit, with lots of opportunity for student participation; uses smaller, homogeneous groups; is provided more frequently; is conducted by instructors with greater expertise; and is implemented for longer duration.	Simply more of the same instruction students received in the core curriculum.
Intended for a specific duration of time using frequent progress monitoring to inform ongoing decisions about placement.	A life sentence.
Part of a recursive RTI process where students move in and out of tiers, depending on their documented need for support. Students are in Tier 1 for most of the school day, even when they receive intervention.	A way to remove challenging students from general education.
Provided to about 5%-10% of students in a school for whom Tier 1 and Tier 2 are not sufficient. These students have intensive academic and/or behavioral needs.	Necessarily special education. Students in Tier 3 may have IEPs, but they do not need to have an IEP to receive intervention. Some RTI models provide services to students with an IEP in a fourth tier of intervention.

are flexible. Student data are reviewed regularly to determine whether students can exit intervention, or if they need to remain in intervention, whether they should stay in Tier 3 or move to Tier 2. Only about 8%–10% of all students at Rodriguez Elementary need Tier 3 interventions; some of these students qualify for special education and have IEPs, and other students do not qualify for special education but need intensive intervention nonetheless.

Tier 2 and Tier 3 interventions will vary by grade level and content areas such as reading, writing, and mathematics. However, there are five key elements for establishing Tier 2 and Tier 3 interventions across grade-level and content areas.

1. Grouping students for intervention
2. Determining who will provide intervention
3. Designing and conducting the intervention, including content and methods
4. Monitoring student progress
5. Monitoring intervention fidelity

In this chapter, these elements are described and examples are provided. We also discuss how they vary between Tier 2 and Tier 3. We have focused this chapter around reading interventions. We do this for two reasons (1) English learners most often struggle in the area of reading and (2) there is more research to support reading interventions for English learners. However, these five elements also apply to writing and math interventions, so the process is similar for these two areas as well. As you go through the chapter, please refer to Figure 5.3 to guide your thoughts on how you will establish Tier 2 and Tier 3 interventions in your school or district.

Figure 5.3   Guide to Effective RTI Implementation: Tier 2 and Tier 3

Guide to Effective RTI Implementation: Tier 2 and Tier 3	Tier 2	Tier 3
Who Is Responsible?		
Necessary Professional Development (For whom, by whom?)		
Modification(s) and/or Interventions		
Length of Time Teacher-Student Ratio		
Assessments		
Frequency of Progress Monitoring		
Treatment Fidelity Observations (How often, by whom?)		
Review of Modification(s) and/or Intervention(s)		
Parent Involvement		
Forms/Resources		

Grouping Students for Intervention

For interventions to be effective they should be conducted in small groups. Groups of four to five are ideal for Tier 2 intervention because they are small enough to meet individual needs and also allow students to learn from each other (Vaughn et al., 2007). This is particularly important for English learners because they must have frequent opportunities for interaction with the teacher and with peers (Echevarria, Vogt, & Short, 2013; 2014a; 2014b). For Tier 3 interventions, groups should be even smaller, typically two to three students per group (Vaughn et al., 2007).

The grade 5 team at Rodriguez Elementary School groups students for intervention based on data from screening measures, as well as students' strengths and needs. Students are grouped by skills and not by language level; the heterogeneity of the language levels is beneficial because students who are at high levels of English proficiency serve as models for students who are at lower levels.

Across the grade 5 classes, there are a total of 12 students in need of Tier 3 intervention. Remember from Chapter 3, that there are two students from Ms. Caliari's class, Francesca and Leann, who need Tier 3 intervention. There are also four students from Ms. Martinez's class who need Tier 3 intervention: Jose, who has a learning disability; Ella, who has a learning disability and ADHD; and Miguel and Luke. There are also three students from Ms. Nyguen's class (Jason, Michael, Brittany) and three from Ms. Catwell's class (Ryan, Veronica, Francisco) who need Tier 3 intervention. Jason, Michael, Francisco, and Brittany have a learning disability. These twelve students are put into four groups for intervention. The team decides that since the students' strengths and areas of need are fairly similar, they will place them so there is a range of English proficiency in each of the four groups. See Table 5.1 for a list of the Tier 3 intervention groups.

The grade 5 team has also determined there are a number of students who need Tier 2 intervention. Ms. Caliari and the other three grade 5 teachers carefully examine the data collected for these students. Recall that in Chapter 3, we discussed the students in grade 5 who have needs in both fluency and comprehension, including vocabulary and comprehension strategies. Other students only have needs in comprehension, again including vocabulary and comprehension strategies. In Ms. Caliari's class, Gabriel, Maribel, and Andy need intervention in both fluency and comprehension, while Andrew, Daniel, Tatyanna, and Triet need comprehension intervention only. Ms. Nyguen has two students, Leticia and Rigo, who have comprehension and fluency needs, and three students, Humberto, Simon, and Lauren, who have comprehension needs.

The teachers decide to combine their students to make two groups. The fluency and comprehension group will have five students and the comprehension group will have seven students. Although the comprehension group is slightly larger than the teachers would like, because of their limited resources, it is necessary. See Table 5.2 for the Tier 2 intervention groups. Ms. Catwell and Ms. Martinez also are able to form two groups of students from their classes as well: one group has fluency and comprehension needs, while the other requires instruction only in comprehension.

Table 5.1 Tier 3 Intervention Groups

Tier 3 Intervention Grade: 5 Intervention Teachers: Ms. Shin, Mr. Correon Paraprofessional: Ms. Rose, Ms. Chavez			
Group 1	**Group 2**	**Group 3**	**Group 4**
Ella	Francesca	Brittany	Michael
Miguel	Jose	Veronica	Jason
Leanne	Luke	Francisco	Ryan

Table 5.2 Ms. Caliari and Ms. Ngyuen's Tier 2 Intervention Groups

Tier 2 Intervention Grade: 5	
Group 1 (Fluency & Comprehension) Intervention Teacher: Ms. Caliari Paraprofessional: Ms. Diaz	**Group 2 (Comprehension)** Intervention Teacher: Ms. Ngyuen
Gabriel	Andrew
Maribel	Daniel
Andy	Tatyanna
Leticia	Triet
Rigo	Humberto,
	Simon
	Lauren

Determining Who Will Provide Intervention

The grade 5 classes have intervention time each day from 10:30–11:30 a.m. At Rodriguez Elementary, one of the special education teachers, the bilingual reading specialist, and three paraprofessionals provide additional support to classroom teachers during intervention time. In this case, Ms. Shin, a special education teacher, Mr. Correon, the bilingual reading specialist, and two paraprofessionals provide Tier 3 intervention to the four groups of grade 5 students. The students receive a full 60 minutes of intervention. Each adult provides 15 minutes of intervention focused on a specific skill: word study, vocabulary, fluency, or comprehension strategies. The students rotate to each adult. The paraprofessionals at Rodriguez Elementary have received extensive professional development in the intervention they provide. (See Figure 5.4 for more information on the role of paraprofessionals in an RTI model.)

To be most effective while delivering Tier 2 intervention, Ms. Caliari and Ms. Nyguen share students; and Ms. Martinez and Ms. Catwell also share students. Ms. Caliari and Ms. Martinez provide intervention that focuses on fluency and comprehension, while Ms. Nyguen and Ms. Catwell deliver intervention that targets comprehension. The teachers work together to plan both the intervention lessons and the activities for the other students in the class during the intervention period.

Figure 5.4 Role of Paraprofessionals in RTI Model

The illustration provided about how the 5th grade team at Rodriguez Elementary School uses paraprofessionals is just one example of the role of paraprofessionals in an RTI model. At some schools with multiple paraprofessionals, these educators are important resources that can provide extra support in an RTI model. Often when schools have multiple paraprofessionals there is a tendency to use these valuable assets to deliver intervention, particularly when the paraprofessionals speak the students' first language. However, it is important to emphasize two points. First, paraprofessionals should never be fully responsible for designing and delivering intervention for students, nor should they be responsible for making instructional decisions about students in the absence of close collaboration with the certified teachers. Second, if paraprofessionals are going to assist in providing interventions, they need specific professional development in the content and methods of the intervention, progress monitoring, and how to collaborate (Hauerwas & Goessling, 2008). Ideally though, we want the expert teachers who know both the content area (e.g., literacy) and EL issues providing the interventions to the students who are in most need.

From the Field   **Interview with an RTI Leader, Principal at an Elementary School**

Interviewer: How do you decide who will provide each tier of intervention? And how do you organize the interventions?

Principal: At our site we have four bilingual paraprofessionals whom we use to help us deliver interventions. We also have two reading specialists whom we use. In our school students who have IEPs receive intervention in Tier 4 from a special education teacher. Students who need Tier 3 intervention receive 45 minutes a day from one of our reading specialists. Classroom teachers deliver Tier 2 intervention for 30 minutes each day. Usually teachers provide intervention to their own students, but at times teachers will share students based on individual needs. During the grade-level intervention time, our four paraprofessionals help monitor the other students in the class while teachers deliver intervention.

Since Tier 2 interventions typically last 30 minutes, the teachers decide they will spend half of the 60 minute intervention block providing intervention while the other students work on independent writing activities. During the other 30 minutes of the allocated time, the teachers differentiate the language arts curriculum for all students, by providing additional support through extension or reteaching. The team also decides that Ms. Caliari should have the support of the bilingual paraprofessional at the school site to help monitor the students who are working independently, since she has many students who have difficulty staying on-task.

This scenario represents just one option for how to determine who will organize and conduct intervention within an RTI model. There are other processes that districts have implemented across the country. See the From the Field feature for another example. However your school or district decides who will conduct the interventions, the duration for Tier 2 should be at least 30 minutes, and for Tier 3 it should be about 60 minutes. This may vary slightly by grade level. For example, a kindergarten teacher might implement two or three 15-minute blocks because 30 minutes is just too long for such young students. At a middle school, if a period is only 50 minutes, that might be as long as is feasible for Tier 3 intervention.

Designing and Conducting Intervention: Content and Methods

In conducting intervention for English learners, consider their academic skill development and language proficiency. Think carefully about the content that will be taught and the methods by which it will be delivered. Intervention provides students with the essential skills and strategies they need to be successful, and teaches these skills to mastery. It does not involve "dumbing down" the curriculum for students, but instead simplifies tasks so that students are able to develop fully the skills critical for academic success. During intervention, teachers continue to use the instructional techniques and methods described in Chapter 4 to make content accessible while developing students' language proficiency.

Often districts and schools choose to use prepackaged intervention programs to simplify planning for teachers and to keep intervention consistent across teachers or other professionals who are delivering it. There are several intervention programs available that can be used for either Tier 2 or Tier 3 interventions. However if your district chooses these programs, consider that the intervention may not have been designed for English learners and therefore adjustments may need to be made. The discussion of the content and methods of intervention later in this section may be helpful as you choose and implement a commercial intervention program.

Although there is not as much research on interventions for English learners as there is for native English speakers, there are several studies that have examined the impact of reading interventions on the achievement of English learners (Baker, Richards-Tutor, Gersten, Baker, & Smith, in press). The majority of these interventions have focused on kindergarten and 1st grade students. For example, Vaughn and colleagues (Vaughn, Cirino, et al., 2006; Vaughn, Linan-Thompson et al., 2006; Vaughn, Mathes, et al., 2006) conducted several studies on the intervention *Enhanced Proactive Reading,* and the results have been very promising for 1st grade English learners. There is also a Spanish version of this intervention (*Lectura Proactiva*) that has been shown to be effective for English learners receiving their language arts instruction in Spanish. These interventions would be considered Tier 2 interventions, or supplemental interventions. As of the writing this book, there has not been any published research that has specifically examined Tier 3 interventions for English learners.

PD **TOOLKIT**™

Click on SIOP Lesson Plans & Activities, then under *RTI Lesson Plans* find the "Lesson Plan for Tier 2 Group" as an example of an intervention lesson at Tier 2.

PD **TOOLKIT**™

Click on SIOP Lesson Plans & Activities, then under *RTI Lesson Plans* find the "Lesson Plan for Tier 3 Group" as an example of an intervention lesson at Tier 3.

Content of Intervention

The content of intervention varies by grade level and student needs, and whether these involve reading, writing, or math. In determining content for intervention, teachers should teach the essential skills necessary for academic achievement that are aligned to the Common Core State Standards or other state standards. It is important for intervention teachers to understand how reading, writing, and mathematics skills and concepts are developed, because struggling students often need instruction in foundational skills. The content of the intervention should be based on student assessment data. For example, screening assessments provide teachers with information on individual strengths and areas of need. It is not within the scope of this chapter or book to describe all the possible content of interventions, but see Figure 5.5 for a sample lesson created for students who are provided Tier 2 intervention by Ms. Caliari. Figure 5.6 includes a sample lesson for the students who receive Tier 3

Figure 5.5 Lesson Plan for Tier 2 Group

Date: Oct. 15
Group: Tier 2—Group 1

Students Present: Gabriel, Andy, Maribel, Rigo, Leticia

Content Objectives:

1. Students will decode and spell multisyllabic words with prefixes (*dis-*, *un-*, *re-*) and root words (*-cover*, *-do*).

2. Students will read a passage with words with these prefixes. The focus is on accuracy, speed, and prosody.

3. Students will summarize a 3-paragraph passage in 3 sentences.

5th grade CCSS:

1. Know and apply grade-level phonics and word analysis skills in decoding words.

2. Use common, grade-appropriate Greek and Latin affixes and roots as clues to the meaning of a word.

3. Read with sufficient accuracy and fluency to support comprehension.

4. Determine two or more main ideas of a text and explain how they are supported by key details; summarize the text.

Language Objective:

1. Students will read words with the prefixes (*dis-*, *un-*, *re-*) to a partner.

2. Students will write definitions to words with these prefixes.

Figure 5.5   (continued)

Materials Needed:
Sticky notes for root words (large yellow sticky notes) and prefixes (small blue sticky notes), words list with selected words with prefixes from the passage, 3-paragraph informational passage (4th grade reading level), highlighters

Introduction (1 Minute)	Word Study (5 Minutes)	Vocabulary Development (6 Minutes)	Fluency Practice (6 Minutes)	Comprehension Strategies (12 Minutes)
Tell students that they will be reading and spelling multisyllabic words with prefixes and then read a passage and write a summary with these words. Write the 3 prefixes on a white board and read them to the students. Have student read the words. Write the 2 root words on the board and read them to the students. Have student spell the root words.	**Multisyllabic words** *Model:* Tell students the small blue sticky notes are for the prefixes and the yellow sticky notes are for root words. Give students the first word and tell them you will model it: *redo.* Clap the syllables: re-do. You will then spell the word. Write the prefix on the blue sticky note and the root word on the yellow one. Say, watch me spell *redo.* *Guided Practice:* Tell students you will do 3–4 together. Tell students a word and ask them to spell the word using the sticky notes. Do it with them using the think-aloud procedure as you spell it. *Independent Practice:* Give students several words to try on their own using choral responding. Then have them each do a different word on their own. Have them spell the word and then read the word to a partner. Have students do a word hunt to highlight words with prefixes in the passage they are reading during fluency practice.	**Vocabulary Flash Cards** *Model:* Provide a word from the word list to the students, *uncover.* What does *uncover* mean? I know that *un-* means "not" and *cover* means "to put something on top of something else." *Uncover* means "to not cover something." "I uncovered what my sister was hiding." I am going to write my word on this index card, and on the back I am going to put the definition and draw a quick picture. *Guided Practice:* Let's do one together, *undo.* *Independent Practice:* Have them do *recover* on their own. Tell them they will finish the other words tomorrow.	**Repeated Reading** *Model:* Read the 3-paragraph passage to the students. *Guided Practice:* Teacher and students read the 3-paragraph passage together. *Independent Practice:* Students read the passage independently. They will practice this passage throughout the week.	**Summarizing** *Model:* First paragraph summary—model using think-aloud. Use a passage from last week's lesson to model summarizing using key words. *First...Next...Finally....* Make sure key words are displayed for students. *Guided Practice:* Let's summarize the first paragraph of this week's passage together. Read the first paragraph from the passage from this week. Have students whisper to their partner what they think the paragraph is mostly about. Provide sentence frame "First, the plant..." *Independent Practice:* Have students read and summarize the second and third paragraphs independently. Provide key words such as *next, then, finally* to all students. Provide sentence frames to students who need it. "Next, the plant..." "Finally, the plant..." Provide time for students to read their summaries to a partner.

Figure 5.6   Tier 3 Intervention Lesson

Number of days for lesson: Minimum 2   **Students Present:** Francesca, Jose, Luke

Date: Oct. 15

Group: Tier 3—Group 2

Word Study—15 minutes

Content Objective:	**5th grade CCSS:**	**Language Objective:**
Students will decode and spell words with the vowel digraphs -ai, -ay, -ee, -ea	Know and apply grade-level phonics and word analysis skills in decoding words.	Students will sort words by vowel digraphs.

Materials Needed: Sticky notes—large yellow sticky notes and small blue sticky notes (with vowel digraphs written on them -ai, -ay, -ee, -ea), word list with words with vowel digraphs

Introduction: Tell students that they will be reading and spelling words with the vowel patterns they have already been introduced to. Write the vowel digraphs on the board and then say the letter of each one makes the sound of the digraph.

Model: Show students the small blue sticky notes that have the following vowel digraphs. The yellow sticky notes are used to spell the rest of the word. Give students the first word and tell them you will model it: *rain.* I am going to spell rain; *r-ai-n.* On the yellow sticky note write *r*; then choose the *-ai-* small blue sticky note; then write the *–n.*

Guided Practice: We will do 5–6 together. Tell students a word and ask them to spell the word using the sticky notes. Do it with them using the think-aloud procedure as you spell it.

Independent Practice: Give each student several different words. Alternate between choral responses and individual responses. Students will then do a word sort with words based on vowel digraphs.

Vocabulary—15 minutes

Content Objective:	**5th grade CCSS:**	**Language Objective:**
Students will use the correct tense (past and present) of regular verbs in a sentence.	Use verb tense to convey various times, sequences, states, and conditions.	Students use sentence frames to write sentences with the correct verb tense (past, present), regular verbs only.

Materials Needed: sentence frames, white boards, markers

Introduction: Tell students that they will be working with verbs and using the correct verb tense in a sentence. Remind students that a verb is an action word. Provide 4–5 sentences on the white board and have students identify the verb in each sentence; use a mix of past, present, and future tenses. Tell the students that after they practice verb tenses they will read a passage that has verbs in the past tense and also has vowel patterns that we are working on in word study.

Model: Sometimes when we write we need to use different forms of a verb. We also see different forms of verbs when we read. These different forms of a verb is called verb tense. For example, if I wanted to talk about how Sara plays today I would talk and write that differently than about how she played yesterday. I might say "She plays with her friends at recess." Or I might say "I play with my friends." I could also say, "Yesterday, she played with her friends at recess." Or "I played with my friends yesterday." Write these sentences on the board and underline the verbs. Highlight that when it's present it is *play* (I, we) or *plays* (she, he) and in the past we add *–ed.* Show all of these examples.

Guided Practice: Let's do a few together. Use think-alouds as you decide which tense to use for the sentence. Use the following verbs: *need, explain, clean.* Write the sentences on the board with blanks for the verbs. Have students write the verb on their white boards.

Independent Practice: Have students do two verbs in both present and past on their own using sentence frames: *wait, agree*
"I_____for my turn to use the computer. "Yesterday I _____ for my turn to use the computer."
"He _____ with her point." "Yesterday he _____ with her point."

Figure 5.6 (continued)

Fluency Practice—15 minutes

Content Objective:	5th grade CCSS:	Language Objective:
Students will read a 2-paragraph passage with words that have vowel digraphs and verbs in past tense. The focus is on accuracy, speed, and prosody.	Read with sufficient accuracy and fluency to support comprehension.	Students will do a "word hunt" highlighting words with vowel digraphs and verbs in past tense in the passage.

Materials Needed: 2-paragraph informational passage (3rd grade reading level), highlighters—two colors for each student

Introduction: Remind students that they are working with words that have vowel combinations -*ai*, -*ay*, -*ee*, -*ea* and regular verbs in the past tense. Write examples of words on the board for the students. Have students do a word hunt for words with these patterns. Highlight vowel patterns in one color and verbs in another.

Model: Read the 2-paragraph passage to the students.

Guided Practice: Teacher and students read the 2-paragraph passage together.

Independent Practice: Students read independently 2-3 times.

Comprehension Strategies—20 minutes

Content Objective:	5th grade CCSS:	Language Objective:
Students will identify the main idea of the passage.	Determine two or more main ideas of a text and explain how they are supported by key details; summarize the text.	Students write the main idea and two supporting details in their own words for the passage using sentence frames as needed.

Materials Needed: Reading passages, highlighters (2 colors per student)

Introduction: Tell students they we will be working to find the main idea and two supporting details of the paragraphs they read in fluency practice. Remind the students what the main idea is and what supporting details are. Post the definitions of these terms with picture cues so that students can refer to them throughout the lesson.

Model: I am going to model how to find the main idea and supporting details using the passage we read last week. Use the think-aloud procedure to show students how to identify the main idea and details. Highlight the main idea with one color and the two details with another color. "I can then write the main idea and supporting details in my own words. Watch me. This passage is about....First..., Then..."

Guided Practice: Do the first paragraph of the passage for this week together. Follow the same procedure as in model.

Independent Practice: Have students complete the second paragraph together. Provide sentence frames for students who need that support.

---

intervention from Ms. Shin, Mr. Correon, and two paraprofessionals. Notice that although the content is not that different in Tier 3, much more time is dedicated to basic word study skills. Also, the level of intensity is different. For example, time is included for peer work in the Tier 2 intervention (less intense); in Tier 3, the teacher is working with the students throughout the intervention period (more intense).

Methods of Delivering Intervention

Tier 2 and Tier 3 interventions are more effective when specific instructional methods are used, regardless of the content being taught (see Gersten et al., 2007). One method for delivering content using explicit instruction is called the Core Intervention Model (CIM) (Gerber

Figure 5.7 Alignment of CIM Principles with SIOP® Components

Six CIM Principles	Eight SIOP® Components and Specific Features
Small groups	Interaction–grouping configurations
Set specific objectives	Lesson Preparation: Content and Language Objectives
Content and materials are appropriate	Lesson Preparation: Supplementary Materials, Adaptation of Content, Meaningful Activities
Explicit and intensive teaching of skills	Building Background–concepts linked to past learning Comprehensible Input–speech, clear explanation of tasks, using a variety of techniques Strategies–teaching learning strategies Practice & Application–hands-on materials and manipulatives, integrating language skills, Lesson Delivery–pacing
Explicit correction procedures	Strategies–Scaffolding strategies Review & Assessment–regular feedback
Opportunities for many correct responses	Interaction–opportunities for interaction with students and teacher Lesson Delivery–student engagement

et al., 2004; Richards & Leafstedt, 2010). In this instructional model the onus is on the intervention teacher's "responsiveness" to students' needs, which places the focus on instruction and not on the student deficits. There are six principles in the CIM, and they are aligned to the eight components of the SIOP® Model (see Figure 5.7).

- **Principle 1: Small Groups.** Remember that for Tier 2 intervention, groups of four to five students are ideal; for Tier 3, groups of two to three are ideal.

- **Principle 2: Setting Objectives.** Setting specific objectives requires that daily lesson goals for students be established for the intervention. Objectives are based on assessed student needs and the critical skills necessary for academic success. According to the SIOP® Model for English learners, both content and language objectives should be developed for intervention, as well as for regular classroom instruction (see Chapter 4 for more information on content and language objectives). In order to have meaningful content and language objectives for intervention, these objectives should be observable and measurable. This means the teacher can observe the student "doing" the behavior and can also determine the extent to which the student has met the objective. Creating and teaching to content and language objectives is important for both Tier 2 and Tier 3 interventions. At Tier 2 the objectives are likely to be highly aligned to grade-level standards. However, objectives for Tier 3 interventions may be more focused on foundational skills that allow students to work toward grade-level standards, and the same objectives may be used for more than one lesson. See the lesson plan examples in Figures 5.5 and 5.6 and notice the differences in the objectives for each tier.

- **Principle 3: Content and Materials Are Appropriate for a Student's Ability.** In planning for intervention, the content and materials selected should target each student's individual needs. At times, this means that individual students in a group may require different content and materials even though they are working toward the same objectives and are participating in the same activities. For example, in the summarizing activity in Ms. Caliari's lesson, all students are working toward the same objective: summarizing the passage. Gabriel, Maribel, Leticia, and Rigo may benefit from modeling and guided practice with using key words such as *first, next, finally.* However, Andy may need more support and may be given written sentence frames such as *First the plant…; Next, it…; Finally, it….* The goal is for all the students to be able to write a brief summary; the scaffolding they receive enables them to be successful in meeting this goal.

- **Principle 4: Skills Must Be Taught Explicitly, Intensively, and at a Rapid Pace.** Explicit teaching involves modeling, breaking tasks and skills into steps, guided practice, and independent practice. Intensive intervention requires attention to group size, pacing, and additional instructional time, as needed. During intervention, group size is small and adequate time is provided for the small group work, in addition to regular classroom instruction. To increase the intensity of intervention, make a group smaller, add additional time, or adjust the content being taught (Vaughn, Wanzek, Woodruff, & Linan-Thompson, 2007). Intensive intervention also needs to be conducted at a rapid pace, so the lessons move quickly. This is critical because students who are struggling have often fallen behind their peers, and therefore, they need to learn much more in less time (Engelmann, Becker, Carnine, & Gersten, 1988). A rapid pace requires students to respond frequently; therefore, there is less time for distraction or inattention, which tend to occur more often with students who need intervention.

- **Principle 5: Students Must Be Provided Opportunities for Many Correct Responses.** During intervention, teachers need to maximize the number of correct response opportunities for each student. Students in need of intervention often do not take the risk to respond, or when they do speak up, their responses are often deemed incorrect. Research suggests that students who respond more often during intervention make more growth than students who respond less, so students need to have as many opportunities to respond meaningfully as possible (Richards, Leafstedt, & Gerber, 2006). Refer back to Ms. Caliari's Tier 2 lesson (Figure 5.5). Note how she maximizes the number of responses by providing opportunities for her students to respond in a variety of ways. She uses choral responses and encourages students to respond individually or with each other. Ms. Caliari includes opportunities for interaction in both the word study (read words to a partner) and comprehension (read summaries to a partner) portions of the intervention. She also reinforces students when they respond correctly. For example, she might say, "Andy that is correct. To spell *redo* we spell the prefix *re, r-e,* and the root word *do, d-o.*" As in the example, it is important that intervention teachers use deliberate, systematic, and specific praise.

- **Principle 6: Corrective Feedback Using the Staircase Approach.** Explicit correction procedures are the crux of the Core Intervention Model. Students are praised for correct responses. When an incorrect answer is given, students are led to the correct answer while the incorrect response is ignored. After an incorrect response, students are provided the opportunity to respond immediately to a simplified question or task. Correction procedures involve using the staircase approach to correct students during instruction. This ensures that students are led to the correct answer and are given the opportunity to respond independently to the original task. Just as a teacher takes the student down the steps in the staircase, he or she must take the student back up. Figure 5.8 shows an example of a staircase for decoding vowel diagraphs. For much more detail on using the staircase approach and the other principles of the CIM, see Richards and Leafstedt (2010).

PD TOOLKIT™

Click on SIOP Resources, then under *RTI and English Learners* find the "Staircase Example" for another example of providing corrective feedback using the staircase method.

Figure 5.8   Example of Staircase Approach

> **Step 1: Original question or task:** "Read this sentence: *The chain was broken.*"
>
> **Step 2: Prompt for a re-read:** "Put your finger on the word that begins with *c*. Read the word again."
>
> **Step 3: Prompt for a specific part/decoding correctly/decoding incorrectly/rule:** "What sound do the letters /ai/ make? Remember that in many words, when two vowels are next to each other, the first one says its name."
>
> **Step 4: Ask yes/no question:** "Does /ai/ make the "ā" sound?"
>
> **Step 5: Tell the answer:** "Does /ai/ makes the sound "ā". What sound?"
>
> **Step 6: Say and have student repeat:** "The word is *chain*. Say it. Read it."

Monitoring Student Progress

As discussed in Chapter 3, student progress must be monitored regularly, particularly if students are in Tier 2 or Tier 3 intervention. Students in Tier 2 typically are monitored every other week, and students in Tier 3 are monitored every week. Often teachers who conduct intervention struggle to find the time to assess the students during their intervention time. Although some schools may have the resources to have another person pull aside students to assess them, most often the teachers who conduct intervention need to do the assessments themselves. For Tier 2, our suggestion is for teachers to take one day every other week for assessing students.

For example, Ms. Caliari conducts intervention Monday through Friday for the first week; then she teaches the intervention on Monday through Thursday for week two. She then uses the Friday of the second week to assess the students. You may feel frustrated that you need to plan time for this assessment. However, it is critical because in an RTI model, progress monitoring is seen as part of the intervention process. Consider that by assessing you are gaining useful information about how well the intervention is working, and by getting this information, you will be able to make some necessary changes, which will actually make your intervention more efficient and effective.

In Tier 3, Ms. Shin, Mr. Correon, and the paraprofessionals need to assess students every week. On Fridays, the two paraprofessionals pull students aside to assess them. Ms. Shin and Mr. Correon have students rotate to them in their groups, and then the students move to independent workstations where they practice reading fluency on the computer for one and do a vocabulary development activity for the other.

Monitoring Intervention Fidelity

Another type of monitoring that schools and districts need to consider within their RTI model is intervention fidelity. What do we mean by intervention fidelity? It is often referred to as *fidelity of implementation* (Gersten, Fuchs, Coyne, Greenwood, & Innocenti, 2005), and it means that the intervention is conducted as intended. Intervention fidelity is important because:

1. If multiple teachers or other educators are conducting intervention, we want to make sure that the intervention is consistent across professionals so we know all students are receiving instruction at the same level of effectiveness.

2. If a student is not making progress, we need to know if the intervention has been delivered as intended; if not, that may explain the student's lack of progress.

As an example, in Chapter 3 we met Andy, who was not making progress in Tier 2. At Rodriguez, fidelity of intervention is monitored regularly, and the teachers know that the intervention Andy received was implemented with high fidelity; therefore, the team's decision to change interventions was warranted. However, if Andy were receiving intervention that lacked fidelity and the team didn't realize this was the problem, then they might have incorrectly moved him to a different intervention tier when really the problem was that the instruction he was receiving was not implemented effectively. Fidelity of intervention is particularly important if a school or district is using the RTI model to determine if a student qualifies for special education services. We would want to know that a student has actually received proper intervention before making this type of decision.

So, how is fidelity monitored? Typically, fidelity is monitored through observations using a checklist or protocol, as is used with the SIOP® Model. An example of the checklist used by Rodriguez Elementary School is found in Figure 5.9. Various people at the school site can conduct fidelity observations, including people from the RTI leadership team, such as a school psychologist, principal, or a reading or math coach. It is VERY important that the person conducting the fidelity observation be familiar with the intervention, as well as trained in how to conduct the observation using the checklist. In our

Figure 5.9 Fidelity Checklist for Core Intervention Model

Core Intervention Model Fidelity Checklist

Observer_____

Teacher/Group_____

Date_____

Component	Present	Absent	Notes
1. Stated the objective for the activity.			
2. Gave clear directions.			
3. Modeled each activity prior to guided practice.			
4. Broke activities down into steps for students.			
5. Provided corrective feedback using staircase.			
6. Provided verbal praise for correct responses.			
7. Provided students many opportunities to respond.			
Percentage of Components Present and Absent			

Source: Modified from Richards & Leafstedt, 2010.

own work with schools, we have found that encouraging teachers to keep a copy of the checklist with them during intervention is a very helpful way for them to conduct the intervention with fidelity.

Final Thoughts

The five key elements of Tier 2 and Tier 3 interventions ensure that students are selected appropriately for intervention, are delivered the intervention they need with specific methods of delivery, and are monitored carefully in their progress. Schools and districts should systematically consider the logistics of intervention, such as who will deliver it, when it will take place, and how teachers will jointly plan their instruction for students, both during intervention and when other students are working independently. When planning interventions for English learners, teacher teams should plan and align them with the input of colleagues with specific backgrounds in second language acquisition and special education.

For Reflection and Discussion

1. How can specialists such as a bilingual teacher and a special education teacher be helpful in the various components of Tier 2 and Tier 3 interventions?

2. Which teaching methods are critical for delivering interventions to struggling English learners? Why?

3. In what ways can we adjust intervention in Tier 3 to make it more intense?

4. Consider how you might monitor intervention fidelity at your site. Why is this critical?

6 How to Distinguish Disability from Linguistic Differences

Monkey Business/Fotolia

The question most often asked of us as we work with teachers across the United States is: How can we tell if a student has some sort of disability or if he or she just needs more time to develop English proficiency? The answer is not simple, and in this chapter we offer guidance for using an RTI process to make just that kind of determination.

Part of the complexity of the issue lies in the fact that English learners are not all alike, although we tend to group them as such. English learners come from a wide range of backgrounds, educational experiences, and English language proficiencies. Some immigrated to the United States when they were very young and others came as adolescents. Many more were born in this country and educated completely in U.S. schools. Although they are a diverse group, the following profiles represent the largest groups of English learners in our schools. These profiles do not depict every English learner, and it is important to remember that each student is a unique individual; however, the following are a few broad categories into which most English learners fall.

- **English learners who are literate and fluent in their home language.** These students' literacy backgrounds afford them the advantage of drawing on their foundation of language and literacy skills. With careful instruction, those skills will transfer to English. However, these students are still learning new concepts, information, and skills in a new language. There may be some areas where they struggle as they process information in this new language. In some cases, as students have reported in our research, they simply do not understand the teacher. As we discuss in Chapter 4, it is critical that teachers use instructional techniques and practices that make both the content and language (English) comprehensible for their students.

- **English learners who speak their native language fluently but are not literate in it.** These students do not have a reservoir of academic skills and concepts on which to draw as they are introduced to literacy development. Imagine how difficult it would be to learn a new concept like nuclear fusion—the process by which multiple like-charged atomic nuclei join together to form a heavier nucleus. It is accompanied by the release or absorption of *energy,* which allows matter to enter a *plasma* state. You have the advantage of using background knowledge and experience to try to make sense of that definition, yet it may still be difficult for you to understand. Now picture having someone explain it to you in a language that you only understand superficially or you understand in conversation but are totally lost at this level of academic discussion. Since you have many successful learning experiences in your background, you would understand that your confusion is because of language, not intelligence, motivation, or having some disability that prevents you from comprehending. However, English learners who have not had successful learning experiences and do not have a reservoir of academic skills and concepts that help them make sense of new information will struggle even more. They would benefit from instruction in their first language to help them develop those critical literacy skills. If bilingual teachers are not available and instruction is in English, we must be extremely careful when attributing poor performance to factors such as low intelligence, lack of motivation, and learning disabilities.

- **English learners who are "limited bilinguals" because they have underdeveloped linguistic skills in both their home language and English.** Most of these students were born in the United States—76% of elementary students and 66% of secondary students—so they have been exposed to a mix of their home language and English for years before they enter school. Because many of these children are poor (Garcia & Jensen, 2007), they most likely do not come from homes where literacy activities are part of the daily fabric of their lives. Almost half of the parents of English learners in elementary school had not completed high school and a quarter had less than a ninth grade education (Ballantyne, Sanderman, & Levy, 2008). As a result, these students have limited literacy experiences and lack exposure to academic language models in either language. These English learners rely on the hours spent in school to provide exposure to literacy, science, and math activities, to learn about a variety of subject areas, and to provide opportunities to hear and use academic language in productive, meaningful ways. The level of English students are exposed to outside of school on television, online, and in conversation is not the kind of language that is useful for completing rigorous, standards-based lessons and for literacy development. When students "speak English," they are often expected to perform at grade level in English. However, they usually have significant gaps in their repertoire of skills, especially if they didn't receive bilingual literacy instruction, and they struggle to understand the type of English that is used in the classroom (Cummins, 2000). Often instruction lacks meaning for them, which can contribute to off-task behavior, low motivation, and apathy toward reading text. These are also some of the characteristics of learning disabilities, so when students are not reaching benchmarks it can be difficult to pinpoint the cause of learning issues.

As you see, each of the profiles discussed presents unique issues and instructional decisions. Now let's turn our attention to the ways that academic language impact learning, keeping in mind the implications for students who fit the profiles discussed above.

The Language Demands of School

There is growing awareness that the type of language used in school differs significantly from the everyday language students use to communicate. Researchers investigating the language demands of school aren't limiting their studies to English learners since most students are challenged by technical and content-specific vocabulary, more complex sentence structures, and rhetorical forms used in academic settings. The Common Core State Standards and Next Generation Science Standards require even more sophisticated use of academic language than was previously the case.

English learners in particular have difficulty when encountering academic language since they lack experience with this more complex type of language and it likely is beyond their level of English proficiency. Academic language is not something that one "picks up" over time because it isn't transparent. This higher level of language use needs to be explicitly taught and practiced through opportunities to use it orally and in writing. Oral language proficiency is especially important because the English oral language skills of English learners correlate with their reading fluency and ability to learn from text (August & Shanahan, 2006).

Academic language presents an acute challenge for English learners in standards-based classrooms where they are learning challenging concepts, skills, and procedures in a language in which they are not yet completely fluent. English learners are capable of participating successfully in lessons that use academic language when their linguistic needs are accounted for. Similarly, English learners do well in some schools and more poorly in others, which confirms that quality of instruction has a significant influence on English learners' achievement (EdSource, 2007).

Learning in a Second Language

We've discussed the language demands that English learners face in school, so it is understandable that many English learners struggle academically, and as a group lag far behind their native English-speaking peers. Disproportionate numbers of English learners are referred to special education, with many either over- or underidentified as having learning disabilities (Trent & Artiles, 2007). It can be quite a challenge to disentangle possible learning disabilities from limited language proficiency, both in English and in their home language. Research provides guidance about what might be expected for students learning in a second language.

- One of the tenets of RTI is early identification of learning problems. The gap between struggling readers and good readers is smallest early on. If a reading problem is addressed early, a lingering problem that results in a history of failure can be avoided. In fact, early identification and intervention can help prevent reading difficulties altogether (Torgesen, 2012). This holds true for English learners and English-speaking students alike.

- Math achievement is significantly impacted by literacy since mathematics is quite language dependent. Aside from English learners needing to understand the teacher's explanation of math concepts and procedures, mathematics uses technical vocabulary particular to math, specific language features for writing explanations and math word problems, and various text types (Schleppegrell, 2007).

- Reading development is similar in L1 and L2 in many ways. However, it differs for second language learners in the following ways: they have limited knowledge of the language of instruction (English); they draw on their first language experiences, knowledge, and skills to make sense of text; and they require accommodations or adjustments to instruction to make it meaningful for them (August & Shanahan, 2006).

- It is unlikely that a reading disability would occur in one language and not the other. English learners with a "true" reading disability will exhibit persistent problems with accurate and fluent word recognition, decoding, and spelling skills even as they become proficient in spoken English (Geva & Farnia, 2012).

- The proportion of English learners with a reading disability is similar to English-speaking students. Approximately 20% of both English learners and native English speakers struggle with decoding and 5%–10% struggle with reading comprehension (August & Shanahan, 2006). When the numbers of English learners suspected of having a reading disability are greater than these percentages, a close look at quality of instruction is indicated.

- More than 80% of English learners are Spanish speakers. Specific evidence-based principles to guide reading instruction for Spanish-speaking students (Vaughn et al., 2006) include:
  - designing programs based on commonalities between reading instruction in English and in Spanish.
  - making connections between students' knowledge in Spanish and its application to English.
  - organizing peer and cooperative groups to enhance learning.
  - providing multiple opportunities for students to use oral language in Spanish or English to respond to higher-order questions.
  - recognizing that English literacy will require more explicit instruction in both phonics and word reading.

- Effective practices for English learners who are receiving special education services include use of visual learning approaches, multisensory teaching approaches, experience-based learning (e.g., language experience approach and discovery learning), process-based teaching approaches (e.g., readers/writers workshop), and technology-based learning (e.g., interactive software and assistive technologies) (Cloud, 2006).

In spite of adequate schooling, some students do not make satisfactory academic progress. Poor performance may be the outcome of various sources of difficulties, with English proficiency being only one of them. When students underperform, school personnel tend to consider learning disabilities or language disorders as the cause.

Distinguishing Disability from Difference

One of the reasons RTI became an option for schools under the Individuals with Disabilities Education Improvement Act of 2004 (IDEA 2004) is that it is difficult to pinpoint with precision high-incidence disabilities such as learning disabilities (LD) or speech and language disorders (SLD). The situation is complicated with English learners since it is often difficult to determine if the student is struggling academically because of low English proficiency, some sort of language or learning disability, or another reason.

In current practice, students who do not achieve the desired level of progress in response to targeted interventions may be considered for eligibility for special education services under the IDEA 2004 (see Appendix A). "Level of progress" would be determined by the student's rate of response to intervention and the size of the gap that exists between the student and the benchmark. In some cases, a student's learning issues are significant enough to warrant more intensive services without spending valuable time going through each step of the school's RTI process (Fuchs, Fuchs, & Compton, 2012). Special education services would also be considered when it has been demonstrated that the intensity or type of intervention required to improve student performance either exceeds the resources in general education or is not available in general education settings.

The data collected during instruction and intervention in Tiers 1, 2, and 3 are included and used to make eligibility decisions. The advantage of using "hard" quantitative data for decision making is that it may be more reliable than "soft" data sources such as teacher referral (Gersten & Dimino, 2006). Teachers might not recognize that English learners' poor academic performance may be the result of any number of factors including: their level of English proficiency made it difficult to keep up with the rest of the class, especially in schools with large classes; they may not have received instruction that supported their linguistic and academic needs in the early grades; or they did not receive sufficient English language development. With RTI, those students can receive the academic intervention they need in a small group setting and avoid unnecessary referral for special education services. Other students like Francesca (student discussed in Chapter 3) who display significant gaps in literacy and general academic skill despite specific instruction would go directly to Tier 3 so that the level of intensity of intervention matches their needs.

It is important to note that at any point in an RTI process, IDEA 2004 allows parents to request a formal evaluation to determine eligibility for special education. An RTI process cannot be used to deny or delay a formal evaluation for special education, nor should special education services be withheld because of a lack of English proficiency when a disability is indicated.

A Learning Disability Is Hard to Define

Assessment and intervention with English learners is complex and has been a vexing issue for decades. There doesn't exist a single specific assessment instrument that can identify with certainty if a student has a language/learning disability, nor is there a specific "treatment" or intervention that works for all students.

Although it is an issue facing many schools, the topic of special education and English learners is a sensitive one, in part because many educators and civil rights advocates have fought long and hard to carefully distinguish English learners as students who require adjustments to instruction because of language and cultural differences from students who have special learning needs because of a language/learning disability. It is an important distinction for reasons of civil rights, ethics, and best educational practice. Nonetheless, there will be English learners who fall into both categories. We can expect approximately the same percentage of individuals with learning disabilities in any population.

Although learning disabilities are common, affecting an estimated 4%–6% of the public school population (Horowitz, 2009), in most situations it can be difficult to identify a specific learning disability since it is not the same as Downs syndrome or visual impairments. Those disabilities have a clear-cut diagnosis and biological characteristics. To date, the same is not true for learning disabilities. In fact, there is some argument that high-incidence disabilities such as learning disabilities (as well as behavior disorders and mild cognitive disabilities) are socially constructed. That is, individual judgment is used to decide what is "normal" along a spectrum of behaviors and to determine at what point an individual is deemed "disabled" (Harry, Klinger, & Cramer, 2007; Ruiz, 1995).

The term *learning disabilities* is used to describe a "mixed bag" of disorders that affect listening, speaking, reading, writing, reasoning, math, and social skills (Horowitz & Stecker, 2007). There isn't one specific characteristic—or even two or three—that typify a student who requires special education services, but it is usually a constellation of behaviors or symptoms, and the constellation changes as the child matures. For example, young children with learning disabilities have weak language functioning and very poor attention. These children are distractable, disorganized, and often off-task (Fuchs, 2009). As they get older, they develop problematic behaviors such as low motivation, poor self-perception, and negative attitudes toward learning.

Identifying a learning disability is even more complicated with English learners. In Figure 6.1, we show a comprehensive checklist of behaviors that provides guidance for determining a learning disability, developed through the National Center for Learning Disabilities (NCLD) (Horowitz & Stecker, 2007). We discuss each domain in the context of language and cultural diversity. As you look over the checklist, you will see that there are many behaviors that apply to most people—even you! Although most people experience problems with learning and behavior from time to time, a person with learning disabilities experiences these difficulties over their life span. When applying the checklist to an individual, the more characteristics you check, the more likely it is that the individual is at risk (or shows signs of) learning disabilities. Family input is critical in getting an accurate picture of an English learner's characteristics. Consider having family members complete the checklist and compare it to one completed by the child's teacher.

Each domain of the checklist is discussed below in the context of language and cultural diversity. One's behavior may be influenced by cultural factors and English learners' performance may be impacted by their language proficiency. As you read through the checklist (Figure 6.1), consider some of the issues discussed below:

1. **Gross and fine motor skills.** Development of these skills would likely not be affected by language differences. However, lack of exposure to activities that demand hand-eye coordination or precision may have an impact on performance. With practice, performance would be expected to improve with skills such as using scissors or playing sports.

Figure 6.1 Learning Disabilities Checklist of Signs and Symptoms

Learning Disabilities Checklist

Domains and Behaviors
Shaded area indicates a characteristic is more likely to apply at that stage of life. Check all that apply.

Columns: Preschool Kindergarten | Grades 1–4 | Grades 5–8 | High School & Adult

Gross and Fine Motor Skills

Behavior	Preschool/K	Grades 1–4	Grades 5–8	HS & Adult
Appears awkward and clumsy, dropping, spilling, or knocking things over				
Has limited success with games and activities that demand eye-hand coordination (e.g., piano lessons, basketball, baseball)				
Has trouble with buttons, hooks, snaps, zippers and trouble learning to tie shoes				
Creates art work that is immature for age				
Demonstrates poor ability to color or write 'within the lines'				
Grasps pencil awkwardly, resulting in poor handwriting				
Experiences difficulty using small objects or items that demand precision (e.g., Legos, puzzle pieces, tweezers, scissors)				
Dislikes and avoids writing and drawing tasks				

Language

Behavior	Preschool/K	Grades 1–4	Grades 5–8	HS & Adult
Demonstrates early delays in learning to speak				
Has difficulty modulating voice (e.g., too soft, too loud)				
Has trouble naming people or objects				
Has difficulty staying on topic				
Inserts invented words into conversation				
Has difficulty re-telling what has just been said				
Uses vague, imprecise language and has a limited vocabulary				
Demonstrates slow and halting speech, using lots of fillers (e.g., uh, um, and, you know, so)				
Uses poor grammar or misuses words in conversation				
Mispronounces words frequently				
Confuses words with others that sound similar				
Inserts malapropisms ('slips of the tongue') into conversation (e.g., a rolling stone gathers no moths; he was a man of great statue)				
Has difficulty rhyming				
Has limited interest in books or stories				
Has difficulty understanding instructions or directions				
Has trouble understanding idioms, proverbs, colloquialisms, humor, and/or puns (note: take into account regional and cultural factors)				

Language (con't)

Behavior	Preschool/K	Grades 1–4	Grades 5–8	HS & Adult
Has difficulty with pragmatic skills (e.g., understands the relationship between speaker and listener, stays on topic, gauges the listeners degree of knowledge, makes inferences based on a speaker's verbal and non-verbal cues)				

Reading

Behavior	Preschool/K	Grades 1–4	Grades 5–8	HS & Adult
Confuses similar-looking letters and numbers				
Has difficulty recognizing and remembering sight words				
Frequently loses place while reading				
Confuses similar-looking words (e.g., beard/bread)				
Reverses letter order in words (e.g., saw/was)				
Demonstrates poor memory for printed words				
Has weak comprehension of ideas and themes				
Has significant trouble learning to read				
Has trouble naming letters				
Has problems associating letter and sounds, understanding the difference between sounds in words or blending sounds into words				
Guesses at unfamiliar words rather than using word analysis skills				
Reads slowly				
Substitutes or leaves out words while reading				
Has poor retention of new vocabulary				
Dislikes and avoids reading or reads reluctantly				

Written Language

Behavior	Preschool/K	Grades 1–4	Grades 5–8	HS & Adult
Dislikes and avoids writing and copying				
Demonstrates delays in learning to copy and write				
Writing is messy and incomplete, with many cross outs and erasures				
Has difficulty remembering shapes of letters and numerals				
Frequently reverses letters, numbers and symbols				
Uses uneven spacing between letters and words, and has trouble staying 'on the line'				
Copies inaccurately (e.g., confuses similar-looking letters and numbers)				
Spells poorly and inconsistently (e.g., the same word appears differently other places in the same document)				

Figure 6.1 (continued)

Learning Disabilities Checklist

Domains and Behaviors *Shaded area indicates a characteristic is more likely to apply at that stage of life. Check all that apply.*	Preschool Kindergarten	Grades 1-4	Grades 5-8	High School & Adult
Written Language (con't)				
Has difficulty proofreading and self-correcting work				
Has difficulty preparing outlines and organizing written assignments				
Fails to develop ideas in writing so written work is incomplete and too brief				
Expresses written ideas in a disorganized way				
Math				
Has difficulty with simple counting and one-to-one correspondence between number symbols and items/objects				
Difficulty mastering number knowledge (e.g. recognition of quantities without counting)				
Has difficulty with learning and memorizing basic addition and subtraction facts				
Has difficulty learning strategic counting principles (e.g. by 2, 5, 10, 100)				
Poorly aligns numbers resulting in computation errors				
Has difficulty estimating (e.g., quantity, value)				
Has difficulty with comparisons (e.g., less than, greater than)				
Has trouble telling time				
Has trouble conceptualizing the passage of time				
Has difficulty counting rapidly or making calculations				
Has trouble learning multiplication tables, formulas and rules				
Has trouble interpreting graphs and charts				
Social/Emotional				
Does not pick up on other people's mood/feelings (e.g., may say the wrong thing at the wrong time)				
May not detect or respond appropriately to teasing				
Has difficulty 'joining in' and maintaining positive social status in a peer group				
Has trouble knowing how to share/express feelings				
Has trouble 'getting to the point' (e.g., gets bogged down in details in conversation)				
Has difficulty with self-control when frustrated				
Has difficulty dealing with group pressure, embarrassment and unexpected challenges				
Has trouble setting realistic social goals				

Domains and Behaviors *Shaded area indicates a characteristic is more likely to apply at that stage of life. Check all that apply.*	Preschool Kindergarten	Grades 1-4	Grades 5-8	High School & Adult
Social/Emotional (con't)				
Has trouble evaluating personal social strengths and challenges				
Is doubtful of own abilities and is prone to attribute successes to luck or outside influences rather than hard work				
Attention				
Fails to pay close attention to details or makes careless mistakes in schoolwork, work, or other activities				
Has difficulty sustaining attention in work tasks or play activities				
Does not follow through on instructions and fails to finish schoolwork, chores, or duties in the workplace				
Has difficulty organizing tasks and activities				
Avoids, dislikes, or is reluctant to engage in tasks that require sustained mental effort such as homework and organizing work tasks				
Loses things consistently that are necessary for tasks/activities (e.g., toys, school assignments, pencils, books, or tools)				
Is easily distracted by outside influences				
Is forgetful in daily/routine activities				
Other				
Confuses left and right				
Has a poor sense of direction; slow to learn the way around a new place; easily lost or confused in unfamiliar surroundings				
Finds it hard to judge speed and distance (e.g., hard to play certain games, drive a car)				
Trouble reading charts and maps				
Is disorganized and poor at planning				
Often loses things				
Is slow to learn new games and master puzzles				
Has difficulty listening and taking notes at the same time				
Performs inconsistently on tasks from one day to the next				
Has difficulty generalizing (applying) skills from one situation to another				

2. **Language.** In the area of language skills, characteristics of second language acquisition often mirror language/learning difficulties. Imagine that you have recently relocated to a non-English speaking country. Take a look at the language characteristics listed in Figure 6.1 and think about how many of those would apply to you. Many English learners lack the auditory acuity to hear new, "foreign" sounds

much like English speakers may have difficulty understanding the name of a person or place that contains sounds with which they are unfamiliar. You would likely have difficulty staying on topic, retelling something said to you, using precise language, or understanding instructions because you would be on cognitive overload. In this scenario, the situation would be language-specific and would get better with time and exposure. Students with learning disabilities manifest many of these characteristics in both languages—their home language and English—consistently and over time.

3. **Reading.** Disentangling language proficiency from reading ability is difficult, and reading is an area that is influenced significantly by language proficiency. On the plus side, research shows that children are able to develop accurate and fluent word-level reading skills in English regardless of English proficiency (Farnia & Geva, 2011). However, generally speaking, lack of English proficiency inhibits reading in a number of ways. English oral language skills correlate with English learners' reading fluency and ability to learn from text (Geva, 2006). Also, it is more difficult to remember letter names, words, or passages that have little or no meaning. We know from schema research that individuals with knowledge of a topic have better recall and are better able to elaborate on the topic than those with limited knowledge of the topic (Chiesi, Spilich, & Voss, 1979). This may account in part for the difficulty English learners have with meaning-based reading skills. For some English learners, their difficulty with reading may be more a function of lack of familiarity with the words and concepts than inability to learn.

4. **Written language.** In young learners and older learners who have had interrupted schooling, some of the characteristics listed in the written language domain may be the result of language differences. For example, difficulty remembering the shape of letters or reversing letters could be attributed to lack of exposure, especially when students are not familiar with the Roman alphabet. Older English learners may have difficulty organizing and expressing their thoughts in a coherent way in writing when they have less than fluent English proficiency.

5. **Math.** Often referred to as the "universal language," in reality math texts and teaching are full of math-specific terminology that can be confusing for English learners (Echevarria, Vogt, & Short, 2010; Hoffert, 2009; NCTM, 2009). In fact, when English learners were presented with visual graphics in math to assist their understanding, the students had difficulty deriving meaning from them (Avalos et al., 2013). Further, what may be interpreted as lack of understanding of a process or operation could actually be the result of the student not understanding the teacher's (or text's) explanation or instructions. In response to the question, "How do teachers sometimes make it difficult for you to learn?" one high school English learner replied, "For me, the hardest part was when they didn't give directions, and specifically in math because I know a lot of math but I didn't understand my teacher." Sometimes it is difficult to determine student knowledge and skill level when a communication gap exists.

6. **Social/emotional.** Behaviors in this domain are particularly culturally laden. Social expectations are dictated by cultural and family practices and differ across cultures. Difficulties in school may be the result of not knowing certain social cues or proprieties and unfamiliarity with subtle language such as what constitutes a joke or "teasing." Further, behaviors in English learners may be a result of frustration or embarrassment over an inability to understand others or to express oneself, especially in older learners.

7. **Attention.** Nearly all the behaviors in the attention domain overlap with characteristics of learning academic material in a second language. The cognitive and linguistic load for English learners is significant and often manifests itself in ways such as difficulty maintaining attention and reluctance to engage in tasks that require sustained mental effort.

8. **Other.** Some of the issues faced by English learners that were discussed in Chapter 2 may account for behaviors found in this category of miscellaneous problematic behaviors. Isolation, fear, chaotic home life, poverty, and other realities might result in students losing things, being disorganized, performing inconsistently on tasks from day to day and so forth. Keep in mind, however, that it is the pervasiveness and preponderance of behaviors that indicates a learning disability, not a handful of the behaviors on the checklist.

The cultural and linguistic factors discussed above would be an important part of the discussion as school-based teams examine data about student performance and behavior. With more exposure to mainstream culture and English, learners will adjust to school expectations and improve academically. In contrast, English learners with learning disabilities will not make quick progress with exposure to English. Learning disabilities are lifelong, and academic progress will be markedly slower for an English learner with a learning disability than for an individual whose only challenge is developing English proficiency. That said, individuals with LD can learn to compensate for areas of weakness, and with early, effective support, they can be highly successful and productive members of society.

Identifying a disability might be considered akin to conducting an experiment on each student to determine what "effective instruction" is for that individual learner. Researcher Lynn Fuchs (2009) suggests that teams look at progress-monitoring data and test the effectiveness of instructional components for a particular child. Then, the components that look effective for that child are incorporated and you drop others. So it is experimental for that child. For English learners this experimental process would include a number of instructional supports such as using the home language for literacy development, or using it for clarification when bilingual instruction isn't possible. Although home language support could be part of Tier 1 instruction and Tier 2 intervention, it is imperative to explore using the first language to see if an English learner's performance improves before any label (i.e., learning disability) is ascribed. Academic improvement when the home language is used indicates that instruction in English was the issue. A student with a learning disability would not make marked improvement since a disability would be evident in both languages.

The writing sample in Figure 6.2 illustrates both the pervasive nature of learning disabilities and the success that individuals with LD can achieve with proper supports. The author of this writing sample is an adult with learning disabilities who, despite her learning challenges and the obstacles she encountered throughout her schooling, attained a master's degree and is employed full time on the staff of a university. As you can see, she continues to struggle with written language. For individuals like her, assistive technologies offer aides such as spell-checking software designed for students with dyslexia, mobile tools for students with learning disabilities, and alternative Web browsers for students with visual disabilities. Further, the National Center for Learning Disabilities has a plethora of useful resources on the topic of learning disabilities, including free literacy and learning resources for Spanish-speaking families (http://getreadytoread.org).

Figure 6.2
Handwriting Sample

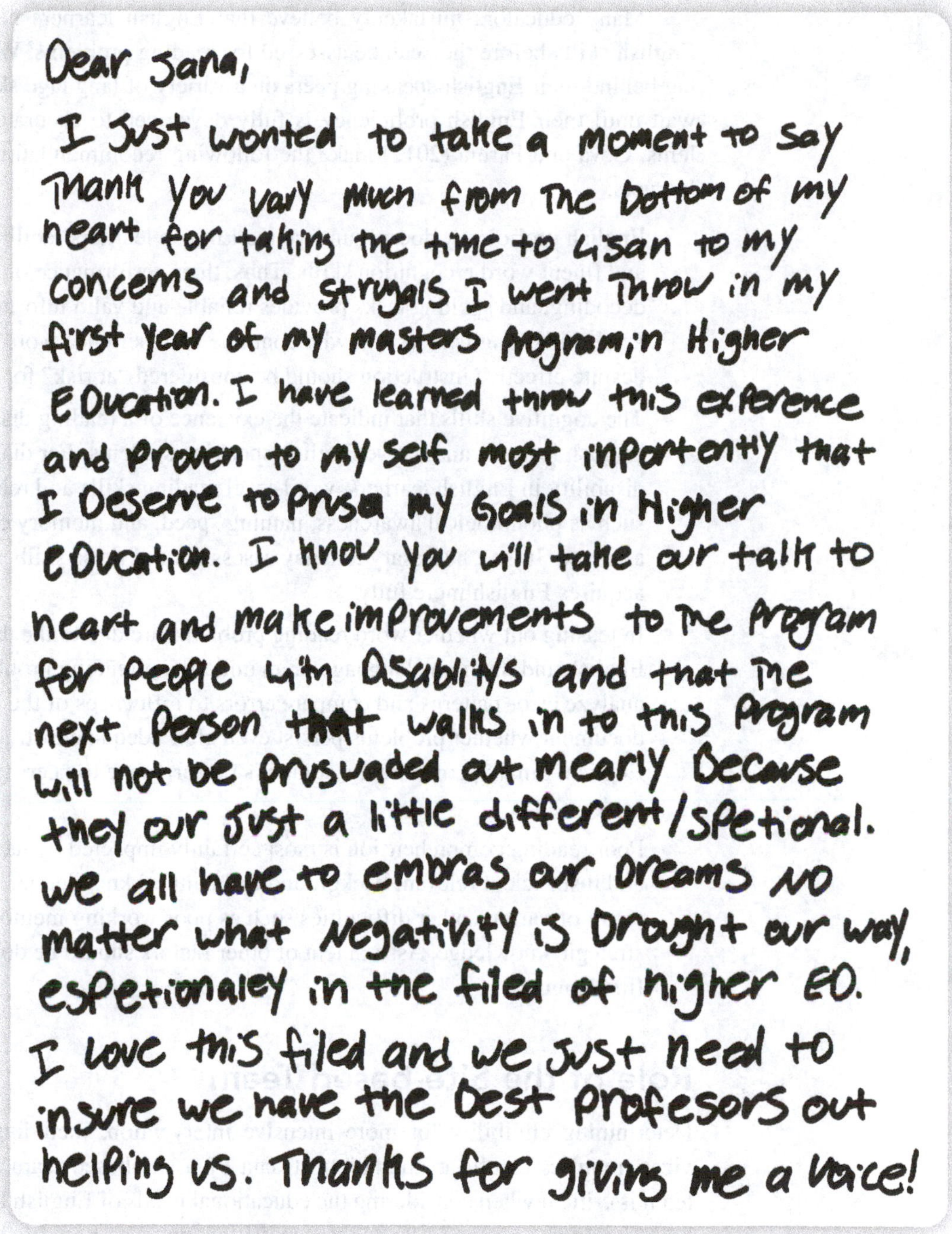

> Dear Jana,
>
> I just wanted to take a moment to say Thank you vary much from the Dottom of my heart for taking the time to Lisan to my concerns and strugals I went Throw in my first year of my masters Progam in Higher EDucation. I have learned throw this exference and proven to my self most inportently that I Deserve to Prusa my Goals in Higher EDucation. I hnow you will take our talk to heart and make improvements to The Program for Peofle wim Disablitys and that The next Person that walks in to this Program will not be Prusuaded out mearly Decause they our Just a little different/sPetional. we all have to embras our Dreams No matter what Negativity is Drought our way, esPetionaley in the filed of higher ED. I love this filed and we Just Need to insure we have the Dest Profesors out helfing us. Thanhs for giving me a Voice!

Source: Candice Chick

Determining Eligibility for Special Education Services

In the previous section, we discussed some issues involved in identifying learning disabilities. In some respects, the most effective way to tell whether a student is struggling because of English learner status or an actual learning impairment is through a process of elimination. This happens during a comprehensive, informed decision-making process conducted by the site-based team. We'll begin by clearing up some misconceptions about assessing English learners and then discuss the role of the team.

Many educators mistakenly believe that English learners need to acquire adequate English skills before they can be assessed for reading problems. While English learners do lag behind their English-speaking peers on a variety of language skills, it isn't necessary to wait until their English proficiency is fully developed to accurately assess reading problems. Geva and Farnia (2012) make the following recommendations for assessing English learners:

- English proficiency doesn't undermine English learners' ability to develop accurate and fluent word recognition skills. Thus, their performance on word reading, decoding, and spelling tasks provides reliable and valid information about their word level skills. English learners who continue to experience word reading difficulties despite effective instruction should be considered "at risk" for reading disability.

- The cognitive skills that indicate the existence of a reading disability are the same for English learners and native English-speaking students. For diagnosing reading disability in English learners, word-level reading skills and related cognitive skills such as phonological awareness, naming speed, and memory can be accurately assessed. It isn't necessary to delay assessment of these skills while the student acquires English more fully.

- In teasing out whether word reading problems are due to the difference between English and the home language or an underlying reading problem, it is important to analyze error patterns and compare errors to influences of the home language. Also, document whether problems persist even after adequate instruction and exposure to English. Finally, compare the student's performance to peers from similar backgrounds.

- Poor reading comprehension is most certainly impacted by lack of English proficiency and insufficient relevant background and cultural knowledge, but it may also be the result of various other difficulties such as poor working memory and inadequate strategic knowledge. Assessment of other factors should be done in English and in the first language.

Role of the Site-based Team

Determining eligibility for more intensive intervention, including special education services, requires careful examination of data by a site-based team. The composition of the team is critical when considering the educational needs of English learners. Individuals who have expertise in second language acquisition must be part of the decision-making process. In addition, professionals who are fluent in the student's language and are familiar with the student's and family's culture are valuable members of the team and provide essential information about the student's academic skills and behavior in both the home language and English. They can also interpret data in culturally and linguistically appropriate ways. The team might also include a family representative and an interpreter, as well as the student, if age appropriate. Also, the school nurse or counselor might attend depending on the issues being discussed. Together, this type of team offers the best chance of examining data and accurately determining if the student's learning difficulties can be explained by sociocultural, linguistic, or learning variables (Salend & Salinas, 2003).

Data that the team examines include more than testing results so that a more complete assessment of the student can be conducted (Kampwirth & Powers, 2012). Other sources of data include the following.

Reviewing Records. A student's cumulative file offers valuable information, including what others have said about her over the years. This information assists in problem solving and provides a history of the student's educational experience. Has the student been referred for special education services previously? What was the outcome? What was the family's input into the decision? What are the student's strengths and areas of difficulty that have persisted over time? Other important information would include how much primary language instruction the student has received, or if there has been adequate English language development provided. In addition, the RTI forms made available in this book (and found online in the PDToolkit) would be valuable documents for showing the kinds of modifications and accommodations that were tried in general education as well as the type and duration of intervention the student received. Other records to examine are health records (Does the student need glasses or hearing aids?) and educational records from the home country, when possible.

Interviews. Parents can be our best informants and may be an underutilized resource. They can provide developmental information, answering questions such as: At what age did the student begin talking? Has his language development been normal? How does his development compare with that of siblings and peers? Has he had any major health concerns or persistent illnesses? How much is the first language used in the home? What are the literacy practices of the family? Also, parents can offer insight into current issues; for example, do the parents perceive that the youngster has difficulties? What is the parent's opinion of the student's academic performance? And do they see the same behaviors at home? In addition to gathering interview data from parents, school staff such as office workers, playground supervisors, and cafeteria workers may offer important insights about the student, especially if they are from the same cultural community. Does the student appear to be a competent individual? Does he show strengths such as leadership qualities or good interpersonal skills? Students may appear quite different outside of the classroom than during instructional time.

Observations. In-class observations are useful for providing a fresh perspective on the student's classroom performance. Further, classroom observation by a team member helps to establish whether the student is being provided high-quality instruction that meets his needs. In Chapter 2 we discussed the impact of teacher attitude on achievement. What is the relationship between the teacher and student? Does the teacher hold high expectations for English learners, nurturing and supporting their language and academic development? How does the teacher promote interest and motivation? Also, observation of behavior outside of the classroom provides a more complete picture of the student's strengths and areas of concern. Observations in the home can be quite informative, if home visits can be arranged.

Testing. Coupled with the information discussed above, test results contribute to a comprehensive profile of a student's strengths and areas of difficulty. Districts vary considerably in the type of assessments and processes used for determining eligibility for special education services. However, no single test should be used to determine intervention intensity or to make eligibility decisions.

It bears repeating here that providing professional development opportunities for the entire staff, including general education and special education teachers (and members of the site-based team), will strengthen the RTI process, particularly when looking for possible causes for an English learner's difficulties. These professional development sessions can focus on second language acquisition, effective instructional practice for English learners, and data collection and interpretation.

For a practitioner's perspective on the issue of language difference versus learning difficulty, we offer the From on the Field feature, where you can find the transcription of an interview with a teacher who taught for 20 years in a low-performing, predominantly low-income (95% free or reduced-price lunch) K–5 elementary school. Of the 1,651 students, 97% are Latino and 60% are English learners. Retired for less than a year at the time of the interview, this teacher reflected on how he distinguished English language proficiency from a learning problem when so many of his students were functioning well below grade-level norms. The second From the Field feature shows the transcript of an interview with a former special education teacher at the same school. These practitioners' perspectives are intended to show how one might meet the needs of English learners and support their learning.

In sum, to distinguish between language differences and learning disabilities, keep in mind that learning disabilities will be manifested in a variety of ways in school and in life, regardless of the language students speak. A student will not likely have a learning disability only in English, nor just in his or her home language. Therefore, some overarching questions to ask about English learners include:

- Does the student differ significantly from others with similar background?
- Does his or her family see a problem?
- What about first language development? Was it normal?
- Does the difficulty the student is experiencing result primarily from cultural, environmental, or economic disadvantage?
- Is the student making steady progress, regardless of how slow?
- Has the student had an opportunity to demonstrate knowledge and skills in his or her home language?
- Has the student had sufficient opportunities to learn by hearing engaging stories, reading interesting texts, and using the home language for literacy development and background information?

The answers to these questions are essential to consider when identifying the source of a student's difficulty in the classroom.

From the Field **A Teacher's Experience**

At my school, almost all students were behind grade level. I always thought of the kids as just having different learning styles. I didn't think about referral to special education because it isn't a magic pill; it is my responsibility to reach the student. I had students read to me and I looked for some sort of pattern in their errors. Can they decode? If they are having problems with comprehension, maybe it is because they don't have strong skills in decoding. The ones who could read when they came from Mexico could transition pretty easily. But most students were born here so they couldn't read in Spanish and they can't read well in English because of the vocabulary. They can't self-correct since they haven't had enough exposure to English. So, if they pronounce knees as k-nees, they don't know to self-correct like an English speaker would.

One time I had two girls in class, Maria and Carmen, who had the same low English proficiency and low reading level. But, I suspected that Carmen had a learning disability by the way she read. I asked the special education teacher to observe them reading and she agreed with me that something more was going on with Carmen. How did we know? When Maria read aloud, she consistently struggled with decoding, made typical errors and seemed used to reading that way. When Carmen read, she seemed nervous, and read erratically, getting the same word right one time and wrong the next. Their English reading level was the same but it was the kind of errors that they made that made the two readers qualitatively different.

In another case, I had a boy in class who had been retained in second grade. In third grade Gilberto still couldn't read although he was around grade level in math. His family was poor, his mother spoke only Spanish, and Gilberto had developed some discipline issues, probably because of his reading problems. I worked with him on the basic components of reading – phonics, phonemic awareness, vocabulary, comprehension, etc. When he slowed down and focused he was able to make steady progress. By the end of the year, he was a reader! He made so much progress academically! Why hadn't he gotten the basics of reading before? Who knows? But with English learners, we start where they are and move them forward. I used whatever I could to get them to read. If they brought something into class, we'd use it as a teachable moment and discuss it, write about it and so forth. You have to use their experiences to engage them in learning.

Small group discussion helped detect if they had low English proficiency or if something else was going on. If they can't follow a discussion because of English proficiency, it is different than a processing problem. When you find a subject that interests a particular student, the EL student will usually persist in order to find alternative vocabulary words. I remember an incident when Luis (a 3rd grader) asked me during a discussion about whales if they were as big as the pyramids we had discussed a few weeks ago. His apparent ability to make this connection from different discussions reinforced my belief that he didn't have a processing problem.

Also, you should always check with the family to see if they notice a problem. One student had trouble expressing himself and had been referred to SST (student study team) and they thought he needed more English language development. I spoke with the mom and she said he was worse in Spanish. Family input is really important.

From the Field A Special Educator's Perspective

When I was a special education teacher, one of the teachers at my school always had two or three students from his class on the SST list. After a while, I got the impression that he wanted the team to refer kids for special education placement so they would be out of his class. (Now all students at the school are included in general education so his strategy wouldn't work!) One day I asked, "Does your credential say that you get to teach only the easy kids? Because mine says I have to teach ALL kids." He got the point. Some teachers think that if a student has learning or behavior challenges then they should be in special education. The reality is that, at best, they will receive more support for part of the day but they will still be a part of the general education classroom. I had an English learner who could fully participate in class discussions, but he couldn't read or write. There are things we can do to support these kids' access to text like using a laptop with software that lets him dictate instead of writing or providing books on tape.

Successful IEP Meetings

Click on SIOP
Resources, then under
*RTI and English
Learners* find the "IEP
for Elementary
Student" form to see
an example of an IEP
for an English learner.

Every student who is deemed eligible to receive special education services has an Individual Education Program (IEP) in which the student's goals and the services provided to assist in meeting the goals are described. The student's special and general education teachers are required to meet with the student's parents and support staff involved in the IEP at least once per year. At this annual IEP meeting the group discusses the student's progress and sets goals for the upcoming year. It is in everyone's best interests to have a successful, productive IEP meeting.

One critical factor in conducting effective IEP meetings begins with the kind of services that are offered at the school and who delivers them. Service providers such as general education teachers, reading specialist, school counselor, speech/language therapist, and occupational therapist need to have the same knowledge base, philosophy, and practice when working with English learners. Services should be coordinated among these professionals and they should use culturally responsive approaches to serving English learners.

Another factor is engaging parents in the process. In order to gain the critical support of and cooperation needed from parents, we should make sure that they are informed partners who are included in the IEP process. They are your best informants about the student. Some suggestions for involving parents of English learners in IEP meetings include reassuring parents that the staff is there to help and assist them. It is important to have an interpreter available at the meeting although for confidentiality it is preferable to have a professional or family member approved by the parents. The meetings should unfold step-by-step so that parents understand what is being said, including what they can do at home to help. The meeting should conclude with an offer of an open-door policy in which parents' questions are welcomed and communication is on-going. Also, they should be provided with a list of community resources that might offer further assistance to the family (Cardenes-Hagan, 2007).

In addition to resources families might find in their community, there are a host of resources available online as well. The National Center for Learning Disabilities (www.ncld.org) recommends that parents know their rights so that they can be more confident during meetings, and that parents should trust their own instincts because they have a unique perspective. They are able to highlight their child's capabilities and talents, which helps education professionals see the student as a whole person—not just someone with a learning disability. A parent guide is found at http://www.ncld.org/publications-a-more/parent-advocacy-guides/idea-parent-guide. Other resources include www.LDOnLine.org and Colorín Colorado (www.ColorinColorado.org, section on learning disabilities). These sorts of resources should be provided to parents so that they are more apt to participate in and be comfortable with the often daunting nature of formal IEP meetings.

Click on SIOP
Resources, then under
*RTI and English
Learners* find the "IEP
for Secondary Student"
form to see an
example of an IEP for
an English learner.

Finally, the team must recommend a program for the student that meets his or her needs—culturally, linguistically, academically, and/or behaviorally. The IEP document may specify the extent to which primary language support will be provided, as well as the amount of explicit English language development the student will receive each day. Other features of a culturally and linguistically appropriate IEP may, for example, specify practices such as preteaching the academic vocabulary terms in a passage prior to reading it and linking a student's background experiences to the text to make it meaningful and improve comprehension. If these practices have been shown to improve the student's performance, then they may be included in the IEP to ensure that instruction supports learning for the student.

Final Thoughts

One of the most perplexing issues in working with struggling English learners is pinpointing the nature of their academic difficulties. As academic standards become more rigorous, it is reasonable to assume that this issue will have greater importance in schools where English learners will be challenged to meet those standards while they are still in the process of learning English. In this chapter we offered some ways to think about the issue and understand the many facets of learning through a second language. One guiding principle is that as English learners acquire more English proficiency, experience high-quality instruction, and learn the expectations of school, their performance will improve over time. Those English learners with a "true" learning disability will not outgrow it. It is our hope that site-based teams will find the information in the chapter useful as they work together making data-based decisions about their students.

For Reflection and Discussion

1. Read through the profiles presented at the beginning of the chapter. Which type of student is most common in your school? How might the English learners at your school differ? What specific information in this chapter most applies to your students?

2. Characteristics of learning disabilities and those of learning a new language overlap to a degree. How would you explain to your colleagues ways to differentiate between the two?

3. Think about how identifying learning disabilities is akin to conducting an experiment on that student. What are some instructional components you might try with a student you suspect of having a learning disability? How would you document the process?

4. Have you been involved in an IEP meeting for an English learner? Discuss with a colleague ways that the meeting might have been more effective, given the suggestions in the chapter.

7 Special Considerations for Secondary English Learners

Monkey Business/Fotolia

Issues for Secondary English Learners

Although the initial focus of RTI was on the elementary grades, particularly grades K–3, many districts are now extending RTI through grade 12. While we must provide intervention as soon as possible for young children, it is of equal importance to provide intensive support, both academically and behaviorally, for students in secondary schools. In some ways, the stakes are even higher for adolescents who lack the necessary knowledge and skills to successfully negotiate secondary curricula because they are at-risk for dropping out of school. The need for intervention at the secondary level is clearly evident, as indicated by the following statistics:

- According to the National Assessment of Educational Progress (NAEP), approximately two-thirds of students in grades 8 through 12 read at less than a "proficient" level (Rampey, Dion, & Donahue, 2009).

- Approximately 40% of high school graduates lack the literacy skills that employers seek (Short & Fitzsimmons, 2006).

- A lingering divide in achievement exists between Caucasian students and those from linguistically and culturally diverse groups (Echevarria, Vogt, & Short, 2010b). National data suggest that there has been not been significant change in the gap in reading scores between English only students and English learners since 1998 (NCES, 2012b).

- The NAEP data also show that only 3% of 8th grade English learners are performing at or above proficient in reading, while 35% of their native English-speaking peers are performing at or above proficient (NCES, 2012a). The same is true in mathematics, with only 5% (down from the previous year) of 8th grade English learners proficient or above while 36% (up from the previous year) of their native English-speaking peers were performing at or above proficient (NCES, 2012b).

- Specifically in vocabulary, NAEP data indicate that in both 2011 and 2009, percentile scores for 8th grade English learners were lower than their native English-speaking peers. For example, native English speakers who scored in the 90th percentile had a standard score of 312, whereas English learners who scored in the 90th percentile had a score of only 260. This pattern was true for 12th grade as well (NCES, 2012c).

- California state testing data in algebra indicate that in 8th grade only 27% of English learners are performing at or above proficient while 52% of native English speakers are performing at that level. In 9th grade the statistics become more dismal for both groups, but the gap still exists, with only 12% of English learners and 21% of native English speakers performing at or above proficient (California Department of Education, 2012).

- The long-term effects of the achievement gap and inadequate instruction are significantly higher drop-out rates for tenth graders whose first language is not English as compared to those who speak English as a first language (Rumberger, 2011).

In this chapter, we discuss the language and academic development of adolescent English learners. We focus on differences in RTI that are unique to English learners at the secondary level (grades 6–12). Finally, we offer recommendations and direction for implementing RTI for English learners in secondary schools.

As we begin, it's important to consider the language and academic development needs of adolescent English learners, including the approximately 66% who are native born (NCELA, 2011). Many of these students, who have been schooled exclusively in the United States, are lacking sufficient proficiency in English to enable them to succeed academically. For a number of reasons, these English learners have become "stalled," meaning that they plateau at the intermediate level of English proficiency. This is insufficient for academic success at the secondary level.

For these adolescents, *prevention,* a frequently used term in the elementary grades and in RTI, may seem to be an odd choice of words. By the time many of these students reach middle school, they already have a history of academic failure that usually becomes worse once they attend high school. Literacy is a key to academic success in the secondary grades, and students who are poor readers and writers are quite likely to perform poorly in high school academic subjects (Ehren, n.d.). In addition, algebra is considered the "gatekeeper" to higher levels of math, and many English learners struggle in algebra, often taking the course multiple times in middle school and high school. By continuing to develop English language proficiency, while at the same time providing academic intervention in critical academic areas, we are "preventing" these same students from experiencing comprehensive school failure.

Why Do Secondary English Learners Struggle Academically?

Adolescent English learners have reading, writing, and math difficulties for some of the following reasons:

- At the secondary level, there is a strong relationship between literacy proficiency and academic achievement because of the need for students to master academic English and use it to meet high standards (e.g., Common Core State Standards). For example, students must use English to read and understand complex expository prose found in textbooks and reference materials, write persuasively, argue and support points of view, take notes from lectures or the Internet, articulate their thinking, generate hypotheses and predictions, express analyses, draw conclusions, and so forth. They must use their emerging English knowledge along with content knowledge to complete assigned tasks. These three knowledge bases—knowledge of English, knowledge of content, and knowledge of how tasks are to be accomplished constitute the major elements of academic literacy (Echevarria, Vogt, & Short, 2010b; Short, 2002). In many classrooms where English learners are present, secondary content teachers do not attend to teaching academic literacy within their subject matter curricula (Short & Fitzsimmons, 2006).

- In classrooms where teachers embed literacy practices in their subject area instruction, the lessons are often mediated by students' expectations and responses to them, and teachers adjust accordingly, perhaps by changing or omitting the literacy-related assignments when students respond negatively to them (O'Brien, Stewart, & Moje, 1995; Vogt, 1989). Students have their own ideas about what constitutes learning in a subject area classroom, and teachers make decisions about teaching practices in conjunction with their students and the culture of secondary schools (Moje, 1996).

- Many schools fail to align their curricula with student interests and out-of-school competencies. Many secondary students who are unwilling to engage in school literacy practices actively engage in out-of-school literacy practices that they believe are important and powerful. Think about your students' use of social networking websites such as Facebook, blogs, and Twitter. Each of these requires a relatively sophisticated level of reading and writing, yet these modes of communication aren't generally considered valid examples of "school writing" (Moje, 2008; Tatum, 2008).

- Many secondary schools do not value an additive literacy curriculum that builds on and further develops English learners' native language literacy skills (Bauer, 2009).

- Literacy development, and therefore academic development in other core areas, is especially challenging for English learners who enter the U.S. educational system in the secondary grades, not only because of the complex course content but also because these students have fewer years to learn English (Short & Fitzsimmons, 2006).

- The sheer number of secondary students needing academic assistance is disproportionate to the number of support personnel, such as reading specialists, who are available to provide needed intensive instruction.

- The configuration of secondary schools with multiple classroom periods and a variety of teachers results in no one "owning" a student academically, as contrasted with elementary, self-contained classrooms with one teacher. Therefore, students with academic difficulties can more easily slip through the cracks until they are experiencing difficulty in or are failing several classes. High school counselors, generally responsible for overseeing many students, are often notified only after a particular student has experienced academic distress or failure.

- Most English learners with intermediate or early advanced proficiency no longer receive intensive English language instruction. Many English learners, including newcomer students, receive little to no ELD or ESL instruction at the secondary level (Gedney, 2009).

- There is a wide range of academic and English proficiency levels in any given secondary classroom. Some adolescent English learners have below grade-level literacy skills in their native language (L1), while others are exceptionally literate in their L1, but struggle to read and write in English. Similarly, some immigrant English learners have had consistent, effective schooling experiences prior to coming to the United States. Others have had interrupted and ineffective schooling, while still others have a background of little or no schooling. Immigrant English learners are also more likely to be poor than non-immigrants (Batalova, Fix, & Murray, 2005). Considering English learners as students who all need the same type of instruction makes no more sense than teaching native speakers exclusively in a whole class configuration, with no attempts at differentiation.

- Many secondary teachers report they are unprepared to meet the language, literacy, and academic needs of their students who are English learners (Echevarria, Vogt, & Short, 2010b; Short & Fitzsimmons, 2006). Therefore, it is not surprising that in recent years English learners have been both over- and underidentified for special education services, resulting in inappropriate placements for many.

- Researchers in the literacy field are advocating the teaching of 21st-century literacy skills to all secondary students in order to prepare them for the technological work of the future (Ajayi, 2009; Black, 2009; Moje, 2008; Sox & Rubenstein-Ávila, 2009; Vogt & Shearer, 2011). This finding has huge implications for how secondary programs are designed, including the texts, materials, and methods that are used for classroom instruction and intervention.

PD **pd** TOOLKIT™

Click on SIOP Videos, then search for "English Learners Discuss What Teachers Do to Make Learning Easier" to watch students discuss ways teachers can support their learning.

- Literacy educators have been concerned for many years about students' motivation to engage in literacy activities, because a lack of motivation negatively impacts reading development. We know that there is a decline in motivation to read as students become older, and older adolescent males are less motivated to read than younger adolescent males (Pitcher et al., 2007). With native-speaking adolescents, a lack of motivation may be manifested as apathy and frustration. Given different topics and materials, these same students may exhibit high motivation. The issue for English learners is that many may be very motivated to read (see Sturtevant & Kim, 2010), but their lack of English proficiency may be perceived as a lack of motivation.

- As with elementary teachers, another major issue for secondary teachers is how to appropriately assess an English learner's literacy and academic strengths and needs, both in English and in the student's home language. It is very challenging for a secondary content teacher to determine whether an English learner's difficulties in class are due to a language proficiency issue, a reading problem, incomplete or insufficient background knowledge about a topic, or limited knowledge of the academic language and vocabulary needed for comprehending the content concepts (Echevarria, Vogt, & Short, 2010b).

The Potential of RTI at the Secondary Level

RTI at the secondary level has the potential be a school-wide approach for assisting adolescent English learners academically. Although at the elementary level the focus is more on preventing students from developing academic difficulties, at the secondary level an RTI approach provides districts and schools a way to systematize screening, progress monitoring, and interventions to help all learners (Reed, Wexler, Vaughn, 2012).

Teachers at the secondary level often are focused on their specific content, but using an RTI model provides the structure for teachers across content areas, including special educators and other professionals, to work collaboratively to meet the needs of all students. A middle school teacher described the change in her and her colleagues: "Before RTI we didn't really feel ownership over our students and did not really feel connected to the other teachers at our site. Now with the RTI model, there is definitely a feeling that we are all responsible for every student in our school. We plan together and have shared academic vocabulary words each month that we all teach and emphasize." The main features of an RTI model at the secondary level are similar to one at the elementary level, that is, universal screening, progress monitoring, tiered levels of intervention, and data-based decision making (Vaughn & Fletcher, 2012). However, RTI at the secondary level "looks" different, and in the next sections we discuss differences in assessment and instruction/intervention at each of the three tiers.

What Is Different about Assessment and Data-Based Decision Making at the Secondary Level?

Both universal screening and progress monitoring are essential in RTI models even at the secondary level. However, there are far fewer valid and reliable assessments at the secondary level than are available at the elementary level, particularly for English learners. Additionally, at the secondary level there are just many more students to assess. The following are a few options for universal screening at the secondary level: (1) use group-administered measures such as the Group Reading Assessment and Diagnostic Evaluation (GRADE) and Group Math Assessment and Diagnostic Evaluation (GMADE); (2) use assessments that are already in place at your site such as state testing data from the prior year (Vaughn & Fletcher, 2012), in conjunction with more short-term benchmark measures that are given several times a year; and (3) use existing data and examine whether students had failed English or algebra courses one or more times to help make decisions about a student (National High School Center et al., 2010).

As at the elementary level, students in Tier 1 should have their progress monitored multiple times each year because students catch up and fall behind at different points in the year. Students in Tier 2 and Tier 3 interventions need to have their progress monitored more regularly; at least monthly in Tier 2 and weekly at Tier 3. Intervention teachers at the secondary level need to schedule time during intervention classes to monitor students' progress. The good news is that many of the progress monitoring measures for students at the secondary level are group administered, and therefore do not take as much time as the ones that are given at the elementary level. This is also true for both reading and math assessments. Again, the availability of more formal assessments for monitoring progress at the secondary level is small. However, there has been research that indicates that both reading fluency measures and maze measures can be effective for monitoring the progress of English learners at the secondary level (Ticha, Espin, & Wayman, 2009). These measures are typically available up to 8th grade, but are not available for grades 9–12. However, many of the students who will need to have their progress monitored regularly will not be reading at grade level and therefore, using CBMs at the 7th or 8th grade level may be appropriate for monitoring student progress during intervention. Additionally, the *CBM Warehouse* (http://www.interventioncentral.org/cbm_warehouse) has a CBM creator for both reading fluency and maze fluency, which allow you to enter a passage and it will create the probe for you. For math at the secondary level, Anne Foegen and her colleagues have worked extensively on developing algebra CBM (Foegen, 2008; Foegen & Morrison, 2010; Foegen, Olson, & Impecoven-Lind, 2008). These measures have been found to be useful for students in both pre-algebra and algebra and for both screening and progress monitoring. Examples of these measures can be found at http://www.education.iastate.edu/c_i/aaims/.

What Is Different about Tier 1 Instruction at the Secondary Level?

In Tier 1 at the secondary level, all students are provided high-quality instruction in all core academic subjects including English Language Arts, Mathematics, Science, and Social Studies/History. The focus is different from Tier 1 at the elementary level where the emphasis is primarily on language arts and mathematics. At the secondary level, teachers across content areas must have the time to engage in conversation about student progress and to design effective instruction to improve outcomes of all students.

Let's take a look at Martin Luther King High School. At MLK they have been implementing RTI for the past three years. All teachers in the core academic subjects have received professional development in the SIOP® Model, and the school uses twice-monthly professional learning communities to meet to discuss students and make data-based decisions. The school uses the SIOP framework for their Tier 1 instruction. Although it is unrealistic to assume that every teacher will teach reading to students, all teachers at MLK receive professional development in literacy instruction for secondary students within their content area.

The teachers know their students' reading levels so they can plan lessons appropriately. Teachers across the content areas are focused on making sure that vocabulary and comprehension of text are taught in all core courses. In fact, teachers in ELA, math, science, and social studies all focus on 2–3 vocabulary words per month to develop students' academic vocabulary, e.g., *contrast, summarize, identify.* In the next several paragraphs we will describe how teachers at MLK High School implement their Tier 1 instruction focused on key principles of adolescent literacy instruction (adapted from Vogt & Shearer, 2011).

Principle 1: Adolescents need an assessment-based literacy program of comprehension instruction embedded in rich content that values peer mediation for comprehension, discussion, collaboration, and social learning. Students with reading problems can read challenging texts given support and instruction in how to: (1) read multisyllabic words and (2) engage in meaningful discussions that challenge them to support positions and argue points of view (Shearer, Ruddell, & Vogt, 2001). Mr. Gonzalez, a 9th grade English teacher at MLK, provides his students with many opportunities to practice and improve their academic English through reading texts that are sometimes adapted to meet their proficiency levels. He has taught his students how to engage in instructional conversations (see Echevarria, Vogt, & Short, 2010b) and refers frequently to classroom posters that list "signal words" (see Vogt & Echevarria, 2008) that enable English learners to use academic vocabulary during discussion and in writing. Mr. Gonzalez's comprehension instruction focuses on developing a variety of learning strategies, as well as exploring differences in how readers comprehend narrative, expository, and informational texts. His assessment of student comprehension is ongoing and continuous, using both informal (e.g., observation, spot-checks, group response) and formal methods (tests, writing assignments, curriculum-based measures).

Principle 2: Adolescents need explicit instruction in domain-specific literacy practices, and critical literacy instruction provided in their content area classrooms to prepare them for college and employment. Domain-specific literacy practices include learning the academic language and vocabulary of the disciplines (e.g., history/social studies, the sciences, literature, and so forth); and critical literacy practices require readers to question author assumptions and biases, check evidence for factual information, and provide counterpoint arguments, as needed. In his classroom, Mr. Gonzalez teaches his English learners and other students to be critical consumers of what they read, whether in print or electronically. For example, his students examine issues of perspective in the local newspaper's opinion page, on television newscasts, and in publications such as *Time, Newsweek,* and the *Wall Street Journal.* In order for his English learners to be successful with these critical literacy tasks, Mr. Gonzalez encourages them to work with partners and small groups, and he provides a variety of scaffolds to support their learning (e.g., as audio recorded articles, marginal notes, and highlighted texts).

Principle 3: Adolescents need a curriculum that honors students' sociocultural contexts and language foundations, capitalizes on individuals' diverse funds of knowledge, and provides literacy support for successful learning. Mrs. Swanson, the 9th grade history teacher, builds on the experiential and knowledge-based learning of her students through activities that promote activation of prior knowledge and that develop background knowledge where gaps exist. For example, she occasionally permits English learners to complete a quick-write activity in their primary language, and orally share the writing in their L1 with other students who speak the same language. Obviously, Mrs. Swanson doesn't speak all of the home languages of her students, but she is able to assess quickly whether her students have background knowledge in a particular topic by watching them write and share information. Too often, teachers think English learners "lack background knowledge," when in reality, the students are unable to share what they know and have experienced in English. When given the opportunity to share their knowledge and experiences in their home language, formerly quiet, disengaged students become more engaged. If it's possible to have another student orally explain or interpret the quick-write in English, the writer's thoughts and background knowledge can be further validated.

Principle 4: Adolescents need rich, engaging, motivating instruction. They need opportunities for self-directed learning and the ability to set achievable goals that promote efficacy. Ms. Rocha, an algebra teacher, values self-directed small group and partner work in her classrooms. She also knows that adolescents are more motivated to carry out their own goals rather than those of a teacher. Although she posts and orally explains the content and language objectives for each lesson, she also encourages her students to write their own personal learning and language goals, especially when beginning a new unit. Ms. Rocha frequently permits student choice of problems, manipulatives, and other materials for solving problems. She has found that when adolescents are given choices and then are provided with scaffolds to enable them to be successful, they can and will complete challenging tasks.

Principle 5: Adolescents need vocabulary instruction that is explicit and contextualized, and that targets strategies that promote independent vocabulary acquisition. Note the words *explicit* and *contextualized.* Mr. Pham, a biology teacher, uses a variety of techniques to bring more context into the teaching of academic vocabulary. These include activities like Four Corners Vocabulary Charts (Vogt & Echevarria, 2008), embedding definitions of key vocabulary into sentences that introduce the words, repetition and review of key vocabulary throughout and across lessons, and explicit teaching of fewer (rather than more) words. He models and uses a think-aloud approach when teaching the words to the students. When selecting vocabulary, he focuses on words that are key to understanding a lesson's content, words that involve language processes and functions in which the students will be engaged, such as the school's key academic vocabulary words of the month (i.e., *summarize, contrast, identify*), and words that enable ongoing learning of new vocabulary (e.g., words with the same root: *photocopy, photography, photosynthesis*) (Echevarria, Vogt, & Short, 2013; 2014a; 2014b).

Principle 6: Adolescents need instruction in technologies that facilitate their ability to use new forms of in-school and out-of-school literacy practices. Mr. Gonzalez strives for relevancy in his teaching, and one way to be relevant to his students is to honor and expand their use of technology resources. In a lesson that explored perspective and persuasive writing techniques, students were expected to blog about particular topics, read each other's blogs, and analyze how the choice of words and phrases can influence and convince. The students then read some historic speeches they found on the Internet and identified the words and phrases used to persuade and influence.

Principle 7: Adolescents benefit from differentiated instruction and intensity of support based on individual needs that are linked to assessment, and are implemented in grouping configurations that range from partners to whole class. Secondary students need opportunities to explore ideas individually and to engage collaboratively in project learning. This leads to differentiated instruction, which is at the heart of effective RTI, whatever the tier or intervention. Mrs. Swanson frequently differentiates classroom tasks, processes, and products according to her students' language proficiency and assessed needs. For example, in one multi-period lesson, she asked a few students to do independent research in several texts and articles she brought to class. This information was shared with another group, who used it to write and perform a skit modeled after a newscast with interviews. Other students with less English proficiency worked with Mrs. Swanson on an Internet search, and together

From the Field **Interview with a High School Principal**

Interviewer: How do you create the time for teachers to collaborate?

Principal: We have set up two types of PLCs at our school. One is a course-specific PLC, so for example, all teachers who teach algebra or all American history teachers. The other is content or department specific, so for example, all math teachers. Teachers meet in each of these PLCs once a month on Wednesdays, which are minimum days. This gives the teachers the time they need to collaborate during their normal instructional day. Teachers typically examine student data and plan lessons collaboratively during this time. Often the intervention teachers will attend the English or Math PLCs to update teachers on students in intervention and to make sure that they understand what is taking place during core instruction.

they summarized their findings and presented them to the class. Mrs. Swanson differentiates in other ways, too, including working with small groups of students to pre-teach a lesson's key concepts and vocabulary, or re-teach a lesson for students needing additional support. This means that even though Ms. Swanson is a History teacher, she knows her students' reading and English proficiency levels. Mrs. Swanson and her 9th grade history team at MLK meet every other week in their content/grade level Professional Learning Communities to look at student data provided by the English Language Arts teachers and plan differentiated lessons for their students. They think about how to modify both the input of the lesson (readings, materials, group configuration) as well as the output of the lesson (how much students will write, number of questions to complete, oral versus written reports, group assignment). For more details, see the From the Field feature.

When creating appropriate classroom instruction for English learners (and all other students), remember the following words of literacy expert Bill Brozo:

> RTI at the secondary level is only as good as its preventive supports. If content teachers fail to offer responsive literacy instruction to benefit every student and differentiated assistance for those in need of extra help, then the preventive potential of RTI is lost. When this happens, RTI at the secondary level becomes little more than a delivery system for remedial reading and, as such, cannot be regarded as a comprehensive program that supports the literacy competencies of all youth (2010, p. 280).

What Is Different about Tier 2 and Tier 3 Interventions at the Secondary Level?

Although at the secondary level interventions are less focused on prevention and more focused on remediation, adolescents do benefit from intervention (Scammacca et al., 2007). Many of the important features of Tier 2 and Tier 3 interventions that were discussed in Chapter 5 will benefit students at the secondary level. For example, providing small group intervention, collecting data on student progress, and using data to make instructional decisions are key principles of intervention at the secondary level (Kamil et al., 2008). Many secondary students who need intervention are going to be several grade levels behind and will need intensive interventions in order for them to make necessary growth. Keeping groups small is one way to create more intensive interventions; other ways include providing interventions that are

45 minutes or longer each day and extending intervention sessions by several weeks longer than what is needed at the elementary level (Denton et al., 2008). These interventions should be delivered by specialists or other trained teachers who understand reading development and struggling readers at the secondary level (Kamil et al., 2008). Interventions that only include limited skill development such as reading fluency are not likely to result in better outcomes for secondary students (Wexler, Vaughn, Roberts, & Denton, 2009). These students need intensive interventions that include the multiple skills they need for academic success, e.g., word level, text level, and strategy instruction (Kamil et al., 2008). In these next sections we will discuss scheduling of Tier2/Tier 3 interventions, time in intervention, and finally content of intervention.

Scheduling

At MLK, Tier 2 and Tier 3 interventions in reading and math are delivered by teachers who have specialist credentials (reading, special education, math) and credentials in the content areas they teach; these teachers also have had extensive professional development in the SIOP® Model. MLK administrators have decided to focus their RTI efforts in 9th grade English and Algebra I because they were informed that students who are successful in these courses have better long-term academic outcomes than students who are not (Christenson et al., 2008; Jimerson, Reshley, & Hess, 2008). Although the school provides supports to students in other courses, the specialists and resources are focused on students in these two courses. Tier 2 interventions are supplemental interventions that students receive in addition to Tier 1.

Since the school uses block scheduling, each period is 90 minutes a day and the students go to each class five days over two weeks, e.g., Algebra on Monday, Wednesday, and Friday one week and Tuesday and Thursday the next. The scheduling allows the school to more easily schedule intervention courses. Students in intervention replace an elective course with an intervention course. See the sample schedule in Figure 7.1 for Elena, who is a student in Tier 2 intervention for both 9th grade English, called Reading Lab C, and Algebra I, called Algebra Lab. Elena moved to the United States from Costa Rica in grade 6. She continued to receive English Language Development as part of her English Language Arts class in 9th grade.

Students in Tier 3 have intervention every day; thus they forgo two elective courses. See the sample schedule in Figure 7.2 for Tran, who is in Tier 3 intervention for both 9th grade English and Algebra. Tran is considered Fluent English Proficient and does not receive specific English Language Development, but since all teachers at MLK use the SIOP® Model, his academic language needs are met throughout the day in his courses. The Tier 3 reading intervention is delivered in two courses, Reading Lab A, which is every day during zero period, and Reading Lab B, which is every other day during the normal school day. The Tier 3 algebra intervention is delivered in a modified course format, Algebra I AB/CD, that is, every day across two years instead of one year, which allows the students more time to master the material. Each quarter the students' schedules change, which allows them to move in and out of intervention as needed.

Group Size and Time in Intervention

At the secondary level small groups are an essential element of effective Tier 2 and Tier 3 intervention. With secondary teachers who are not accustomed to organizing small groups, the question comes up: How small is small? We suggest you make your groups as small as is feasible given your resources. In a study conducted in middle school, researchers found that

Figure 7.1 Elena's Schedule, Tier 2 Intervention for Both 9th Grade English and Algebra I

Time	Monday	Tuesday	Wednesday	Thursday	Friday
8:00–9:30	Algebra I	Algebra Lab	Algebra I	Algebra Lab	Algebra Lab
9:40–11:10	Reading Lab C	English with ELD	Reading Lab C	English with ELD	English
11:20–12:50	History	Spanish I	History	Spanish I	Spanish I
12:50–1:30	Lunch	Lunch	Lunch	Lunch	Lunch
1:40–3:10	Science	PE	Science	PE	PE

Source: Based on Lenz, Ehren, & Deshler, 2005.

Figure 7.2 Tran's Schedule, Tier 3 Intervention for Both 9th Grade English and Algebra I

Time	Monday	Tuesday	Wednesday	Thursday	Friday
7:10–7:55	Reading Lab A	Reading Lab A	Reading Lab A	Reading Lab A	Reading Lab A
8:00–9:30	Algebra AB	Algebra AB	Algebra AB	Algebra AB	Algebra AB
9:40–11:10	Spanish	PE	Spanish	PE	PE
11:20–12:50	Reading Lab B	English	Reading Lab B	English	English
12:50–1:30	Lunch	Lunch	Lunch	Lunch	Lunch
1:40–3:10	History	Science	History	Science	Science

students did not make significant gains in groups of 10–12 for 50 minutes per day and suggest that smaller group sizes and more time may be necessary for students at the secondary level (Vaughn et al., 2010). However, having only 5–6 students in an intervention class may not be a realistic option at the secondary level. At MLK the intervention classes for Tier 2 have 20 students and for Tier 3 the classes have 10–12 students. Ms. Taylor, a Tier 2 intervention teacher, uses a combination of whole group and small groups during the 90-minute block. For example, in her Tier 2 Reading Lab C, Ms. Taylor has 18–20 students in each intervention class and has one paraprofessional, who has had extensive professional development, to provide support. Ms. Taylor delivers 30 minutes of direct instruction to all students and explains the independent work for the day. Then she divides the students into four smaller groups and for the rest of the class period she and her instructional assistant each see two groups for 30 minutes to provide more intensive instruction. Students in Tier 2 receive about 75 minutes of instruction in whole group plus 75 minutes of instruction in small groups each week, in addition to their regular English class. A comparable model is used in the Algebra Lab course.

Tier 3 intervention uses a similar structure. In Reading Lab B, Mr. Johnson provides direct instruction for 30 minutes to all 10–12 students and then divides the students into two smaller groups for more intensive intervention. During the small group time, he and the instructional assistant see each group for 30 minutes, for a total of 60 minutes of intensive intervention. Additionally, students in Tier 3 attend Reading Lab A during zero period for 45 minutes each day; during this time the students are mainly provided direct instruction in whole group with 10–12 other students. In a given week students in Tier 3 reading intervention receive about 330 minutes of instruction in groups of 10–12 students plus 150 minutes of intervention in small groups in addition to their regular English class. The amount of time and group size makes Tier 3 much more intense than Tier 2 intervention. A similar model is used in the modified algebra course, but the students receive this class every day for two years.

Content of Intervention

For secondary English learners we want to remember that even during intervention they need to be given opportunities to develop reading, writing, listening, and speaking skills. The intervention teachers at MLK write both content and language objectives each day to help students work on these language proficiency skills. As described in Chapter 5, the content of the intervention for Tier 2 and Tier 3 differ slightly; this is true at the secondary level as well. At MLK, the Tier 2 interventions are aligned to the 9th grade level CCSS for language arts. There is a small amount of time spent on reviewing decoding multisyllabic words and fluency practice, but the majority of the time is spent on comprehension strategies and vocabulary development. Algebra instruction in Tier 2 is also aligned to the CCSS; however, teachers provide additional support to students in more basic algebra skills such as distributive property and integers, and they give students opportunities to learn with algebra tiles. For Tier 3, these students are typically several grade levels behind, and therefore there is much more focus on foundational skills such as phonics and decoding in the reading interventions. For Tier 3, MLK chose a published intervention curriculum that has an emphasis on phonics and decoding skills but also teaches fluency, vocabulary, comprehension strategies, and writing. (See What Works Clearinghouse for a list of intervention programs that have been found to be effective at the high school level.) This program does not include language and content objectives so the Tier 3 teachers write these objectives for each lesson and modify lessons to meet the needs of the English learners in the class. For Tier 3 the algebra lab uses a published curriculum that provides students with the foundation skills needed for algebra and offers more lessons on each topic since the students have two years rather than one to master the content.

Secondary RTI for English Learners: Putting It All Together

In this final section, we examine four options for organizing a secondary RTI program for English learners. The first suggests a five-tiered approach to meeting individual students' literacy and academic needs with increasing levels of intensity (see Figure 7.3). Please note that we do not intend to imply that students should be tracked throughout the school day in a particular level. Instead, in line with RTI and SIOP principles that decry fixed ability groups for instruction, these options provide for flexibility, depending on a student's language, literacy, behavioral, and academic needs. The amount of time needed in each level or tier should be determined by in-depth assessment and consistent, effective progress monitoring.

The Pennsylvania Department of Education (2008) has been in the forefront of providing its educators with guidelines and recommendations for implementing RTI programs, including those at the secondary level. We have adapted these guidelines for English learners and, depending on your context, we believe that any one of these options can be viable for middle and high schools where English learners are present (see Figure 7.4). Our primary adaptations are the addition of SIOP® Model instruction for all Tier 1 teachers of English learners (and ideally for all intervention providers) and English language development (ELD or ESL), depending on students' English proficiency needs. You will notice that Option 3 is very similar to the option used by MLK and described in this chapter section. You will find a wealth of information about RTI and other initiatives at the Pennsylvania Department of Education website for the Pennsylvania Training and Technical Assistance Network (www.pattan.net).

In each of these two models, as well as the one described in this chapter that is used at MLK, collaboration across teachers is essential. For example, teachers at each grade level, particularly within language arts and math, will need time to collaborate with each other and

Figure 7.3 Secondary RTI Option 1 for English Learners

Tier 1	Use of instructional methods in core content subjects that develop language, literacy, and content proficiency for all students, regardless of literacy levels, and that provides students the competitive skills they need for post-graduate success
Tier 2	Use of instructional methods in and across content classes that provide practice in the use of learning strategies in whole-class configurations that allow access to college-ready curriculum
Tier 3	Use of instructional methods that develop mastery of specific learning strategies for students needing short-term instruction of the strategies embedded throughout classroom lessons
Tier 4	Use of instructional methods that develop mastery of entry-level language and literacy skills for students needing intensive, accelerated language and literacy intervention
Tier 5	Use of instructional methods that develop mastery of language and literacy foundations related to the content and learning strategies that occur in classroom instruction for language-disabled students

Source: Based on Lenz, Ehren, & Deshler, 2005.

Figure 7.4   Secondary RTI Options 2, 3, 4 for English Learners

Option 2	Option 3	Option 4
ELD/ESL, depending on student's English proficiency	ELD/ESL, depending on student's English proficiency	ELD/ESL, depending on student's English proficiency
Tier 1 and 2 students receive grade-level instruction in heterogeneous classes.	Tier 1 and 2 students receive grade-level instruction in heterogeneous classes.	All language arts classes are homogenously grouped in two period blocks.
Tier 2 students receive an extra period of strategic intervention.	Tier 2 students receive an extra period of strategic intervention in homogeneous classes.	Tier 1 and 2 students receive grade-level instruction plus an extra period for enrichment or strategic instruction.
Students receive Tier 3 interventions for two periods.	Tier 3 students receive two periods of intensive instruction that is either in addition to or replaces the core and an elective class.	Tier 3 students receive two periods of intensive intervention that is either in addition to or replaces grade-level instruction and an elective class. Classes are parallel scheduled to allow student movement based on data.
Classes occur throughout the day.	Reading/language arts classes are parallel scheduled.	

Source: Based on information from the Pennsylvania Department of Education, 2008, p. 11.

Click on SIOP Videos, then search for "Secondary Administrator Addresses RTI" to hear a secondary principal describe his school's RTI schedule.

the intervention teachers to examine data and make decisions about who needs intervention and to design the intervention.

Furthermore, schools will need to examine how classes will be scheduled to ensure that students get the needed intervention, but also have the opportunity to exit intervention during various points in a semester. One of the biggest challenges at the secondary level is the master schedule, which generally requires a semester-long commitment to a class. Therefore, a number of options need to be considered in order for interventions to assist students in meeting graduation requirements. Some possibilities include (National Center for Learning Disabilities, 2008):

- Offer an intensive learning strategies course for credit—this is not study skills, but is a class that teaches students strategies for accessing text.

- Create summer school "bridge" programs to help students transition from elementary to middle school, and middle school to high school.

- Offer before- and after-school intervention programs; when considering this option, however, remember issues such as busing. A lack of transportation between school and home can sabotage even the most promising intervention program, as evidenced by a situation encountered by one of the authors (MaryEllen), who created a middle school intensive reading intervention with 90+ students who were referred by their teachers. The intervention teachers were trained and materials were purchased for the in-school class. Because of scheduling issues, the intervention class was moved to after school. However, only one student was able to attend because the other students had transportation problems.

- Offer a "class" within a class. This option is possible within a middle school block schedule for Language Arts, especially if an instructional aide is available to monitor and assist the other students.

- Recommend extended graduation, allowing five years for students who need more time.

- Examine intervention models that are effective across content areas. Age and developmentally appropriate interventions that work for adolescents in all subject areas prompt more buy-in from teachers for RTI.

- Examine the need, when working with secondary adolescents, to put additional behavioral interventions in place, such as mentoring, peer support programs, and systems to reward positive behaviors through incentives and structured advisories (Pennsylvania Department of Education, 2008).

Final Thoughts

After reading numerous publications with recommendations about what RTI for secondary schools should include, we realized that not one of the suggestions came from those who matter the most: the students. When asked, adolescent English learners will respond with pinpoint clarity about what their teachers need to do to help them be effective. Similarly, they can quickly identify exactly what teachers do to make their job as students very challenging. As Allington states (2008, p. 1), "Most struggling readers never catch up with their higher-achieving classmates because schools create school days for them where they struggle all day long." For these students, English learners and native speakers alike, the SIOP® Model offers the best chance to receive the instruction in content and language that they need to make academic progress toward meeting rigorous content standards. For those who need more, effective RTI instruction in Tiers 2 and 3, with English language support, provides the last chance for many to achieve high school graduation.

For Reflection and Discussion

1. Many screening instruments and other assessments used at the elementary level (see Chapter 3) are also appropriate for secondary students, but perhaps not for English learners. What assessment information do you need to gather to adequately assess English learners' language and academic strengths and needs?

2. Many of the intervention features that are described in Chapter 5 are relevant for interventions at the secondary level but RTI does "look" different for secondary schools. What are the features described in Chapter 5 that are relevant for your school site, and which do you need to modify based on the suggestions from this chapter?

3. As you consider the recommendations from this chapter, which are relevant to and feasible for your present secondary school configuration? Consider your school's master schedule, staffing, support personnel, curriculum initiatives, and so forth. Which of the recommendations would require some systemic changes for your school?

4. What are the first steps you need to take as you begin a secondary RTI plan for English learners? Who needs to be involved in determining these first steps?

Sec. 300.307 Specific learning disabilities

(a) General. A State must adopt, consistent with Sec. 300.309, criteria for determining whether a child has a specific learning disability as defined in Sec. 300.8(c)(10). In addition, the criteria adopted by the State–

   (1) Must not require the use of a severe discrepancy between intellectual ability and achievement for determining whether a child has a specific learning disability, as defined in Sec. 300.8(c)(10);

   (2) Must permit the use of a process based on the child's response to scientific, research-based intervention; and

   (3) May permit the use of other alternative research-based procedures for determining whether a child has a specific learning disability, as defined in Sec. 300.8(c)(10).

(b) Consistency with State criteria. A public agency must use the State criteria adopted pursuant to paragraph (a) of this section in determining whether a child has a specific learning disability.

(Authority: 20 U.S.C. 1221e-3; 1401(30); 1414(b)(6))

Sec. 300.309 Determining the existence of a specific learning disability

(a) The group described in Sec. 300.306 may determine that a child has a specific learning disability, as defined in Sec. 300.8(c)(10), if–

   (1) The child does not achieve adequately for the child's age or to meet State-approved grade-level standards in one or more of the following areas, when provided with learning experiences and instruction appropriate for the child's age or State-approved grade-level standards:

   (i)   Oral expression.
   (ii)   Listening comprehension.
   (iii) Written expression.
   (iv)   Basic reading skill.
   (v)   Reading fluency skills.
   (vi)   Reading comprehension.
   (vii) Mathematics calculation.
   (viii) Mathematics problem solving.

   (2)

   (i) The child does not make sufficient progress to meet age or State-approved grade-level standards in one or more of the areas identified in paragraph (a)(1) of this section when using a process based on the child's response to scientific, research-based inter-vention; or

   (ii) The child exhibits a pattern of strengths and weaknesses in performance, achievement, or both, relative to age, State-approved grade-level standards, or intellectual development, that is determined by the group to be relevant to the identification of a specific learning disability, using appropriate assessments, consistent with Sec. Sec. 300.304 and 300.305; and

(3) The group determines that its findings under paragraphs (a)(1) and (2) of this section are not primarily the result of–

    (i)   A visual, hearing, or motor disability;

    (ii) Mental retardation;

    (iii) Emotional disturbance;

    (iv) Cultural factors;

    (v) Environmental or economic disadvantage; or

    (vi) Limited English proficiency.

(b) To ensure that underachievement in a child suspected of having a specific learning disability is not due to lack of appropriate instruction in reading or math, the group must consider, as part of the evaluation described in Sec. Sec. 300.304 through 300.306–

(1) Data that demonstrate that prior to, or as a part of, the referral process, the child was provided appropriate instruction in regular education settings, delivered by qualified personnel; and

(2) Data-based documentation of repeated assessments of achievement at reasonable intervals, reflecting formal assessment of student progress during instruction, which was provided to the child's parents.

(c) The public agency must promptly request parental consent to evaluate the child to determine if the child needs special education and related services, and must adhere to the timeframes described in Sec. Sec. 300.301 and 300.303, unless extended by mutual written agreement of the child's parents and a group of qualified professionals, as described in Sec. 300.306(a)(1)–

(1) If, prior to a referral, a child has not made adequate progress after an appropriate period of time when provided instruction, as described in paragraphs (b)(1) and (b)(2) of this section; and

(2) Whenever a child is referred for an evaluation.

(Authority: 20 U.S.C. 1221e-3; 1401(30); 1414(b)(6))

Source: http://idea.ed.gov/explore/view/p/%2Croot%2Cregs%2C300%2CD%2C300%252E307%2C.

Although there are no single answers to these questions, or quick and easy solutions, there are some common approaches that schools use to deal with the logistical concerns of RTI. The following represent a sampling of the most common questions we are asked as we conduct professional development on the topic of RTI and English learners:

1. **What is the right way to implement RTI for English learners?**

   There is no one particular approach to or definition of RTI; the literature on RTI covers several core features that constitute an RTI framework (see the components in Figure 1.1 in Chapter 1, and the principles of a successful RTI program and guiding questions for English learners in that chapter). RTI involves a significant change from the way schools have done business in the past, and if schools are going to make AYP targets and meet the needs of all students, then the way RTI will be implemented in a given district or building will depend on the issues discussed in this book and the plan that is developed.

2. **What is the role of special education teachers in RTI?**

   Teachers certified to work with students with mild to moderate disabilities, including learning disabilities, would continue to provide direct and indirect services to those students with IEPs. Ideally, however, the special education teacher would also have training in understanding the educational needs of English learners. With RTI, their expanded role would include providing consultation to teams (grade level, multidisciplinary, or RTI teams) and sharing their expertise with colleagues as school personnel work together in a school-wide effort.

3. **How do we get started with putting RTI in place? Do we begin with a whole building or the whole district?**

   The decision of how to begin implementation of RTI depends largely on buy-in from stakeholders. If there is strong administrative support and the planning stage involved members from a variety of constituencies, then district-wide implementation may be effective. However, if there is a lot of resistance, consider starting small, with one grade level in elementary or one content area (reading or math) in secondary. It is important to implement RTI well and experience success. Once RTI is in place, the process serves as a model for getting others on board. Increased student achievement through effective RTI is the best "seller" of the program to others.

4. **Can RTI be used for determining special education eligibility?**

   Yes. IDEA 2004 makes it clear that states are required to permit the use of RTI in determining special education eligibility (see Appendix A). However, the statute and its regulations don't specify RTI implementation (Zirkel & Krohn, 2008). RTI changes the nature of the comprehensive evaluation away from testing for eligibility and toward examining data that were collected on the student's instructional progress (including English language proficiency) for planning increasingly intense interventions. Some experts believe that testing for special education eligibility is unnecessary with

RTI. Since districts can choose RTI or a discrepancy model, "there is no point in a discrepancy model if RTI is in place" (East, 2006).

5. **Who will conduct the intervention?**

Delivery of intervention varies widely and differs in Tier 2 and Tier 3 intervention. With a school-wide or grade-level model, scheduling is done at the administration level. Typically, school administrators determine what can be done given their personnel, resources, and master schedule. In most cases, the general education teacher conducts small group Tier 2 intervention during class time while other students are working independently. In other cases, intervention for students is provided during the time their class is elsewhere participating in programs such as P.E., art, music, foreign language, and computer lab. In secondary settings, a period of intervention may be part of a student's class schedule. (Keep in mind that intervention is designed to be temporary so that students receiving services do not miss out on these special programs or electives the entire year.) In other situations, someone other than the classroom teacher provides Tier 2 intervention. One creative district employs retired teachers to work with students before school and after school, other districts use existing personnel such as literacy coaches or reading specialists, and still others hold Saturday school taught by teachers or specialists.

For Tier 3 intervention, the increased intensity requires a greater level of expertise. The teacher or specialist providing Tier 3 intervention should be well trained and have background in both literacy and teaching English learners effectively. So, it may be a special education teacher with knowledge of second language acquisition or a bilingual teacher or ESL specialist with expertise in literacy.

In terms of what research supports, the jury is still out. Most early reading studies with English learners that resembled Tier 2 interventions had interventions that were supplementary to general classroom instruction and were delivered in small groups by instructors other than the general classroom teacher (McMaster, Kung, Han, & Cao, 2008). As the research base on intervention grows, we will know more about ways to conduct interventions most effectively. In the meantime, district planning teams should make decisions that fit best with their local conditions.

6. **Why is collaboration with colleagues important, and how do we do it?**

Collaboration in grade-level teams, subject-area teams, or cross-disciplinary teams, commonly called a Professional Learning Community (PLC), has benefits that are undisputed, yet many schools struggle with getting teachers to embrace the idea as a priority in their professional lives. Danielson (2007) discusses the importance of collaboration with colleagues. "During conversations about practice, particularly when such conversations are organized around a common framework, teachers are able to learn from one another and to thereby enrich their own teaching. It is this joint learning that makes the conversations so rich—and so valued." In our research on professional development for improving practice with English learners (Echevarria, Short, & Vogt, 2008), we also found that this process of collaboration and discussion is critical both to enriching the professional lives of educators and to ensuring that the components used in a given setting (SIOP components for instruction and RTI components) are applied with fidelity.

Lack of time is the most common barrier to collaboration, which prevents teachers from exchanging ideas, jointly planning lessons, evaluating individual student progress on a regular basis, and discussing appropriate adaptations, modifications, and interventions. This barrier is real and not easily remedied. Some teams meet before or after school, during lunch, or during common planning periods. Some schools dismiss students early one day a week for meetings, whereas others use funding sources to pay for substitutes, for example, one day per month. Each school or district needs to create ways to increase time for collaboration, which should be part of an overall professional development program since the activities of these groups provide feedback to teachers around common goals and components of their RTI program.

In their book on collaboration, Honigsfeld and Dove (2010) suggest that teachers use the acrostic ESCROW to guide their PLC meetings:

Establish and stick to set meeting times.

Start by discussing big ideas and set essential learning goals.

Concentrate on areas of special difficulty for English learners: scaffolding learning, adapting content, modifying assignments, increasing oral language opportunities, and differentiating tasks.

Review previous lessons based on student performance data.

Overcome the need to always be in control.

Work toward common understanding of English learners' needs.

Some collaborative groups actually observe one another's teaching or provide feedback on each other's videotaped lessons. However in-depth, some level of collaboration is recommended in order to enhance professional growth and improve instruction for English learners—and all students.

7. **What do we do if more than 50% of our school population qualifies for Tier 2 and Tier 3 instruction?**

There are some districts with high numbers of English learners in predominantly low-income, underperforming schools. The majority of students are performing below grade level for many of the reasons discussed in Chapter 2. However, even in these challenging schools, instructional programs should offer high-quality teaching that connects with what students know and is meaningful to them and that provides many opportunities to be exposed to interesting, relevant text and discussions using academic language. There are many schools committed to high-quality instruction that are model programs and "beat the odds." We highlight one such class in Appendix D.

If schools are using funds to support costly Tier 2 and Tier 3 services for more than the expected number of students, then those schools might consider investing the funds in effective professional development in Tier 1. Unusually high numbers of students in Tiers 2 and 3 raise a red flag that Tier 1 general education instruction needs to be seriously evaluated. As mentioned in other chapters, all students can and will learn under the right circumstances; the emphasis needs to be on meeting English learners' language and academic needs in the general education classroom. Administrative support and commitment to improved instruction is imperative.

8. **How do RTI and SIOP "dovetail"?**

The SIOP® Model is a framework for making instruction comprehensible for English learners. Its emphasis on academic language development, differentiated instruction, and providing access to the core make it applicable in all tiers of the RTI process. The features of the SIOP® Model are integrated throughout the components of RTI. For example, if ELs are to learn the components of reading, reach grade-level standards in all content areas, and develop English proficiency, Tier 1 instruction should reflect the features of the SIOP® Model consistently. Content and language objectives are posted to guide instruction and learning. Also, Tier 1 teachers give specific attention to vocabulary development, provide information in multiple ways (visual clues, physical gestures), present ideas verbally and in writing, create frequent opportunities for meaningful oral language practice including working with peers, make instructions and expectations extremely clear (e.g., through modeling a procedure or completing together part of a task), differentiate instruction based on language proficiency or academic skill level, and provide additional opportunities for practice. Many of these same features are necessary for making Tier 2 intervention effective for English learners. Even if Tier 2 intervention is a specific curriculum, teachers need to reflect on the SIOP features to make sure that they are providing optimal instruction at Tier 2, instruction that is understandable and that develops students' English language proficiency during intervention. At Tier 3, intervention is more intensive, and is provided in groups of 1–3 students. However, English learners still benefit from the features of the SIOP® Model within the context of Tier 3 intervention. An English learner needs to understand the teacher's expectations and the language she uses, as well as have sufficient opportunity to practice skills and have a chance to use academic language in meaningful ways. So, the RTI process and the SIOP® Model work together, hand in glove, to support the learning of English learners.

9. Does an ideal RTI model exist?

There are a number of states and districts that have implemented effective RTI approaches. A single ideal RTI model will probably never exist because research comparing different ways of reforming service delivery systems in schools is complex and may not be relevant as conditions vary from state to state and region to region. One of the reasons we included the Guide to Effective RTI in this book is so that readers can consider their own particular situation, take the information provided in each chapter, and develop an RTI plan that suits the needs of their schools' and districts' student population.

For specific examples of RTI approaches, we direct readers to two excellent websites that feature RTI programs. One, from the National Center on Response to Intervention, includes an RTI state database that provides a snapshot of each state's RTI implementation to date and is found at http://state.rti4success.org/. The other website is from the Pennsylvania Training and Technical Assistance Network, http://www.pattan.net/teachlead/ResponsetoIntervention.aspx, and provides many resources including an RTI Implementation Guide.

Finally, in the PDToolkit for SIOP we highlight several programs that have implemented an RTI model well and have seen positive results.

10. How does the ESL program work within an RTI process for English learners?

RTI is a comprehensive school-wide service delivery model designed to offer evidence-based instruction to students and, based on assessment data, adjustments are made to increase academic success for all students. In the past, programs within schools (e.g., ESL, special education, Title 1) have operated as silos, separate from one another with little interaction or collaboration. Sometimes, in fact, school personnel feel threatened that a process like RTI may minimize their role or even eliminate their position. Quite the opposite is true. With RTI, the role of the ESL teacher could be expanded. He or she would continue to provide much-needed English language development services to students (even if they receive Tier 2 or Tier 3 literacy intervention) but might also serve as a team member on the problem-solving team. Their expertise makes a valuable contribution to discussions about struggling English learners. Bottom line: The idea of RTI is to provide the services students need, so English learners would continue to receive specialized ESL instruction as needed.

11. **What are some questions to guide implementation?**

    The extent to which the following questions guide program development results in either successful RTI implementation or the creation of barriers to effective RTI implementation. As teams develop their RTI plan, make decisions about implementation, discuss resource allocation, and consider professional development priorities, they should ask themselves the following:

    - Have English learners had sufficient opportunity to learn (time and quality of instruction)?
    - Does Tier 1 instruction reflect best practice, and is it being implemented to a high degree?
    - Are our teachers respectful of and supportive of English learner students' cultures and language learning needs?
    - Are we committed to using only evidence-based intervention and curriculum?
    - How will we oversee fidelity of implementation?
    - Are we giving our English learners enough time in Tiers 2 and 3 before considering special education services?
    - Are teachers highly qualified in their content areas and also in effective teaching for English learners?
    - Are we utilizing the expertise of our staff in a collaborative way to provide a comprehensive instructional program for all students, including English learners (ESL, bilingual, general education teachers, specialists, administrators)?
    - Are we asking every member of the staff to contribute some time to RTI so that it is in fact a school-wide initiative?
    - What are we willing to give up in order to free up time for RTI?

    These kinds of questions are important for strategic planning and improving implementation of an RTI process.

Appendix C   SIOP Protocol (Abbreviated)

The Sheltered Instruction Observation Protocol (SIOP)®
(Echevarria, Vogt, & Short, 2000, 2004, 2008, 2013, 2014a, 2014b)

Observer(s): _____

Date: _____

Grade: _____

ESL Level: _____

School: _____

Teacher: _____

Class/Topic: _____

Lesson: Multi-day Single-day (circle one)

Total Points Possible: 120 (Subtract 4 points for each NA given) _____

Total Points Earned: _____   Percentage Score: _____

Directions: Circle the number that best reflects what you observe in a sheltered lesson. You may give a score from 0–4 (or NA on selected items). Cite under "Comments" specific examples of the behaviors observed.

	Highly Evident		Somewhat Evident		Not Evident	
Lesson Preparation	4	3	2	1	0	
1. **Content objectives** clearly defined, displayed, and reviewed with students	☐	☐	☐	☐	☐	
2. **Language objectives** clearly defined, displayed, and reviewed with students	☐	☐	☐	☐	☐	
3. **Content concepts** appropriate for age and educational background level of students	☐	☐	☐	☐	☐	
4. **Supplementary materials** used to a high degree, making the lesson clear and meaningful (e.g., computer programs, graphs, models, visuals)	☐	☐	☐	☐	☐	N/A
5. **Adaptation of content** (e.g., text, assignment) to all levels of student proficiency	☐	☐	☐	☐	☐	☐
6. **Meaningful activities** that integrate lesson concepts (e.g., surveys, letter writing, simulations, constructing models) with language practice opportunities for reading, writing, listening, and/or speaking	☐	☐	☐	☐	☐	

Comments:

	Highly Evident		Somewhat Evident		Not Evident	N/A
Building Background	4	3	2	1	0	N/A
7. **Concepts explicitly linked** to students' background experiences	☐	☐	☐	☐	☐	☐
8. **Links explicitly made** between past learning and new concepts	☐	☐	☐	☐	☐	
9. **Key vocabulary** emphasized (e.g., introduced, written, repeated, and highlighted for students to see)	☐	☐	☐	☐	☐	

Comments:

	Highly Evident		Somewhat Evident		Not Evident
Comprehensible Input	4	3	2	1	0
10. **Speech** appropriate for students' proficiency level (e.g., slower rate, enunciation, and simple sentence structure for beginners)	☐	☐	☐	☐	☐
11. **Clear explanation** of academic tasks	☐	☐	☐	☐	☐
12. **A variety of techniques** used to make content concepts clear (e.g., modeling, visuals, hands-on activities, demonstrations, gestures, body language)	☐	☐	☐	☐	☐

Comments:

	Highly Evident		Somewhat Evident		Not Evident	
Strategies	4	3	2	1	0	
13. Ample opportunities provided for students to use **learning strategies**	☐	☐	☐	☐	☐	
14. **Scaffolding techniques** consistently used assisting and supporting student understanding (e.g., think-alouds)	☐	☐	☐	☐	☐	
15. A variety of **questions or tasks that promote higher-order thinking skills** (e.g., literal, analytical, and interpretive questions)	☐	☐	☐	☐	☐	

Comments:

	Highly Evident		Somewhat Evident		Not Evident	
Interaction	4	3	2	1	0	
16. Frequent opportunities for **interaction** and discussion between teacher/student and among students, which encourage elaborated responses about lesson concepts	☐	☐	☐	☐	☐	
17. **Grouping configurations** support language and content objectives of the lesson	☐	☐	☐	☐	☐	
18. Sufficient **wait time for student** responses consistently provided	☐	☐	☐	☐	☐	N/A
19. Ample opportunities for students to **clarify key concepts in L1** as needed with aide, peer, or L1 text	☐	☐	☐	☐	☐	☐

Comments:

	Highly Evident		Somewhat Evident		Not Evident	N/A
Practice & Application	4	3	2	1	0	N/A
20. **Hands-on materials and/or manipulatives** provided for students to practice using new content knowledge	☐	☐	☐	☐	☐	☐
21. Activities provided for students to **apply content and language knowledge** in the classroom	☐	☐	☐	☐	☐	☐
22. Activities integrate all **language skills** (i.e., reading, writing, listening, and speaking)	☐	☐	☐	☐	☐	

Comments:

	Highly Evident		Somewhat Evident		Not Evident	
Lesson Delivery	4	3	2	1	0	
23. **Content objectives** clearly supported by lesson delivery	☐	☐	☐	☐	☐	
24. **Language objectives** clearly supported by lesson delivery	☐	☐	☐	☐	☐	
25. **Students engaged** approximately 90% to 100% of the period	☐	☐	☐	☐	☐	
26. **Pacing** of the lesson appropriate to students' ability level	☐	☐	☐	☐	☐	

Comments:

	Highly Evident		Somewhat Evident		Not Evident	
Review & Assessment	4	3	2	1	0	
27. Comprehensive **review of key vocabulary**	☐	☐	☐	☐	☐	
28. Comprehensive **review of key content concepts**	☐	☐	☐	☐	☐	
29. Regular **feedback** provided to students on their output (e.g., language, content, work)	☐	☐	☐	☐	☐	
30. **Assessment of student comprehension and learning** of all lesson objectives (e.g., spot checking, group response) throughout the lesson	☐	☐	☐	☐	☐	

Comments:

Appendix D   Case Study Activity

Select one of the following case studies for an English learner in elementary, middle, or high school. Based on the profile presented, be prepared to discuss the following questions with a group of educators.

Case Study #1: Marisela (third grade)

Marisela is a nine-year-old girl who attends ABC Elementary School. She is a high-risk student who was born prematurely and was in the hospital for three months due to low birth weight. She attended a parochial school kindergarten and repeated kindergarten in public school. A native-Spanish speaker, at the end of kindergarten Marisela did not recognize any of the letters of the English alphabet and was only able to identify her name in print. She had difficulty retaining information and needed a great deal of teacher redirection to complete tasks. She ended first grade as a non-reader who, while able to recognize consonant sounds, did not recognize vowels, and could not segment or blend CVC words. Marisela had a bank of ten high-frequency words, and was beginning to establish one-to-one word pointing and to focus on the print in text. Marisela became very frustrated when any new concept was introduced and refused to participate or try to do her work without one-on-one teacher help or extra support from the bilingual aide.

Based on the information provided above, discuss the following questions:

- What might be some possible causes for a mismatch between Marisela's personal and educational background and the content she is being taught?

- What questions would you want to ask Marisela's teacher about the instructional approaches that are being used in the classroom?

- What information should you seek before determining that the current classroom instruction is inappropriate for Marisela's needs? Re-examine the figure "Clarifying RTI Terms" on page 10 in this book. Which, if any, of the recommendations might be appropriate for Marisela? How could the teacher monitor Marisela's progress on the accommodations you have selected?

- Many teachers have difficulty using reading assessment findings to tailor instruction for groups of students who are struggling. As a peer coach or administrator for Marisela's teacher, what advice, assistance, or recommendations might you provide in order to help the teacher better utilize the information he or she already has about Marisela?

- Revisit the SIOP® Model features in the SIOP protocol found in Appendix C. Based on Marisela's profile, which of the features are especially important if she is to be successful in the classroom setting?

Case Study #2: Jacinto (sixth grade)

Jacinto is an eleven-year-old boy who has lived and attended school in the United States for the past three years. He has been receiving intensive ESL instruction and support for one hour each day during each school year. Jacinto's older brother, Gaspar, who is fourteen and in ninth grade, has adjusted well to his teachers and classes, and seems to be thriving both academically and in learning English. Gaspar attended ESL classes during sixth and seventh grades. The boys' parents, although not fluent in English, are very concerned about and involved in their sons' schooling. They do what they can to help with homework assignments and make it clear that the boys are to be respectful to their teachers and do what they say.

Jacinto, unlike his older brother, has struggled academically since his family arrived from Guatemala when he was nine. His teachers have reported distractibility, an unwillingness to participate in class activities, and a reluctance to learn and practice English, as well as serious academic gaps in reading and math. In fifth grade, Jacinto nearly failed several subjects. However, his teacher, feeling that the boy's English language proficiency was limited, gave Jacinto a D on his report card for both science and social studies, and a C- in math because he seemed to try hard during the math period.

Now that Jacinto is in sixth grade, the reading and content demands have substantially increased, and Jacinto is again performing poorly. He seldom completes homework assignments, frequently telling his parents that his teachers don't assign homework. He is no longer receiving intensive English instruction with the ESL teacher, and he's beginning to talk with his friends about dropping out of school as soon as he reaches his sixteenth birthday.

Based on the information provided about Jacinto, discuss the following questions:

- What might be some possible causes for a mismatch between Jacinto's personal and educational background and the content he is being taught?

- What questions would you want to ask Jacinto's teachers about the instructional approaches that are being used in the classroom?

- What information should you seek before determining that the current classroom instruction is inappropriate for Jacinto's needs?

- Re-examine the figure "Clarifying RTI Terms" on page 10 of this book. Which, if any, of the recommendations might be appropriate for Jacinto? How could the teacher monitor Jacinto's progress on the accommodations/ modifications you have selected?

- Many teachers have difficulty using reading assessment findings to tailor instruction for groups of students who are struggling. As a peer coach or administrator for Jacinto's teacher, what advice, assistance, or recommendations might you provide in order to help the teacher better utilize the information he or she already has about Jacinto?

- Revisit the SIOP® Model features in the SIOP protocol found in Appendix C. Based on Jacinto's profile, which of the features are especially important if he is to be successful in the classroom setting?

Case Study #3: Tran (ninth grade)

Tran is a second-generation Vietnamese American who was born in southern California. While Vietnamese is his first language, Tran is fluent conversationally in English. A gregarious boy with an infectious smile, he is well liked by his peers and teachers alike. Because he has attended his local neighborhood schools since kindergarten, Tran is comfortable navigating through high school and he is somewhat a "big man on campus," primarily because of his leadership skills and engaging personality.

Academically, Tran is having difficulties in his ninth grade classes, especially in those that require a great deal of reading. For many years, he has been able to "coast," periodically succumbing to "fake reading," whereby he pretends to read assignments both in class and at home, but in reality he's simply picking out words he recognizes. He frequently talks to his friends about their assignments and up to this point he has been able to glean key information and concepts where he can, in order to maintain a C average. But, this year Tran's inability to read comprehensively has caught up with him and he's in danger of failing. Several of his teachers have expressed concern about how Tran is performing, yet Tran dismisses their concerns, telling them that he'll start studying harder to improve his grades.

Based on the information provided about Tran, discuss the following questions:

- What might be some possible causes for a mismatch between Tran's personal and educational background and the content he is being taught?

- What questions would you want to ask Tran's teachers about the instructional approaches that are being used in the classroom?

- What information should you seek before determining that the current classroom instruction is inappropriate for Tran's needs?

- Re-examine the figure "Clarifying RTI Terms" on p. 10 of this book. Which, if any, of the recommendations might be appropriate for Tran? How could the teacher monitor Tran's progress on the accommodations/modifications you have selected?

- Many teachers have difficulty using reading assessment findings to tailor instruction for groups of students who are struggling. As a peer coach or administrator for Tran's teacher, what advice, assistance, or recommendations might you provide in order to help the teacher better utilize the information he or she already has about Tran?

- Revisit the SIOP® Model features in the SIOP protocol found in Appendix C. Based on Tran's profile, which of the features are especially important if he is to be successful in the classroom setting?

Academic language: Language proficiency associated with schooling, and the abstract language abilities required for academic work; a more complex, conceptual, linguistic ability that includes analysis, synthesis, and evaluation. Academic language and vocabulary can be generic across content areas, or unique for each type of content, and both represent considerable challenges for English learners and struggling readers.

Additive bilingualism: Rather than neglecting or rejecting students' home language and culture, additive bilingualism promotes building on what home language knowledge the child brings to the classroom and adding to it.

Adequate Yearly Progress (AYP): Integral to the No Child Left Behind (NCLB) legislation, this term refers to the annual minimum growth needed to meet the requirements of NCLB within a specified timeframe.

Assessment: The orderly process of gathering, analyzing, interpreting, and reporting student performance, ideally from multiple sources over a period of time; also, the broad process of obtaining information used in decision making about a student, group of students, curriculum, program, or educational policy.

Baseline data: Basic information on a student's current performance level, which is gathered before a program or intervention begins. It is the starting point to be used to compare a student's learning before a program of instruction begins.

Benchmark: The expected grade-level performance of the student.

Benchmark assessment: The periodic assessment (a minimum of three times a year) of all students compared to age or grade-level standards.

Bilingual instruction: School instruction using two languages, generally the native language of a student and a second language. The amount of time that each language is used depends on the type of bilingual program, its specific objectives, and students' levels of language proficiency.

Collaborative team: A group of people at a school or district who meet on a scheduled or as-needed basis to fulfill a specific purpose or function. Collaborative teams in RTI may include teachers, parents, administrators, and other interested community members who work in cooperation, with shared goals and perceived outcomes occurring in a climate of trust.

Communicative competence: The combination of grammatical, discourse, strategic, and sociolinguistic competence that allows the recognition and production of fluent and appropriate language in all communication settings.

Content-based ESL: An instructional approach in which content topics are used as the vehicle for second language learning. A system of instruction in which teachers use a variety of instructional techniques as a way of developing second language, content, cognitive, and study skills.

Content standards: Definitions of what students are expected to know and be capable of doing for a given content area; the knowledge and skills that need to be taught in order for students to reach competency; what students are expected to learn and what schools are expected to teach. There may be national, state, or local-level standards.

Core curriculum: The planned instruction in a content area, which is central and usually mandatory for all students of a school (e.g., reading, math, science).

Culturally and linguistically diverse (CLD) learners: Term that encompasses more than English learners. It may also describe a student who speaks a dialect or dialect-influenced form of Standard American English (SAE) or a student who comes from a nonmainstream culture.

Curriculum Based Measurements (CBM): A concise method used to find out how students are progressing in basic academic areas such as math, reading, writing, and spelling; CBM are widely available and well-researched tools for collecting ongoing assessment data during intervention.

Data-based decision making: The use of student assessment data to guide the design, implementation, and adjustment of instruction; considered by some to be synonymous with progress monitoring because both require the collection and use of data.

Differentiated instruction: Instruction that matches the specific strengths and needs of each learner; includes providing alterations to curriculum, instruction, and assessment that recognize students' varying background knowledge, language proficiency, and academic abilities.

Early intervention services: A set of coordinated services for students in kindergarten through grade 12 (with particular emphasis on students in kindergarten through grade 3) who are not currently identified as needing special education or related services, but who need additional academic and behavioral support to succeed in general education.

Elementary and Secondary Education Act (ESEA) Title I: The nation's major federal law related to education in grades pre-kindergarten through high school (the most recent version is known as No Child Left Behind). Title I of ESEA provides funding for high-poverty schools to help students who are behind academically or at risk of falling behind.

Engagement: When students are fully taking part in a lesson, they are said to be engaged. This is a holistic term that encompasses listening, reading, writing, responding, and discussing. The level of students' engagement during a lesson may be assessed to a greater or lesser degree.

English learners (ELs): Children and adults who are learning English as a second or additional language. This term may apply to learners across various levels of proficiency in English. ELs may also be referred to as English language learners (ELLs), non-English speaking (NES), limited-English speaking (LES), and a non-native speaker (NNS).

ESL: English as a second language; used to refer to programs and classes to teach students English as a second (or additional) language.

Evaluation: Judgments about students' learning made by interpreting and analyzing assessment data; the process of judging achievement, growth, product, processes, or changes in these; judgments of education programs. The process of assessment and evaluation can be viewed as progressive: first, assessment; then, evaluation.

Explicit instruction: Instruction that is clear, deliberate, and visible.

Fidelity of implementation: Instructional programs, methods, or models are implemented with intensity, accuracy, and consistency; using a program or method of instruction as it was intended to be used. An RTI process must be implemented with fidelity.

Five "Big Ideas" or Pillars of Reading: Critical aspects of reading for all RTI tiers: phonemic awareness, phonics, fluency, vocabulary, and comprehension; many reading experts believe the "big ideas" represent a narrow view of the process of reading. Allington (2008) recommends an additional five "big ideas" that are particularly relevant to RTI: (1) classroom organization; (2) matching pupils to texts; (3) access to interesting texts, choice, and collaboration; (4) writing and reading as natural, reciprocal processes; and (5) expert tutoring.

Grouping: The assignment of students into groups of classes for instruction, such as by age, ability, or achievement; or within classes, such as by reading ability, proficiency, language background, or interests. Flexible grouping enables students to move among different groups based on their performance and instructional strengths and needs.

Home language: The language or languages spoken in the student's home by people who live there; also referred to as first language (L1), primary language, mother tongue, or native language.

Individuals with Disabilities Education Act (IDEA): The federal law dealing with the education of children with disabilities. IDEA requires all states that accept IDEA federal funds to provide a free appropriate public education to all children with disabilities in the state.

Instructional intervention: Clear, deliberate, and carefully planned instruction delivered by trained personnel tailored to meet the identified needs of struggling students.

Intensive intervention: Explicit and systematic instruction delivered by highly skilled teacher specialists that provides students with increased opportunities for guided practice and teacher feedback. This instruction is targeted and tailored to meet the needs of struggling learners in small groups.

Intervention: A change in instructing a student in an area of learning or behavioral difficulty to try to improve performance and achieve adequate progress.

Levels of language proficiency: Students learning language progress through stages. The stages or levels may be labeled differently across states. In seminal work in this area, Krashen and Terrell (1983, 1984) described the stages as the following: Preproduction, Early production, Speech emergence, Intermediate fluency, and Advanced fluency. At present, many states have levels similar to those in the WIDA (World-class Instructional Design and Assessment) English language proficiency standards (WIDA, 2007):

Entering (Level 1): Lowest level, essentially no English proficiency. Students are often newcomers and need extensive pictorial and nonlinguistic support. They need to learn basic oral language and literacy skills in English.

Beginning (Level 2): Second lowest level. Students use phrases and short sentences and are introduced to general content vocabulary and lesson tasks.

Developing (Level 3): Next level of proficiency. Students can use general and specific language related to the content areas; they can speak and write sentences and paragraphs although with some errors, and they can read with instructional supports.

Expanding (Level 4): Akin to an intermediate level of proficiency. Students use general, academic, and specific language related to content areas. They have improved speaking and writing skills and stronger reading comprehension skills (compared to the Developing level).

Bridging (Level 5): Akin to advanced intermediate or advanced level of proficiency. Students use general academic and technical language of the content areas. They can read and write with linguistic complexity. Students at this level have often exited the ESL or ELD program, but their language and academic performance is still monitored.

Reaching (Level 6): At or close to grade-level proficiency. Students' oral and written communication skills are comparable to native English speakers at their grade level. Students at this level have exited the ESL or ELD program but their language and academic performance is still monitored.

Measurement: Refers to the procedure of assigning scores or numbers to describe the degree to which a student has acquired a particular skill or attribute.

Native English speaker: An individual whose first language is English. Native language is an individual's first, primary, or home language (L1).

No Child Left Behind Act of 2001 (NCLB): Also known as the reauthorization of the Elementary and Secondary Education Act (ESEA); under this legislation, all children must reach proficiency, as defined by each state's proficiency measures; requires annual testing in grades 3–8 and 11 in reading and mathematics; also requires disaggregated reporting of scores on an annual basis to the federal government.

Outcome assessment: The measurement of how students perform academically at the end of planned instruction or at the end of the year.

Proficiency for English learners as listed in Vogt & Echevarria (2008, pp. 51–52): Remember that students at lower levels of English proficiency are not necessarily functioning at lower levels of cognitive ability. Frequently, these students are able to use higher level thinking skills in their primary language but have a more difficult time understanding academic content and expressing their knowledge in English.

1. Beginning (Pre-Production): English learners in this stage have little comprehension of oral and written English, and are unable to produce much, if any, English.

2. Beginning (Early Production): In this stage English learners have limited English comprehension but can now give one- or two-word oral responses.

3. Intermediate (Early): Students at this stage have some proficiency in communicating simple ideas and can comprehend contextualized information.

4. Intermediate: At this stage, English learners have proficiency in communicating ideas and comprehending contextualized information in English.

5. Early Advanced: These English learners can communicate well, have good comprehension of information, and have adequate vocabulary to achieve academically.

6. Advanced: Students at this stage have near native speech fluency, very good comprehension of information in English, and expanded vocabulary to achieve academically.

Progress monitoring: A scientifically based practice used to assess students' academic performance and evaluate the effectiveness of instruction. Progress monitoring can be implemented with individual students or an entire class.

Scaffolding: Adult (e.g., teacher) support for learning and student performance of tasks through instruction, modeling, questioning, feedback, graphic organizers, and more, across successive lessons. These supports are gradually withdrawn ("gradual release of responsibility"), thus transferring more and more autonomy to the child. Scaffolding activities provide support for learning that should be removed as learners are able to demonstrate strategic behaviors in their own learning.

School-based team: A group of school personnel who work collaboratively to address the needs of struggling students. Schools use a variety of terms for school-based teams such as educational support team, student study team, instructional intervention team, multidisciplinary team, problem-solving team, student assistance team, or student progress monitoring team.

Scientifically based interventions: Scientifically based means research that involves the application of rigorous, systematic, and objective procedures to obtain reliable and valid knowledge relevant to educational activities and programs. Also referred to as *evidence based interventions*.

Scientific, research-based instruction: Curriculum and educational interventions that are research based and have been proven to be effective for most students.

Sheltered instruction (SI): A means for making content comprehensible for English learners while they are developing English proficiency. Sheltered classrooms, which include a mix of native English speakers and English learners or only English learners, integrate language and content while infusing sociocultural awareness. SDAIE, Specially Designed Academic Instruction in English, is a term for sheltered instruction that is used in several states. It features strategies and techniques for making content understandable for English learners. Although some SDAIE techniques are research-based, SDAIE itself has not been scientifically validated.

SIOP® (Sheltered Instruction Observation Protocol): A scientifically validated model of sheltered instruction designed to make grade-level academic content understandable for English learners while at the same time developing their English language. The Protocol and lesson planning guide ensure that teachers are consistently implementing practices known to be effective for English learners.

Special education: Instruction that is specially designed to meet the individual needs of a child with a disability, according to the federal special education law, the Individuals with Disabilities Education Act (IDEA 2004).

Standard protocol: Intensive, short-term instructional interventions conducted with a small group of targeted students that follow a specified script and have research to support their effectiveness. The materials used supplement the general education curriculum.

Subtractive bilingualism: The learning of a new language at the expense of the primary language. Learners often lose their native language and culture because they don't have opportunities to continue learning or using it, or they perceive that language to be of lower status. Loss of the primary language often leads to cultural ambivalence.

Supplemental intervention: Additional Tier 1 instruction targeted to meet specific language and literacy needs of individual students. Supplemental materials may be used that are aligned with and support the core instructional program.

Universal screening (school-wide screening): A quick-check assessment of all students' current level of performance in a content or skill area. This is administered three times per year.

Note: Some of the terms and definitions in this Glossary have been adapted from the following sources: Echevarria, Vogt, & Short, 2008, pp. 244–247; RTI for English Learners Institute Participant Workbook (developed for Pearson by J. Echevarria & M.E. Vogt), 2009, pp. 77–79; and Pennsylvania Department of Education: Response to Intervention. Framework for Secondary Schools: Guidelines and Recommendations, 2008, pp. 23–26.

Adger, C., & Locke, J. (2000). *Broadening the base: School/community partnerships serving language minority students at risk.* Santa Cruz, CA: Center for Research on Education, Diversity & Excellence.

Ajayi, L. (2009). English as a second language learners' exploration of multimodal texts in a junior high school. *Journal of Adolescent & Adult Literacy, 52*(7), 585–595.

Allington, R. L. (2008). *What really matters in Response to Intervention: Research-based designs.* Boston, MA: Allyn & Bacon.

Allington, R. L., & Johnston, P. H. (2002). *Reading to learn: Lessons from exemplary fourth-grade classrooms.* New York, NY: Guilford.

Artiles, A. J., Kozleski, E., Trent, S., Osher, D., & Ortiz, A. (2010). Justifying and explaining disproportionality, 1968–2008: A critique of underlying views of culture. *Exceptional Children, 76,* 279–299.

Artiles, A. J., & Trent, S. (1994). Overrepresentation of minority students in special education: A continuing debate. *Journal of Special Education, 27,* 410–437.

August, D., Beck, I. L., Calderón, M., Francis, D. J., Lesaux, N. K., & Shanahan, T. (2008). Instruction and professional development. In D. August & T. Shanahan (Eds.), *Developing reading and writing in second-language learners* (pp. 131–250). New York, NY: Routledge; Washington, DC: Center for Applied Linguistics; Newark, DE: International Reading Association.

August, D., Carlo, M., Dressler, C., & Snow, C. (2005). The critical role of vocabulary development for English language learners. *Learning Disabilities Research and Practice, 20,* 50–57.

August, D., & Shanahan, T. (Eds.). (2006). *Developing literacy in second-language learners: A report of the National Literacy Panel on Language-Minority Children and Youth.* Mahwah, NJ: Lawrence Erlbaum Associates.

August, D., & Shanahan, T. (Eds.). (2008). *Developing reading and writing in second-language learners: Lessons from the Report of the National Literacy Panel on Language-Minority Children and Youth.* New York, NY: Routledge; Washington, DC: Center for Applied Linguistics; Newark, DE: International Reading Association.

August, D., & Shanahan, T. (2010). Effective literacy instruction for English learners. In California Department of Education (Ed.), *Improving education for English learners: Research-based approaches* (pp. 209–249). Sacramento, CA: CDE Press.

Avalos, M., Bengochea, A., & Medina, E. (2013, March 9). Reading, writing, viewing and speaking math: Fostering mathematical literacy. Paper presented at the REL-SE Research to Practice Bridge Event, Miami, FL.

Baca, L., & Cervantes, H. (1984). *The bilingual special education interface.* St. Louis, MO: Times Mirror/Mosby.

Baker, D. L., Richards-Tutor, C., Gersten, R., Baker, S. K., & Smith, J. L. (in press). Reading interventions for at-risk English learners. In E. Lopez, S. Nahari, & S. Proctor (Eds.), *Handbook of multi-cultural school psychology: An interdisciplinary perspective* (2nd ed.). New York, NY: Routledge.

Ballantyne, K. G., Sanderman, A. R., & Levy, J. (2008). *Educating English language learners: Building teacher capacity.* Washington, DC: National Clearinghouse for English Language Acquisition. Available at http://www.ncela.gwu.edu/practice/mainstream_teachers.htm.

Barton, P., & Coley, R. (2009). Those persistent gaps. *Educational Leadership 67*(4), 18–23.

Batalova, J., Fix, M., & Murray, J. (2005). *English language learner adolescents: Demographics and literacy achievements.* Report to the Center for Applied Linguistics. Washington, DC: Migration Policy Institute.

Batsche, G., Elliott, J., Graden, J., Grimes, J., Kovaleski, J., Parsse, D., Reschly, D., Schrag, J., & Tilly, W. D. (2008). *Response to intervention: Policy considerations and implementation.* Alexandria, VA: National Association of State Directors of Special Education.

Bauer, E. B. (2009). Informed additive literacy instruction for ELLs. *The Reading Teacher, 62*(5), 446–448.

Bear, D., Helman, L., Templeton, S., Invernizzi, M., & Johnston, F. (2007). *Words their way for English learners: Word study for phonics, vocabulary, and spelling instruction.* Upper Saddle River, NJ: Pearson/Merrill Prentice Hall.

Beck, L., McKeown, M., & Kucan, L. (2002). *Bringing words to life: Robust vocabulary instruction.* New York, NY: Guilford.

Biancarosa, G., & Snow, C. (2004). *Reading next: A vision for action and research in middle and high school literacy.* Report to the Carnegie Corporation of New York. Washington, DC: Alliance for Excellent Education.

Blachowicz, C. L. Z., Fisher, P., Ogle, D., & Watts-Taffe, S. (2006). Vocabulary: Questions from the classroom. *Reading Research Quarterly, 41,* 524–539.

Black, R. W. (2009). English-language learners, fan communities, and 21st-century skills. *Journal of Adolescent and Adult Literacy, 52*(8), 688–697.

Bottoms, G. (2007). Treat all students like the "best" students. *Educational Leadership, 64*(7), 30–37.

Brooks, K., & Thurston, L. (2010). English language learner academic engagement and instructional grouping configurations. *American Secondary Education, 39*(1), 45–60.

Brophy, J., & Good, T. (1970). Teacher's communication of differential expectations for children's classroom performance: Some behavioral data. *Journal of Educational Psychology, 61,* 365–374.

Brozo, W. G. (2010). Response to Intervention or responsive instruction? Challenges and possibilities of Response to Intervention for adolescent literacy. *Journal of Adolescent & Adult Literacy, 53*(4), 277–281.

California Department of Education. (2012). *2012 STAR Test Results.*

Capps, R., Fix, M., Murray, J., Ost, J., Passel, J., & Herwantoro, S. (2005). *The new demography of America's schools: Immigration and the No Child Left Behind Act.* Washington, DC: The Urban Institute.

Cardenes-Hagan, E. (2007). *English language learners with learning disabilities.* Webcast retrieved on January 25, 2010 from www.colorincolorado.org/powerpoint/web cast2007.ppt.

Carlo, M. S., August, D., McLaughlin, B., Snow, C. E., Dressler, C., Lippman, D. N., Lively, T. J., & White, C. E. (2004). Closing the gap: Addressing the vocabulary needs of English-language learners in bilingual and mainstream classrooms. *Reading Research Quarterly, 39*(20), 188–215.

Chiesi, H., Spilich, G., & Voss, J. (1979). Acquisition of domain-related information in relation to high- and low-domain knowledge. *Journal of Verbal Learning and Verbal Behavior, 18,* 257–274.

Christenson, S. L., Reschly, A. L., Appleton, J. J., Berman-Young, S., Spanjers, D. M., & Varno, P. (2008). Best practices in fostering student engagement. In A. Thomas & J. Grimes (Eds.), *Best practices in school psychology* (5ᵗʰ ed., pp. 1099–1119). Bethesda, MD: National Association of School Psychologists.

Clarke, B. Lembke, E. S., Hampton, D. D., & Hendricker, E. (2011). What we know and what we need to know about measuring student response in mathematics. In R. Gersten & R. Newman-Gonchar (Eds.), *Understanding RTI in Mathematics: Proven Methods and Applications.* Baltimore, MD: Paul H. Brookes Publishing.

Cloud, N. (1993). Language, culture & disability: Implications for instruction and teacher preparation. *Teacher Education and Special Education, 16*(1), 60–72.

Cloud, N. (2006). How can we best serve English language learners who have special needs, such as a disability? In E. Hamayan & R. Freeman (Eds.), *English language learners at school: A guide for administrators* (pp. 208–209). Philadelphia, PA: Caslon Publishing.

Cochran-Smith, M., & Zeichner , K. (2009). *Studying Teacher Education.* Mahwah, NJ: Lawrence Erlbaum Associates, Inc.

Council for Exceptional Children. (2008). New strategies to help students succeed. *CEC Today.* Retrieved from http://www.cec.sped.org/AM/.

Council for Exceptional Children. (2009). Special Issue: Evidence-based practices for reading, math, writing and behavior. *Exceptional Children, 75,* 3.

Coxhead, A. (2000). A new academic word list. *TESOL Quarterly, 34*(2), 213–238.

Crossley, S., McCarthy, P., Louwerse, M., & McNamara, D. (2007). A linguistic analysis of simplified and authentic texts. *The Modern Language Journal, 19*(2), 15–30.

Crosson, A. C., & Lesaux, N. K. (2011). Revisiting assumptions about the relationship of fluent reading to comprehension: Spanish-speakers' text-reading fluency in English. *Reading & Writing: An Interdisciplinary Journal, 23,* 475–494.

Cummins, J. (1984). *Bilingualism and special education: Issues in assessment and pedagogy.* Clevedon, England: Multilingual Matters.

Cummins, J. (2000). *Language, power and pedagogy.* Clevedon, England: Multilingual Matters.

Cunningham, P. (2006). High-poverty schools that beat the odds. *The Reading Teacher, 60*(4), 382–385.

Danielson, C. (2007). *Enhancing professional practice: A framework for teaching* (2nd ed.). Alexandria, VA: Association for Supervision and Curriculum Development.

Darling-Hammond, L. (2000). Teacher quality and student achievement: A review of state policy evidence. *Education Policy Analysis, 8*(1).

Darling-Hammond L., & Sykes G. (2003). Wanted: A national teacher supply policy for education: The right way to meet the "Highly Qualified Teacher" challenge. *Education Policy Analysis Archives, 11*(33).

Deno, S. L. (1985). Curriculum-based measurement: The emerging alternative. *Exceptional Children, 52*(3), 219–232.

Denton, C. A., Wexler, J., Vaughn, S., & Bryan, D. (2008). Intervention provided to linguistically diverse middle school students with severe reading difficulties. *Learning Disabilities Research & Practice, 23*(2), 79–89.

Diller, D. (2007). *Making the most of small groups: Differentiation for all.* Portland, ME: Stenhouse.

Dole, J., Duffy, G., Roehler, L., & Pearson, P. D. (1991). Moving from the old to the new: Research in reading comprehension instruction. *Review of Educational Research, 61,* 239–264.

Donnelly, W. B., & Roe, C. J. (2010). Using sentence frames to develop academic vocabulary for English learners. *The Reading Teacher, 64*(2), 131–136.

Dudley-Marling, C., & Michaels, S. (2012). *High-expectation curricula: Helping all students succeed with powerful learning.* New York, NY: Teachers College Press.

Duffy, G. (2002). The case for direct explanation of strategies. In C. C. Block & M. Pressley (Eds.), *Comprehension instruction: Research-based practices.* New York, NY: Guilford Press.

Duffy, H. (n.d.). *Meeting the needs of significantly struggling learners in high school: A look at approaches to tiered intervention.* Washington, DC: National High School Center, U.S. Department of Education. Retrieved from www.rti4success.org.

Dymock, S., & Nicholson, R. (2010). High 5! Strategies to enhance comprehension of expository text. *The Reading Teacher, 64*(3), 166–178.

East, B. (2006). *Myths about Response to Intervention (RTI) implementation.* Retrieved from http://www.rtinetwork.org/Learn/What/are/MythsAboutRTI.

Echevarría, J. (1995). Interactive reading instruction: A comparison of proximal and distal effects of instructional conversations. *Exceptional Children, 61*(6), 536–552.

Echevarría, J. (2012). *Effective practices for increasing the achievement of English learners.* Washington, DC: Center for Research on the Educational Achievement and Teaching of English Language Learners. Retrieved from http://www.cal.org/create/resources/pubs/.

Echevarría, J., & Graf, V. (1988). California bilingual special education model sites (1984–1986): Programs and research. In A. Ortiz & B. Ramirez (Eds.), *Schools and the culturally diverse student: Promising practices and future directions* (pp. 104–111). Reston, VA: Council for Exceptional Children.

Echevarría, J., & Graves, A. (2014). *Sheltered content instruction: Teaching English learners with diverse abilities* (5th ed.). Boston, MA: Allyn & Bacon.

Echevarría, J., & Hasbrouck, J. (2009). *Response to intervention and English learners* (CREATE Brief). Washington, DC: Center for Research on the Educational Achievement and Teaching of English Language Learners.

Echevarría, J., Richards-Tutor, C., Canges, R., & Francis, D. (2011). Using the SIOP Model to promote the acquisition of language and science concepts with English learners. *Bilingual Research Journal, 34*(3), 334–351.

Echevarría, J., Richards-Tutor, C., Chinn, V., & Ratleff, P. (2011). Did they get it? The role of fidelity in teaching English learners. *Journal of Adolescent and Adult Literacy, 54*(6) 425–434.

Echevarría, J., & Short, D. (2010). Programs and practices for effective sheltered content instruction. In California Department of Education (Ed.), *Improving education for English learners: Research-based approaches.* (p. 250–321). Sacramento, CA: CDE Press.

Echevarría, J., & Short, D. (2011). *The SIOP® Model: A professional development framework for comprehensive schoolwide intervention.* Washington, DC: Center for Research on the Educational Achievement and Teaching of English Language Learners. Retrieved from http://www.cal.org/create/resources/pubs/professional-development-framework.html.

Echevarría, J., Short, D., & Powers, K. (2006). School reform and standards-based education: An instructional model for English language learners. *Journal of Educational Research, 99*(4), 195–211.

Echevarría, J., Short, D., Richards-Tutor, C., & Himmel, J. (in press). Using the SIOP® Model as a professional development framework for comprehensive schoolwide intervention. In J. Echevarría, S. Vaughn, & D. Francis (Eds.), *English learners in content area classes: Teaching for achievement in the middle grades.* Boston, MA: Pearson.

Echevarría, J., Short, D., & Vogt, M.E. (2008). *Implementing the SIOP® Model through effective professional development and coaching.* Boston, MA: Allyn & Bacon.

Echevarría, J., Vogt, M.E., & Short, D. (2010). *The SIOP® Model for teaching mathematics to English learners.* Boston, MA: Pearson.

Echevarría, J., Vogt, M.E., & Short, D. (2013). *Making content comprehensible for English learners: The SIOP® Model* (4th ed.). Boston, MA: Pearson.

Echevarría, J., Vogt, M.E., & Short, D. (2014a). *Making content comprehensible for elementary English learners: The SIOP® Model.* Boston, MA: Pearson.

Echevarría, J., Vogt, M.E., & Short, D. (2014b). *Making content comprehensible for secondary English learners: The SIOP® Model.* Boston, MA: Pearson.

EdSource. (2007). *Similar English learner students, different results: Why do some schools do better?* EdSource Report. Mountainview, CA: Author.

Ehren, B. J. (2013). Expanding pockets of excellence in RTI. *The Reading Teacher 66*(6) 449–453.

Ehren, B. J. (n.d.). *Response to Intervention in secondary schools: Is it on your radar screen?* Retrieved from www.rtinetwork.org.

Engelmann, S., Becker, W. C., Carnine, D. W., & Gersten, R. (1988). The Direct Instruction Follow Through Model: Design and outcomes. *Education & Treatment of Children, 11*(4), 303–317.

Ervin, R. A., Schaughency, E., Goodman, S. D., McGlinchey, M. T., & Matthews, A. (2006). Merging research and practice agendas to address reading and behavior school-wide. *School Psychology Review, 35,* 198–223.

Farina, F., & Geva, E. (2011). Cognitive correlates of vocabulary growth in English language learners. *Applied Psycholinguistics 32*(4), 711–738.

Figueroa, R. (2002). Assessment and identification: Toward a new model of assessment. In A. Artiles & A. Ortiz, (Eds.), *English language learners with special education needs.* Washington, DC: Center for Applied Linguistics.

Figueroa, R. (2007). Assessment and identification. In A. Artiles & A. Ortiz, (Eds.), *English language learners with special education needs.* Washington, DC: Center for Applied Linguistics.

Foegen, A. (2008). Algebra progress monitoring and interventions for students with learning disabilities. *Learning Disability Quarterly, 31,* 65–78.

Foegen, A., & Morrison, C. (2010). Putting algebra progress monitoring into practice: Insights from the field. *Intervention in School and Clinic, 46,* 95–103.

Foegen, A., Olson, J. R., & Impecoven-Lind, L. (2008). Developing progress monitoring measures for secondary mathematics: An illustration in algebra. *Assessment for Effective Intervention, 33,* 240–249.

Fuchs, D. (2009). *Determining which students will receive Tier 3 intervention.* Iris Center. Retrieved from http:// iris.peabody.vanderbilt.edu/rti05_tier3/rti_tier3_04 .html.

Fuchs, D., & Deshler, D. (2007). What we need to know about responsiveness to intervention (and shouldn't be afraid to ask). *Learning Disabilities Research & Practice, 22*(2), 129–136.

Fuchs, D., Fuchs, L., & Compton, D. (2012). Smart RTI: A next-generation approach to multilevel prevention. *Exceptional Children, 78*(3), 263–279.

Fuchs, L. (2009). *How can Tier 3 intervention be implemented?* Retrieved from http:// iris.peabody.vanderbilt. edu/rti05_tier3/rti_tier3_05 .html.

Fuchs, L., & Fuchs, D. (2007). The role of assessment in the three-tier approach to reading instruction. In D. Haager, J. Klinger, & S. Vaughn (Eds.), *Evidence-based reading practices for response to intervention.* Baltimore, MD: Paul H. Brookes Publishing Co.

Fuchs, L. S., Fuchs, D., & Hamlett, C. L. (1993). Formative evaluation of academic progress: How much growth can we expect? *School Psychology Review, 22*(1), 27–48.

Futrell, M., & Gomez, J. (2008). How tracking creates a poverty of learning. *Educational Leadership, 65*(8), 74–78.

Garcia, E., & Hamayan, E. (2006). What is the role of culture in language learning? In E. Hamayan & R. Freeman (Eds.), *English language learners at school: A guide for administrators* (pp. 61 –64). Philadelphia, PA: Caslon Publishing.

Garcia, E., & Jensen, B. (2007). Helping young Hispanic learners. *Educational Leadership, 64*(6), 34–39.

Gedney, S. (Ed.). (2009). *Structuring language instruction to advance stalled English learners.* Aiming High. Santa Rosa, CA: Sonoma County Office of Education (www .scoe.org).

Genesee, F., Lindholm-Leary, K., Saunders, B., & Christian, D. (2006). *Educating English language learners: A synthesis of research evidence.* New York, NY: Cambridge University Press.

Gerber, M., Jimenez, T., Leafstedt, J., Villaruz, J., Richards, C., & English, J. (2004). English reading effects of small-group intensive intervention in Spanish for K–1 English learners. *Learning Disabilities Research and Practice, 19*(4), 239–251.

Gersten, R., Baker, S. K., Shanahan, T., Linan-Thompson, S., Collins, P., & Scarcella, R. (2007). *Effective literacy and English language instruction for ELs in the elementary grades: A practice guide* (NCEE 2007-4011). Washington, DC: National Center for Education Evaluation and Regional Assistance, Institute of Education Sciences, U.S. Department of Education. Retrieved from http://ies.ed.gov/ncee.

Gersten, R., Brengelman, S., & Jiminez, R. (1994). Effective instruction for culturally and linguistically diverse students: A reconceptualization. *Focus on Exceptional Children, 27,* 1–16.

Gersten, R., & Dimino, J. (2006). RTI (Response to Intervention): Rethinking special education for students with reading difficulties (yet again). *Reading Research Quarterly, 41,* 99–108.

Gersten, R., Fuchs, L. S, Compton, D., Coyne, M. D., Greenwood, C., & Innocenti, M. S. (2005). Quality indicators for group experimental and quasi-experimental research in special education. *Exceptional Children, 71,* 149–164.

Geva, E. (2006). Second language oral proficiency and second language literacy. In D. August & T. Shanahan (Eds.), *Developing literacy in second language learners: Report of the National Literacy Panel on Language Minority Children and Youth* (pp. 123–141). Mahwah, NJ: Lawrence Erlbaum Associates.

Geva, E., & Farnia, F. (2012). Assessment of reading difficulties in ESL/ELL learners: Myths, research evidence, and implications for assessment. *Encyclopedia of Language and Literacy Development* (pp. 1–9). London, ON: Western University. Retrieved from http:// www.literacyencyclopedia.ca/pdfs/topic.php?topId=310.

Glenn, C., & de Jong, E. (1996). *Educating immigrant children: Schools and language minorities in twelve nations.* New York, NY: Garland Publishing.

Goldenberg, C. (2004). *Successful school change.* New York, NY: Teachers College Press.

Goldenberg, C. (2006). Involving parents of English learners in their children's schooling. *Instructional Leader,* Texas Elementary Principals and Supervisors Association.

Goldenberg, C. (2008). Teaching English language learners: What the research does—and does not—say. *The American Educator, 32*(2), 8–23.

Goldenberg, C., Rueda, R. S., & August, D. (2008). Socio-cultural contexts and literacy development. In D. August & T. Shanahan (Eds.), *Developing reading and writing in second-language learners: Lessons from the Report of the National Literacy Panel on Language-Minority Children and Youth.* New York, NY: Routledge, Washington, DC: Center for Applied Linguistics, and Newark, DE: International Reading Association.

Goldenberg, C., & Saunders, W. (In press). Research to guide English language development instruction. In California Department of Education (Eds.), *Improving education for English learners: Research-based approaches.* Sacramento, CA: CDE Press.

Graves, A., Plasencia-Peinado, J., Deno, S., & Johnson, J. (2005). Formatively evaluating the reading progress of first-grade English learners in multiple-language classrooms. *Remedial and Special Education, 26*(4), 215–225.

Gresham, F. M., MacMillan, D. L., Beebe-Frankenberger, M. E., & Bocian, K. M. (2000). Treatment integrity in learning disabilities intervention research: Do we really know how treatments are implemented? *Learning Disabilities Research & Practice, 15*(4), 198–205.

Haager, D., & Mahdavi, J. (2007). Teacher roles in implementing interventions. In D. Haager, J. Klinger, & S. Vaughn (Eds.), *Evidence-based reading practices for Response to Intervention* (pp. 245–264). Baltimore, MD: Paul H. Brookes Publishing.

Hale, J. (2001). *Learning while black: Creating educational excellence for African American children.* Baltimore, MD: Johns Hopkins.

Hamayan, E. (2006). What is the role of culture in language learning? In E. Hamayan & R. Freeman (Eds.), *English language learners at school: A guide for administrators.* Philadelphia, PA: Caslon Publishing

Harry, B., Klinger, J., & Cramer, E. (2007). *Case studies of minority student placement in special education.* New York, NY: Teacher College Press.

Hasbrouk, J., & Tindal, G. (2006). Oral reading fluency norms: A valuable assessment tool for reading teachers. *The Reading Teacher, 59,* 636–644.

Hauerwas, L. B., & Goessling, D. P. (2008). Who are the interventionists? Guidelines for paraeducators in RTI. *Teaching Exceptional Children Plus, 4*(3) Article 4.

Retrieved from http://escholarship.bc.edu/ education/tecplus/vol4/iss3/art4.

Hiebert, E., Stewart, J., & Uzicanin, M. (2010, July 10). *A comparison of word features affecting word recognition of at-risk beginning readers and their peers.* Paper presented at the annual meeting of the Society for the Scientific Study of Reading on July 10, Berlin.

Hoffert, S. B. (2009). Mathematics: The universal language? *The Mathematics Teacher, 103*(2), 130–139.

Hollins, E., & Guzman, M. T. (2009). Research for preparing teachers for diverse populations. In M. Cochran-Smith & K. Zeichner (Eds.), *Studying Teacher Education.* Mahwah, NJ: Lawrence Erlbaum Associates, Inc.

Honigsfeld, A., & Cohan, A. (2008). The power of two: Lesson study and SIOP® help teachers instruct ELLs. *Journal of Staff Development, 29*(1), 24 –28.

Honigsfeld, A., & Dove, M. (2010). *Collaboration and co-teaching: Strategies for English learners.* Thousand Oaks, CA: Corwin Press.

Horowitz, S. (2009). *Learning disabilities: What they are, and what they are not.* National Center for Learning Disabilities. Retrieved from http://www.ncld.org/ld-basics/ld-explained/basic-facts/learning-disabilities-what-they-are-and-what-they-are-not.

Horowitz, S., & Stecker, D. (2007). *Learning disabilities checklist of signs and symptoms.* National Center for Learning Disabilities. Retrieved from http://www.ncld.org/publications-a-more/checklists-worksheets-a-forms/ld-checklist-of-signs-and-symptoms.

Hosp, M. K., Hosp, J. L., & Howell, K. W. (2007). The ABCs of CBM: A practical guide to curriculum based measurement. New York, NY: Guilford Press.

Hosp, J., & Madyun, N. (2007). Addressing disproportionality with response to intervention. In S. Jimerson, M. Burns, & A. VanDer Heyden (Eds.), *Handbook of Response to Intervention.* New York, NY: Springer.

International Reading Association. (February/March, 2010). Six guiding principles for Response to Intervention. *Reading Today,* 1.

Jensen, E. (2005). *Teaching with the brain in mind* (2nd ed.). Alexandria, VA: Association for Supervision and Curriculum Development.

Jiménez, R. T., Garcia, G. E., & Pearson, P. D. (1996). The reading strategies of bilingual Latina/o students who are successful English readers: Opportunities and obstacles. *Reading Research Quarterly, 57*(6), 576–578.

Jimerson, S., Hong, S., Stage, S., Gerber, M. (2013). Examining oral reading fluency trajectories among English language learners and English speaking students. *Journal of New Approaches in Educational Research, 2.* Retrieved from http://naerjournal.ua.es/article/view/v2n1-1.

Jimerson, S. R., Reschly, A.L., & Hess, R. (2008). Best practices in increasing likelihood of high school completion. In A. Thomas & J. Grimes (Eds.), *Best practices in school psychology* (5th ed., pp. 1085–1097). Bethesda, MD: National Association of School Psychologists.

Johns, J. (2008). *Basic reading inventory: Pre-primer thorough grade twelve and early literacy assessments* (10th ed.). Dubuque, IA: Kendall Hunt.

Kamil, M. L., Borman, G. D., Dole, J., Kral, C. C., Salinger, T., & Torgesen, J. (2008). *Improving adolescent literacy: Effective classroom and intervention practices: A Practice Guide* (NCEE #2008-4027). Washington, DC: National Center for Education Evaluation and Regional Assistance, Institute of Education Sciences, U.S. Department of Education. Retrieved from http://ies.ed.gov/ncee/wwc.

Kampwirth, T., & Powers, K. (2012). *Collaborative consultation in the schools* (4th ed.). Boston, MA: Pearson.

Kelly, P., Gomez-Bellenge, F., Chen, J., & Schultz, M. (2008). Learner outcomes for English language learner low readers in an early intervention. *TESOL Quarterly, 42*(2), 225–260.

Klinger, J., & Edwards, P. (2006). Cultural considerations with Response to Intervention models. *Reading Research Quarterly, 41*(1), 108–117.

Klinger, J., Sorrells, A., & Barrera, M. (2007). Considerations when implementing Response to Intervention with culturally and linguistically diverse students. In D. Haager, J. Klinger, & S. Vaughn (Eds.), *Evidence-based reading practices for response to intervention.* Baltimore, MD: Paul H. Brookes Publishing Co.

Langdon, H. (1989). Language disorder or difference? Assessing the language skills of Hispanic students. *Exceptional Children, 56,* 2, 160–167.

Lenz, B. K., Ehren, B. J., & Deshler, D. D. (2005). The content literacy continuum: A school reform framework for improving adolescent literacy for all students. *Teaching Exceptional Children, 37*(6), 60–63.

Lesaux, N., & Giva, E. (2008). Development of literacy in second-language learners. In D. August & T. Shanahan (Eds.), *Developing reading and writing in second-language learners: Lessons from the Report of the National Literacy Panel on Language-Minority Children and Youth.* New York, NY: Routledge, Washington, DC: Center for Applied Linguistics, and Newark, DE: International Reading Association.

Lesaux, N. K., Kieffer, M. J., Faller, S. E., & Kelley, J. G. (2010). The effectiveness and ease of implementation of an academic vocabulary intervention for linguistically diverse students in urban middle schools. *Reading Research Quarterly, 45*(2), 196–228.

Marston, D., Reschly, A., Lau, M., Muyskens, P., & Canter, A. (2007). Historical perspectives and current trends in problem solving. In D. Haager, J. Klinger, & S. Vaughn (Eds.), *Evidence-based reading practices for response to intervention.* Baltimore, MD: Paul H. Brookes Publishing Co.

Marzano, R. (2004). *Building background knowledge for academic achievement.* Alexandria, VA: ASCD.

Marzano, R., Pickering, D., & Pollock, J. (2001). *Classroom instruction that works.* Alexandria, VA: ASCD.

McCardle, P., Mele-McCarthy, J., Cutting, L., Leos, L., & D'Emilio, T. (2005). Learning disabilities in English language learners: Identifying the issues. *Learning Disabilities Research & Practice, 20*(1), 1–5.

McIntyre, E., Kyle, D., Chen, C., Munoz, M., & Beldon, S. (2010). Teacher learning and ELL reading achievement in sheltered instruction classrooms: Linking professional development to student development. *Literacy Research & Instruction, 49*(4), 334–351.

McMaster, K., Kung, S., Han, I., & Cao, M. (2008). Peer-assisted learning strategies: A tier 1 approach to promoting English learners' response to intervention. *Exceptional Children, 74*(2) 194–214.

Moje, E. B. (1996). "I teach students, not subjects": Teacher-student relationships as contexts for secondary literacy. *Reading Research Quarterly, 31*(2), 172–195.

Moje, E. B. (2008). Foregrounding the disciplines in secondary literacy teaching and learning: A call for change. *Journal of Adolescent & Adult Literacy, 52*(2), 96–107.

Moll, L., Amanti, C., Neff, D., & Gonzalez, N. (1992). Funds of knowledge for teaching: Using a qualitative approach to connect homes and classrooms. *Theory Into Practice. 31*(2), 132–141.

Nagy, W. (2012) Words as tools: Learning academic vocabulary as language acquisition. *Reading Research Quarterly, 47,* 91–108.

National Assessment of Educational Progress (NAEP). (2008). *The nation's report card.* Retrieved from http://nationsreportcard.gov.

National Center for Education Statistics. (2002). *1999–2000 Schools and staffing survey.* Washington DC: U.S. Department of Education, Office of Educational Research and Improvement.

National Center for Education Statistics. (2012a). *The nation's report card: Mathematics 2011* (NCES 2012–458). Washington, DC: Institute of Education Sciences, U.S. Department of Education.

National Center for Education Statistics. (2012b). *The nation's report card: Reading 2011* (NCES 2012–458). Washington, DC: Institute of Education Sciences, U.S. Department of Education.

National Center for Education Statistics. (2012c). *The Nation's Report Card: Vocabulary Results From the 2009 and 2011 NAEP Reading Assessments* (NCES

2013–452). Institute of Education Sciences, U.S. Department of Education, Washington, D.C.

National Center for Learning Disabilities. (2008). *RTI gets promoted to secondary schools: An interview with Barbara J. Ehren & Kathleen Whitmire.* Retrieved from http://ncldtalks.org.

National Center on Student Progress Monitoring. (2009). *Common questions about progress monitoring.* Retrieved from http://www.studentprogress.org/progresmon.asp#1.

National Clearinghouse for English Language Acquisition (NCELA). (2011). The growing numbers of English learner students. Retrieved from www.ncela.gwu.edu/files/uploads/9/growingLEP_0809.pdf.

National Council of Teachers of Mathematics (NCTM). *Principles and standards for school mathematics.* Reston, VA: Retrieved http://www.nctm.org/standards/default. aspx?id=58.

National Governors Association. Center for Best Practices and Council of Chief State School Officers. (2010). *Common core state standards for English language arts and literacy in history/social studies, science, and technical subjects.* Washington, DC: Author.

National High School Center, National Center on Response to Intervention, and Center on Instruction. (2010). *Tiered intervention in high schools: Using preliminary "lessons learned" to guide ongoing discussion.* Washington, DC: American Institutes for Research.

National Reading Panel. (2000). *Teaching children to read: An evidence-based assessment of the scientific research literature on reading and its implications for reading instruction.* Washington, DC: National Institute of Child Health and Human Development, National Institutes of Health.

Nutta, J., Mokhtari, M., & Strebel, C. (2012) *Preparing every teacher to reach English learners.* Boston, MA: Harvard Education Press.

O'Brien, D. G., Stewart, R. A., & Moje, E. B. (1995). Why content literacy is difficult to infuse into the secondary school: Complexities of curriculum, pedagogy, and school culture. *Reading Research Quarterly, 30*(3), 442–463.

O'Malley, J. J., & Chamot, A. U. (1990). *Learning strategies in second language acquisition.* Cambridge: Cambridge University Press.

Oakes, J. (1985). *Keeping track: How schools structure inequality.* New Haven, CT: Yale University Press.

Oakes, J. (1987). Tracking in secondary schools: A contextual perspective. *Educational Psychologist, 22*(2), 129–153.

Oh, D., Haager, D., & Windmueller, M. (2007). A longitudinal study predicting reading success for English language learners from kindergarten to grade one. *Multiple Voices, 10,* 107–124.

Ortiz, A. (1997). Learning disabilities occurring concomitantly with linguistic differences. *Journal of Learning Disabilities, 30,* 321–332.

Ortiz, A., & Yates, J. (2002). Considerations in the assessment of English language learners referred to special education. In A. Artiles & A. Ortiz, (Eds.), *English language learners with special education needs.* Washington, DC: Center for Applied Linguistics.

Padron, Y., Waxman, H., & Rivera, H. (2002). *Educating Hispanic students: Obstacles and avenues to improved academic achievement.* Santa Cruz, CA: Center for Research on Education, Diversity & Excellence.

Payne, R. (2008). Nine powerful practices. *Educational Leadership, 65*(7), 48–52.

Pennsylvania Department of Education. (2008). *Response to Intervention (RtI). Framework for secondary schools: Guidelines and recommendations.* Pennsylvania Training and Technical Assistance Network. Retrieved from www.pattan.net.

Perie, M., Grigg, W. W., & Donahue, P. L. (2005). *The nation's report card: Reading 2005* (NCES 2006-451). National Center for Educational Statistics, U.S. Department of Education. Washington, DC: Government Printing Office.

Pitcher, S. M., Albright, L. K., DeLaney, C. J., Walker, N. T., Seunarinesingh, K., & Mogge, S. (2007). Assessing adolescents' motivation to read. *Journal of Adolescent & Adult Literacy, 50*(5), 378–396.

Pressley, M. (2005). *Literacy-instructional effective classrooms and schools... And why I am so worried about comprehension instruction even in places like these!* Keynote address presented to the Research Institute of the 51st International Reading Association Annual Convention, Chicago, IL.

Ramirez, D., Yuen, S., Ramey, D., & Pasta, D. (1991). *Executive summary: Final report: Longitudinal study of structured English immersion strategy, early-exit and late-exit transitional bilingual education programs for language minority children.* Submitted to the U.S. Department of Education. San Mateo, CA: Aguirre International.

Rampey, B. D., Dion, G. S., & Donahue, P. L. (2009). *The nation's report card: Trends in academic progress in reading and mathematics 2008.* Retrieved from www.nces.ed.gov/nationsreportcard/pubs/main2008/2009479.asp.

Reed, D. K., Wexler, J., & Vaughn, S. (2012). *RTI for reading at the secondary level: Recommended literacy practices and remaining questions.* New York, NY: Guilford Press.

Reeves, D. (December 2008/January 2009). Looking deeper into the data. *Educational Leadership, 66*(4), 89–90.

Richards, C., & Leafstedt, J. (2010). *Early reading intervention: Strategies and methods for struggling readers.* Boston, MA: Allyn & Bacon.

Richards, C., Leafstedt, J. M., Gerber, M. M. (2006). Qualitative and quantitative examination of four low performing kindergarten English learners: Characteristics of responsive and non-responsive students. *Remedial and Special Education, 27,* 218–234.

Richards-Tutor, C., Solari, E. J., Leafstedt, J. M., Gerber, M. M., Filippini, A., & Aceves, T. (2013). Response to Intervention for English learners: Examining models for determining response and non-response. *Assessment for Effective Intervention, 38,* 172–184.

Riches, C., & Genesee, F. (2006). Literacy: Crosslinguistic & crossmodal issues. In F. Genesee, K. Lindholm-Leary, W. Saunders, & D. Christian (Eds.), *Educating English language learners: A synthesis of research evidence.* New York, NY: Cambridge University Press.

Rodriguez, A. (2010). Start with the adults. *Educational Leadership, 68,* 2, 74–75.

Ronfeldt, M., Loeb, S., & Wyckoff, J. (2013). How teacher turnover harms student achievement. American *Education Research Journal, 50*(1), 4–36.

Rothsten, D., & Santana, L. (2011). *Make just one change: Teach students to ask their own questions.* Boston, MA: Harvard Education Press.

Ruddell, M. R. (2007). *Teaching content reading and writing* (5th ed.). Hoboken, NJ: Wiley Jossey-Bass Education.

Rueda, R. (1989). Defining mild disabilities with language minority students. *Exceptional Children, 56*(2), 131–128.

Ruiz, N. (1989). An optimal learning environment for Rosemary. *Exceptional Children, 56*(2), 130–144.

Ruiz, N. (1995). The social construction of ability and disability: Profiles types of Latino children identified as language learning disabled. *Journal of Learning Disabilities, 28,* 476–490.

Rumberger, R. (2011). *Dropping out: Why students drop out of high school and what can be done about it.* Cambridge, MA: Harvard University Press.

Rumberger, R., Gandara, P., & Merino, B. (2006). Where California's English learners attend school and why it matters. *UC Linguistic Minority Research Institute Newsletter, 15*(2), 1–3.

Salend, S., & Salinas, A. (2003). Language differences or learning difficulties. *Teaching Exceptional Children, 35*(4), 36–43.

Saunders, W. M., Foorman, B. R., & Carlson, C. D. (2006, November). Do we need a separate block of time for oral English language development in programs for English learners? *Elementary School Journal, 107*(2), 181–198.

Saunders, W. M., & Goldenberg, C. N. (2010). ELD chapter in *Improving Education for English Learners: Research-Based Approaches.* Sacramento, CA: CDE Press.

Saunders, W. M., & Goldenberg, C. N. (2010). Research to guide English language development instruction. In California Department of Education (Ed.), *Improving education for English learners: Research-based approaches* (pp. 21–81). Sacramento, CA: CDE Press.

Saunders, W. M., Goldenberg, C. N., & Gallimore, R. (2009). Increasing achievement by focusing grade level teams on improving classroom learning: A prospective, quasi-experimental study of Title I schools. *American Educational Research Journal, 46*(4), 1006–1033.

Scammacca, N., Roberts, G., Vaughn. S., Edmonds, M., Wexler, J., Reutebuch, C. K., & Torgesen, J. K. (2007). *Interventions for adolescent struggling readers: A meta-analysis with implications for practice.* Portsmouth, NH: RMC Research Corporation, Center on Instruction.

Scarcella, R. (2003). *Academic English: A conceptual framework* (Technical report 2003-1). Santa Barbara, CA: Linguistic Minority Research Institute.

Schleppegrell, M. (2007). The linguistic challenge of mathematics teaching and learning. *Reading and Writing Quarterly, 23,* 139–159.

Schmoker, M. (2007). Reading, writing and thinking for all. *Educational Leadership, 64*(7) 63– 66.

Schmoker, M. (2011). *Focus: Elevating the essential to radically improve student learning.* Alexandria, VA: Association of Supervision and Curriculum Development.

Shanahan, T. (December 2012/January 2013). The Common Core ate my baby and other urban legends. *Educational Leadership, 70*(4), 10–16.

Shannon, B. S., & Bylsma, P. (2007). *Nine characteristics of high performing schools.* Olympia, WA: Office of Superintendent of Public Instruction. Retrieved from http://www.k12.wa.us/research/default.aspx.

Shearer, B. A., Ruddell, M. R., & Vogt, M.E. (2001). Successful middle school intervention: Negotiated strategies and individual choice. In T. Shanahan & F. V. Rodriguez (Eds.), *National Reading Conference Yearbook, 50* (pp. 558 –571), National Reading Conference.

Short, D. (2002). Language learning in sheltered social studies classes. *TESOL Journal, 11*(1), 18–24.

Short, D., Cloud, N., Morris, P., & Motta, J. (2012). Cross-district collaboration: Curriculum and professional development. *TESOL Journal, 3*(3), 402–424.

Short, D., Echevarría, J, & Richards-Tutor, C. (2011). Research on academic literacy development in sheltered instruction classrooms. *Language Teaching Research, 15*(3), 363–380.

Short, D. J., Fidelman, C. G., & Louguit, M. (2012). Developing academic language in English language learners through sheltered instruction. *TESOL Quarterly, 46*(2), 334–361.

Short, D., & Fitzsimmons, S. (2006). *Double the work: Challenges and solutions to acquiring language and academic literacy for adolescent English language learners*. A Report to the Carnegie Corporation. New York, NY: Alliance for Education.

Simon, C., Lewis, S., Uro, G., Uzzell, R., Palacios, M., & Casserly, M. (2011). Today's promise, tomorrow's future: The social and educational factors contributing to the outcomes of Hispanics in urban schools. The Council of the Great City Schools.

Smith, D. D., & Tyler, N. C. (2010). *Introduction to special education: Making a difference* (7th ed.). Columbus, OH: Pearson/Merrill.

Snow, M. A., & Katz, A. (2010). English language development: Issues and implementation at grades K through 5. In California Department of Education (Ed.), *Improving education for English learners: Research-based approaches* (pp. 83–143). Sacramento, CA: CDE Press.

Sobel, A., & Kugler, E. (2007). Building partnerships with immigrant parents. *Educational Leadership, 64*(6), 62–66.

Sox, A., & Rubinstein-Ávila, E. (2009). WebQuests for English-language learners: Essential elements for design. *Journal of Adolescent & Adult Literacy, 53*(1), 38–48.

Stecker, P. M., & Lembke, E. S. (2005). *Advanced applications of CBM in reading: Instructional decision making strategies manual*. National Center on Student Progress Monitoring. Retrieved from http://www.studentprogress.org/library/Training/CBMmath/AdvancedReading/AdvRdgManual-FORMATTEDSept29.pdf.

Sturtevant, E. G., Boyd, F. B., Brozo, W. G., Hinchman, K. A., Moore, D. W., & Alvermann, D. E. (2006). *Principled practices for adolescent literacy. A framework for instruction and policy*. Mahwah, NJ: Lawrence Erlbaum Associates.

Sturtevant, E. G., & Kim, G. S. (2010). Literacy motivation and school/non-school literacies among students enrolled in a middle-school ESOL program. *Literacy Research and Instruction, 49*(1), 68–85.

Suarez-Orozco, C., Suarez-Orozco, M., & Todorova, I. (2008). *Learning a new land: Immigrant students in American society*. Cambridge, MA: Harvard University Press.

Tatum, A. (2008). Toward a more anatomically complete model of literacy instruction: A focus on African American male adolescents and texts. *Harvard Educational Review, 78*(1), 155–182.

Thompson, G. (2004). *Through ebony eyes: What teachers need to know but are afraid to ask about African American students*. San Francisco, CA: Jossey-Bass.

Thompson, G. (2008). Beneath the apathy. *Educational Leadership 65*(6), 50–54.

Ticha, R., Espin, C. A., & Wayman, M. M. (2009). Reading progress monitoring for secondary-schools: Reliability, validity, and sensitivity of growth of reading-aloud and MAZE-selection measures. *Learning Disabilities Research & Practice, 24*(3), 132–142.

Tomlinson, C. A. (1999). *The differentiated classroom: Responding to the needs of all learners*. Alexandria, VA: ASCD.

Torgesen, J. K. (2000). Individual differences in response to early interventions in reading: The lingering problem of treatment resisters. *Learning Disabilities Research & Practice, 15,* 55–64.

Torgesen, J. K. (2012). Catch them before they fall: Identification and assessment to prevent reading failure in young children. *Reading Rockets*. Retrieved from http://www.readingrockets.org/article/225/.

Trent, S. C., & Artiles, A. (2007). Today's multicultural, bilingual, and diverse schools. In R. Turnbull, A. Turnbull, M. Shank, & S. J. Smith (Eds.), *Exceptional lives: Special education in today's schools* (5th ed., pp. 56–79). Upper Saddle River, NJ: Pearson.

Trent, S. C., Kea, C., & Oh, K. (2008). Preparing preservice educators for cultural diversity: How far have we come? *Exceptional Children, 74*(3), 328–350.

Tucker, J., & Sornson, R. (2007). One student at a time; one teacher at a time: Reflections on the use of instructional support. In S. Jimerson, M. Burns, & A. VanDer Heyden (Eds.), *Handbook of Response to Intervention* (pp. 269–278). New York, NY: Springer.

Valdes, G. (2001). *Learning and not learning English: Latino students in American schools*. New York, NY: Teachers College Press.

Vanderwood, M., & Nam, J. (2007). Response to intervention for English language learners: Current development and future directions. In S. Jimerson, M. Burns, & A. Van Der Heyden (Eds.), *Handbook of Response to Intervention* (pp. 408–417). New York, NY: Springer.

Vanderwood, M. L., Kinklater, D., & Healy, K. (2008). Predictive accuracy of nonsense word fluency for English language learners. *School Psychology Review, 37,* 5–17.

Vaughn, S., Cirino, P. T., Linan-Thompson, S., Mathes, P. G., Carlson, C. D., Hagan, E. C., et al. (2006). Effectiveness of a Spanish intervention and an English intervention for English-language learners at risk for reading problems. *American Educational Research Journal, 43*(3), 449–479.

Vaughn, S., & Fletcher, J.M. (2012). Response to intervention with secondary school students. *Journal of Learning Disabilities, 45*(3), 244–256.

Vaughn, S., Gersten, R., & Chard, D. (2000). The underlying message in LD intervention research: Findings from research syntheses. *Exceptional Children, 67,* 99–114.

Vaughn, S., & Klinger, J. (2007). Overview of the three-tier model of reading intervention. In D. Haager, J. Klinger, & S. Vaughn (Eds.), *Evidence-based reading practices for response to intervention* (pp. 3–10). Baltimore, MD: Paul H. Brookes Publishing Co.

Vaughn, S., Linan-Thompson, S., Mathes, P. G., Cirino, P. T., Carlson, C. D., Pollard-Durodola, S. D., et al. (2006). Effectiveness of Spanish intervention for first grade English language learners at risk for reading difficulties. *Journal of Learning Disabilities, 39,* 56–73.

Vaughn, S., Mathes, P., Linan-Thompson, S., Cirino, P., Carlson, C., Pollard-Durodola, S., et al. (2006). Effectiveness of an English intervention for first-grade English language learners at risk for reading problems. *Elementary School Journal, 107*(2), 153–181.

Vaughn, S., Wanzek, J., Wexler, J., Barth, A., Cirino, P. T., Fletcher, J. M., Romain, M. A., Denton, C. A., Roberts, G., & Francis, D. J. (2010). The relative effects of group size on reading progress of older students with reading difficulties. *Reading and Writing: An Interdisciplinary Journal 23*(8), 931–956.

Vaughn, S., Wanzek, J., Woodruff, A., & Linan-Thompson, S. (2007). Prevention and early identification of students with reading disabilities. In D. Haager, J. Klingner, & S. Vaughn (Eds.), *Evidence-based reading practices for Response to Intervention* (pp. 11–27). Baltimore, MD: Paul H. Brookes.

Vellutino, F., Scanlon, D., & Zhang, H. (2007). Identifying reading disability based on response to intervention: Evidence from early intervention research. In S. Jimerson, M. Burns, & A. VanDer Heyden (Eds.), *Handbook of Response to Intervention.* New York, NY: Springer.

Villegas, A. M., & Lucas, T. (2007). The culturally responsive teacher. *Educational Leadership, 64*(6), 28–33.

Vogt, M. E. (1989). *A study of the congruence between pre-service teachers' and cooperating teachers' attitudes and practices toward high and low achievers.* Unpublished doctoral dissertation submitted to the University of California, Berkeley.

Vogt, M. E. (2009). Teachers of English learners: Issues of preparation and professional development. In F. Falk-Ross, S. Szabo, M. B. Sampson, & M. M. Foote (Eds.), *Literacy issues during changing times: A call to action.* Texas A & M University, Commerce: College Reading Association Yearbook, 30, pp. 22–36.

Vogt, M. E. (2012). English learners: Developing their literate lives. In R. M. Bean & A. S. Dagen (Eds.), *Best practices of literacy leaders: Keys to school improvement* (pp. 248–260). New York, NY: Guilford Press.

Vogt, M. E., & Echevarría, J. (2008). *99 ideas and activities for teaching English learners with the SIOP® Model.* Boston, MA: Allyn & Bacon.

Vogt, M. E., & Shearer, B. A. (2011). *Reading specialists and literacy coaches in the real world* (3rd ed.). Boston, MA: Allyn & Bacon.

Wallace, T., Espin, C. A., McMaster, K., Deno, S. L., & Foegen, A. (2007). CBM progress monitoring within a standards-based system. *The Journal of Special Education, 41*(2), 66–67.

Waxman, H., Gray, J., & Padron, Y. (2003). *Review of research on educational resilience.* Santa Cruz, CA: Center for Research on Education, Diversity & Excellence.

Wayman, M. M., Wallace, T., & Wiley, H. I. (2007). Literature synthesis on curriculum-based measurement in reading. *The Journal of Special Education, 41*(2), 85–120.

Weinstein, R. S. (1985). Student mediation of classroom expectancy effects. In J. Dusek (Ed.), *Teacher expectancies.* Hillsdale, NJ: Lawrence Erlbaum Associates.

Wexler, J., Vaughn, S., Roberts, G., & Denton, C. A. (2010). The efficacy of repeated reading and wide reading practice for high school students with severe reading disabilities. *Learning Disabilities Research & Practice, 25*(1), 2–10.

Zirkel, P. A., & Krohn, N. (2008). RtI after IDEA: A survey of state law. *Teaching Exceptional Children, 40*(3), 71–73.

Zwiers, J. (2008). *Building academic language: Essential practices for content classrooms.* San Francisco, CA: Jossey-Bass; Newark, DE: International Reading Association.